JN326285

Discovering JAPAN
A New Regional Geography

TEIKOKU-SHOIN

Contents

Contents 2
Preface 4

Part 1

Chapter 1 The structure and nature of Japan 5
    1 Location of Japan 6
    2 The varied landforms of Japan 7
    3 Climate of Japan 14
    4 Natural disasters and the endowments of nature 18

Chapter 2 An Outline of Japanese History 20
    1 Prehistoric Japan 20
    2 Ancient Japan 20
    3 Medieval Japan 22
    4 Feudal Japan 23
    5 Modern Japan 25

Chapter 3 Various perspectives of Japan 26
    1 Life-style and culture of Japan 26
    2 Population distribution and population change of Japan 28
    3 Increasing ties within the Japanese Archipelago 30
    4 Industrial perspective of Japan 32

Chapter 4 The regional geography of Japan 36

Part 2

Chapter 1 Kyūshū Region 40
    1 Looking at the map 42
    2 The Kyūshū Region's strong ties with other Asian nations 44
    3 North and South Kyūshū : Contrasts in agriculture and in life-styles 46
    4 From steel manufacture to automobile and IC production 49
    5 Gifts of nature and the development of tourism 51
    6 The southern islands, Okinawa 52
    — Japan seen through its regions —
       History of Minamata disease and Ecotown initiatives 55

Chapter 2 Chūgoku / Shikoku Region 56
    1 Looking at the map 58
    2 Industries and life in Setouchi 60
    3 Industries and life in San'in 65
    4 Industries and life in Southern Shikoku 67
    — Japan seen through its regions —
       Initiatives to cope with rural depopulation 69

Chapter 3 Kinki Region 70
    1 Looking at the map 72
    2 The Keihanshin Metropolitan Area and Ōsaka 74
    3 Industries around the coast of Ōsaka Bay
       and Kansai International Airport 77

	4	The ancient capitals and tourism 80
	5	Contrasts between Northern and Southern Kinki.. 83

◆ Japan seen through its regions
— Lake Biwa and environmental problems 85

Chapter 4 Chūbu Region.. **86**
1. Looking at the map 88
2. Industry and transport in the Tōkai Area.. 90
3. Nature, economy and life in the Central Highlands....................................... 94
4. Life and economy in snowy Hokuriku 97

◆ Japan seen through its regions
— The light and shadow of nuclear power... 101

Chapter 5 Kantō Region.. **102**
1. Looking at the map 104
2. Tōkyō in Japan, Tōkyō in the world 106
3. Life in the Tōkyō Metropolitan Area 110
4. The Keihin Industrial District
    and its surrounding industries.. 112
5. Agriculture serves the Tōkyō Metropolitan Area 114
6. The leisure industry and nature conservation 116

◆ Japan seen through its regions
— Initiatives for internationalism and multiculturism 117

Chapter 6 Tōhoku Region.. **118**
1. Looking at the map 120
2. Transport development and urban growth.. 122
3. Farmers and fishermen respond to challenges... 123
4. Traditional industries and new industries 126

◆ Japan seen through its regions
— The role of professional sports in regional revival.............................. 129

Chapter 7 Hokkaidō Region... **130**
1. Looking at the map 132
2. The history of Hokkaidō's development
    and the growth of cities.. 134
3. Agriculture and stock raising in Hokkaidō's broad acres............................ 136
4. Changes in Hokkaidō's fishing industry... 138
5. The rise and fall of Hokkaidō's mining and industry 139
6. Tourism that support the region 140

◆ Japan seen through its regions
— "The Paradise of the Wild"- the ideal and reality of Shiretoko................ 141

Viewing Japan 142
Statistics of Japan.. 146
Index 150

Preface

Since the 1980s, the wave of globalization that has affected most of the world has also swept across Japan. Along with this development, more and more foreign companies have established a presence in Japan, a trend that has resulted in a rapid increase in the number of foreigners working, residing and studying throughout the country. Furthermore, the Japanese government is experimenting with various policies to attract more tourists as part of a national policy of the 21st century that is aimed at establishing Japan as a nation well equipped to cater for tourists from other countries. Thanks to worldwide interest in Japan, the perception of the country has changed greatly from "an exotic country steeped in mystery," to "a country playing an important role in supporting the industry and economy of the world" to "a country creating and transmitting modern culture to the world" as represented by cultural features such as Japanese cuisine and Japanese *manga* and *anime*.

The original version of this book was initially published with the aim of helping Japanese junior high school students to understand their country within the context of globalization. In translating the book into English, we hope to help foreigners who are working, residing or studying in Japan, and those who are visiting Japan for sightseeing or for business purposes. As international exchange increases through continuing globalization, it becomes all the more necessary to gain a more accurate and deeper understanding of Japan that is not distorted by ill-informed prejudice or exoticism. At the same time, we hope that this book will be useful to students who are studying in Japanese schools abroad, as well as young Japanese people studying in Japan who wish to take off into a world in which they can talk about their country in English, the new global language. We hope this book will enjoy a wide readership and that it will provide new and useful insights into today's Japan.

PART 1

Chapter 1
The structure and nature of Japan

KARAFUTO (SAHALIN)
KAMCHATKA PEN.
SEA OF OKHOTSK
Amur R.
KUNASHIRI I.
ETOROFU I.
L. Khanka
HOKKAIDŌ
SEA OF JAPAN
SADO I.
HONSHŪ
KOREAN PEN.
OKI Is.
IZU Is.
PACIFIC OCEAN
TSUSHIMA I.
SHIKOKU
GOTŌ Is.
KYŪSHŪ
EAST CHINA SEA
YAKU I.   TANEGA-SHIMA I.
ŌSHIMA (AMAMIŌSHIMA I.)

▲① **Japan viewed through satellite imagery** While it may seem like a photograph of the Earth taken from a spaceship, this is an image taken from a satellite, and has been made to look three-dimensional through the addition of landform data. It has also been processed so as to show the curvature of the Earth.<©TRIC>

◀ ① **Location of Japan**
Japan's neighbors include South Korea, North Korea, China, Russia and the Philippines. Using an atlas, try to find countries that are similar to Japan in latitude and longitude.

1 Location of Japan

Japan, an island nation beside a continent

As we can see from the satellite image shown in Figure 1, Japan is an island nation surrounded by seas. The island nation consists of four large islands-Honshū, Hokkaidō, Kyūshū, and Shikoku, as well as numerous small islands. These islands form a chain, or archipelago, that stretches from north to south, and is arranged like an arch with its outer curve facing the Pacific Ocean.

With an area of approximately 380,000km^2, Japan is far from being a large country by world standards. Yet, with its numerous islands, Japan covers a territory that is wide and extensive, stretching in all directions. There is a 25 degree difference in latitude between the northernmost point, Etorofu Island, and the southernmost point, Okinotori Island. Additionally, between the westernmost point, Yonaguni Island, and the easternmost point Minamitori Island there is a 30 degree difference in longitude. If a railway were to be built across the sea and if the *shinkansen* "*Nozomi*" were to run to the extreme points of Japan's territory, how long would it take to reach these places from Tokyo? Even with a *shinkansen* that travels to Shin'ōsaka in 2 hours and 30 minutes, to reach Yonaguni Island or Minamitori Island, islands that lie approximately 2,000km from Tokyo, it would take as much as 9 hours.

In addition, Japan is located close to the eastern edge of Eurasia, which is the world's largest continent. As a result, Japan has always been heavily influenced not only by continental elements in the climate, but also by lifestyles and cultures that have come across the sea from the Asian mainland.

▲ ① **Scenery viewed from the Tōkaidō *Shinkansen*** The left photograph shows a plain seen between Shin'yokohama and Odawara, the central one shows Lake Hamana seen between Hamamatsu and Toyohashi, and the right one shows mountains and orchards between Toyohashi and Mikawa-Anjō.

▲ ② **Landscapes viewed from Australia's intercontinental railroad train, "The Gun"**(the left shows part of Northern Territory, the right was taken in South Australia). A seemingly endless vista of reddish-brown land stretches from horizon to horizon.

2 The varied landforms of Japan

Landforms of Japan

Figure 1 consists of three photographs taken from the train window while riding the Tōkaidō *Shinkansen* "*Kodama*" from Tōkyō to Nagoya. The landforms seen from the window change quickly, from plains, to coastal stretches, to mountains, and these different views, from residential areas to fields to forests show changes in the way people live. By contrast, continental railroads, such as those of Australia or Siberia, pass through landscapes that can be the same for days on end, and which are generally not as varied as those in Japan. The wealth in variations and changes in landscape, with plains, coasts and mountains following one another, is one of the distinct characteristics of the geography of Japan. How did these characteristics come to be the way they are?

The surface of the Earth is thought to have been shaped by movements of thick rock plates, that are arranged in a giant jigsaw pattern across the surface of the earth. Where the plates are pressed against each other, the land sometimes rises and sometimes sinks. Japan is located at a point where four plates are pressed against each other, and this has led to frequent rising and sinking of the land. Mountains and mountain ranges are made of the risen parts, and basins and plains from the sunken parts. This rising and sinking of land has been frequent throughout Japan over a long period of geological time, and has produced a pattern of landforms that has a rich variety.

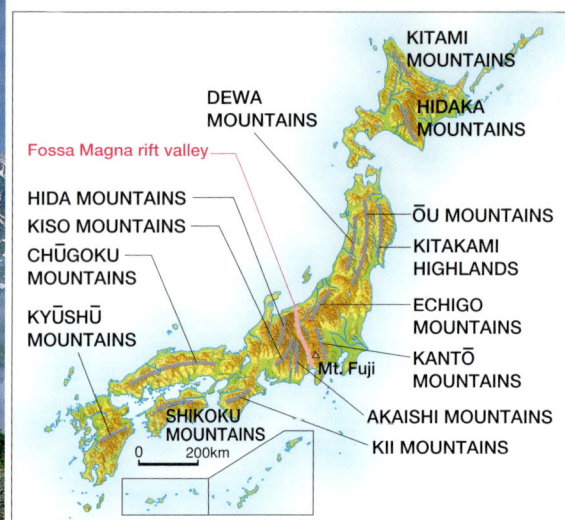

▲ ① **Sharply eroded mountains** (Nagano Prefecture) The peak of Mt. Shirouma in the Hida Mountains of the Japan Alps is more than 2900m above sea level.

▲ ② **Major mountains of Japan and Fossa Magna**

◂ ③ **Mt. Fuji** (Yamanashi Prefecture) Places which provide beautiful views of Mt. Fuji are popular as locations for the tourist industry.

▸ ④ **Seishin New Town** (Kōbe City, Hyōgo Prefecture) This is a new town created by the large-scale leveling of a hill.

Mountains of Japan

As seen in Figure 2, Japan is a mountainous country. The highest point above sea level is Mt. Fuji, 3,776m high, a mountain located on the borders of Shizuoka and Yamanashi Prefectures. Mt. Fuji is a volcano that has repeatedly erupted through hundreds of thousands years. With its beautiful form that resembles a perfect cone, no matter what angle it is seen from, Mt. Fuji has always been a symbol of Japan.

On the other hand there are mountains almost as high as Mt. Fuji in the Hida, Kiso, and Akaishi Mountains in the central region of Honshū. With their sharp, snow-capped mountain peaks and often pure white scenery, these mountain ranges have been called the Nihon Alps (Japan Alps) because of their similarities with the European Alps. Unlike volcanic mountains such as Mt. Fuji, these mountains have been created through the rising of rock beds that accumulated on the seabed many millions of years ago. In addition, fed by abundant rain and snow, the rivers have carved out deep valleys. This is how the mountainous regions with steep slopes have been formed. Yet, the mountain ranges of Japan also contain areas such as the Kitakami Highlands and Chūgoku Mountains, which have broad gentle slopes rather than sharply carved ones. Today, these are used for the grazing of livestock such as cattle.

Distinct from the mountainous regions and generally much lower in altitude, are numerous natural hills from soft rocks. These can be easily worked by bulldozers, and are therefore suitable for development. In various parts of Japan, industrial complexes and new towns have been built on hills of this kind.

▲ ⑤ **Shinano River** (Niigata City, Niigata Prefecture)　There are orchards along the river, with paddy fields beyond.

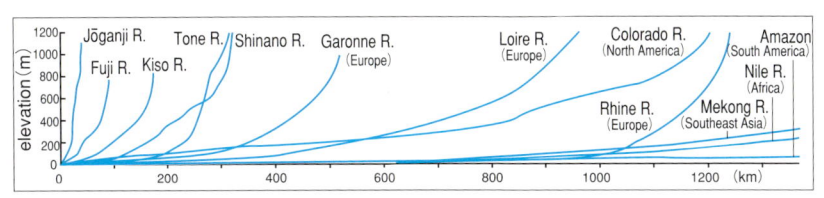

▲ ⑥ **Comparison of major rivers overseas and in Japan** (taken from Chronological Scientific Tables 2007 and other sources)　The cross section depicts the areas up to 1200m above sea level, and the length up to 1370km Rivers beyond these limits are not included.

▲ ⑦ **Kurobe Dam** (Toyama Prefecture)

Rivers of Japan

　With its source located approximately 3,000m above sea level, and its length of 367km, the Shinano is Japan's longest river. Flowing through numerous basins and plains on its way to the sea, the Shinano has supported the lives of a great number of people who live close to it. Several rivers flowing from the Hida Mountains join each other in the Matsumoto Basin, becoming the river Sai. The Sai then flows into the Nagano Basin and joins with the Chikuma, whose source is in the Kantō Mountains. The water from the river is used for all kinds of purposes and makes possible the cultivation of fruit in the basins through which the Chikuma flows. When it arrives in Niigata Prefecture, the Chikuma changes its name to the Shinano, waters the vast Echigo Plain, then flows out into the Sea of Japan.

　Yet, looking at Figure 6, we can see that the Shinano is much shorter and steeper than major rivers elsewhere in the world. It is said that a Dutch civil engineer who came to Japan from the flat lowlands of Holland, upon viewing the Jōganji River of Toyama Prefecture said, " This isn't a river, it's a waterfall! ". With gentle rivers, it takes time for the rainfall to reach the river mouth, making it possible to use the river water for a fairly long period, but in the case of the steep rivers of Japan, the rainfall passes almost immediately to the sea. That said, water shortages can occur at times of drought. Although Japan has abundant rainfall by world standards, it is also a nation low in water resources. So as to use rainfall without waste, water is saved by damming up the rivers in the mountains. In addition, dams play a useful role in preventing floods at times of heavy rainfall.

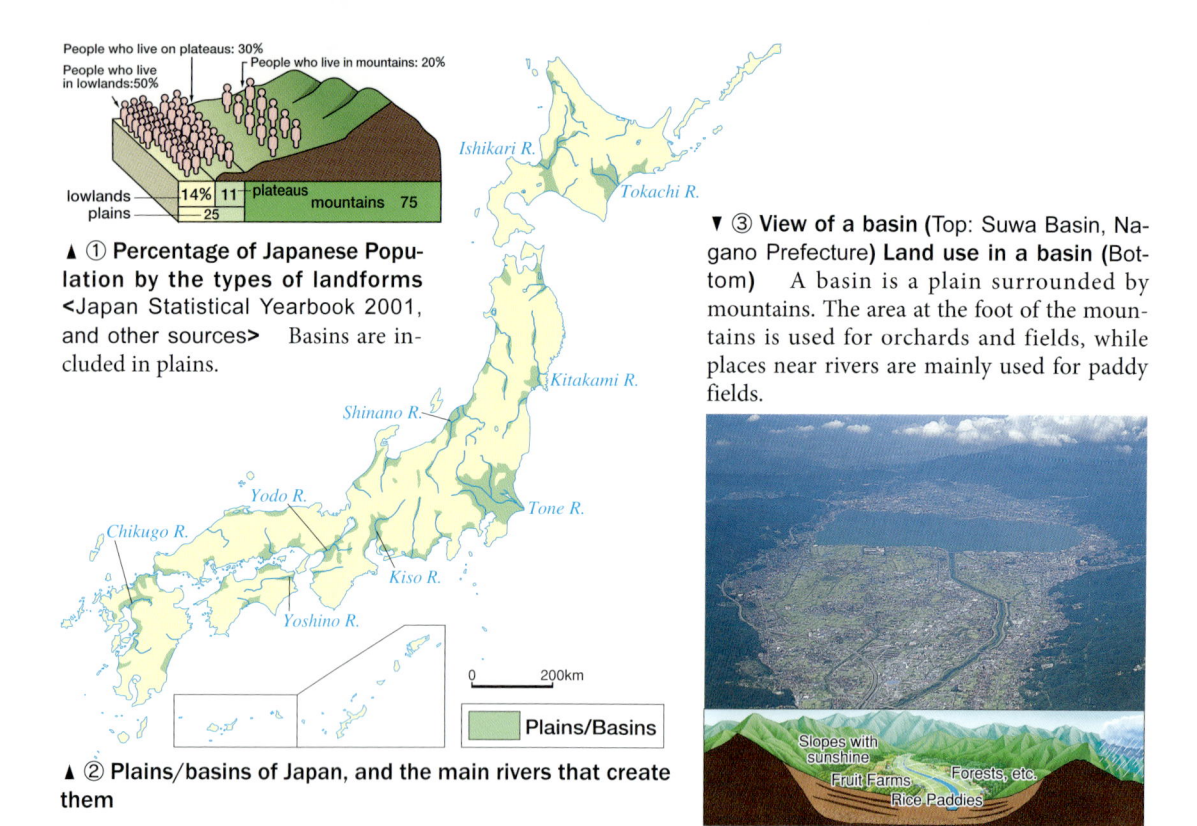

▲ ① **Percentage of Japanese Population by the types of landforms** <Japan Statistical Yearbook 2001, and other sources> Basins are included in plains.

▼ ③ **View of a basin** (Top: Suwa Basin, Nagano Prefecture) **Land use in a basin** (Bottom) A basin is a plain surrounded by mountains. The area at the foot of the mountains is used for orchards and fields, while places near rivers are mainly used for paddy fields.

▲ ② **Plains/basins of Japan, and the main rivers that create them**

Plains of Japan generated by rivers

Rivers that rise in the mountains flow vigorously in the upper part of their courses and as a result, carve the mountains into deep valleys. This process is called erosion. Additionally, there are mudslides in times of heavy rain, and these can pour large amounts of earth and sand into the river. The earth and sand produced by erosion and by mudslides are carried to the river's lower course and settle at places where the speed of the flow decreases, such as at the foot of a mountain and the river's mouth. The plains of Japan are made from the accumulation of the earth and sand that have been brought down by the rivers. Looking at Figure 2, we can see that plains have been formed immediately downstream from where the large rivers leave the mountains. Furthermore, the plains of Japan are mostly very small in surface area compared to plains in other countries. Yet given Japan's mountainous geography, these small plains are crucially important as living places for people. As Figure 1 shows, while plains account for only 25% of the surface area of Japan, they contain approximately 80% of the Japanese population.

Types of plains

Plains can be classified as basins, or lowland areas surrounded by mountains, alluvial fans, deltas formed by earth and sand carried by rivers, and plateaus. Alluvial fans are landforms created by the rivers which, after flowing from mountains, waver to the right and left at the upper edge of the plain, and through this process eventually pile earth and sand into a fan-shaped landform, that spreads out from the foot of the mountain slope. The central part of the alluvial fan has rapid drainage due to the accumulation of stones and large grains of sand, and the river channel and rainfall are often taken underground, leaving the surface dry. This feature allows parts of alluvial fans within the Kōfu and Yamagata Basins

► ④ Landforms created by rivers

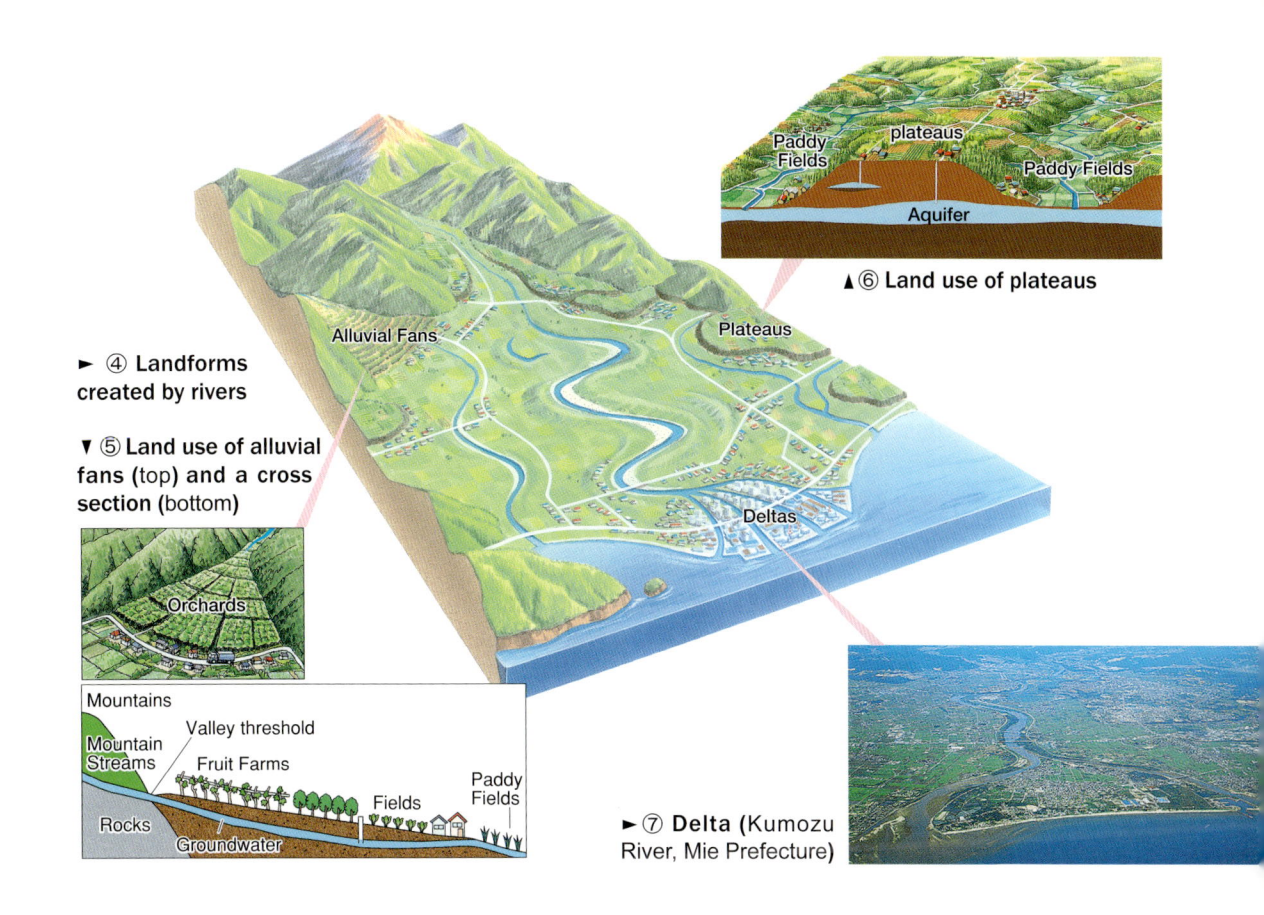

▼ ⑤ Land use of alluvial fans (top) and a cross section (bottom)

▲ ⑥ Land use of plateaus

► ⑦ Delta (Kumozu River, Mie Prefecture)

to be used as orchards. The water taken underground later reappears as water springs at the edges of the alluvial fans. These springs have always been a valuable source of water for drinking and for irrigation, and people have consequently built villages and towns around them.

Deltas are created by the accumulation of fine sand and mud carried by rivers, at the point where rivers flow into the seas or lakes. With their fertile soil and tendency to retain water, deltas have always been used as paddy fields[1]. These landforms are called deltaic plains, and they lie at, or slightly below, river or sea level.

Plateaus exist at a higher level than the aforementioned plains. In that it has a level surface, a plateau is a type of plain, and perhaps the most typical example of a plateau in Japan is the Kantō Plain. Plateaus are formed by the rise of former sea-beds or riverbeds. In the Kantō Region, some places, such as the Shimōsa Uplands, with its thick accumulation of volcanic ash, carry a mantle of red soil[2]. With rapid water drainage resulting from the accumulation of beds of sand and stones, these places are often used as cultivated land[3]. Just as with alluvial fans, water springs appear at the margins of the plateaus. Additionally, between plateaus, there are strips of long and narrow valleys carved by small rivers. In these valleys and along the margins of the plateaus, where there are springs, the soil contains enough moisture for paddy rice cultivation.

Notes (P.11)
[1] Due to today's urban and industrial development, deltas are also being used for residential and industrial land.
[2] This is referred to as the "Kantō Plain loam layer.", or simply the Kantō loam.
[3] Plateaus are nowadays often used as residential land, and for the construction of urban buildings such as factories, schools and hospitals, as well as for golf courses.

▲ ② **Coast with continuous beaches** (Kujūkuri Coast, Chiba Prefecture)

▲ ① **Ria coast** (Sanriku Coast, Iwate Prefecture)

▲ ③ **Coast with coral reefs** (Minna Island, Okinawa Prefecture)

The abundantly varied coasts of Japan

The coastal scenery of the Japanese archipelago is rich in variety. In many parts of the coast, mountains rise sharply from the sea revealing their rocky sides. Ria coasts are coasts with many small headlands and inlets, arranged in a pattern that resembles the shape of saw blades. Deep ria inlets are easy for boats to enter, and have thus been suitable for the development of fishing ports. Moreover at Shima Peninsula and at along the Sanriku Coast, marine farming of pearls and scallops is possible, taking advantage of the sheltered and relatively still waters of the ria inlets.

In other parts of Japan, there are also smooth coastlines with long continuous beaches, as is the case along the Kujūkuri Coast. In addition, sand dunes can be found along coasts where beach sand has been accumulated by wind action. In large-scale sand dunes, such as those along the coast of Tottori Prefecture, such plants as Japanese shallots (Chinese allium) and watermelons are raised by irrigation.

In the southern part of Japan, there are also coasts created by living organisms. These are the coral reefs seen around the coasts of the Nansei Islands which are warmed by the waters of the Kuroshio (Japan Current). With many people visiting the region to enjoy sea bathing and diving, these seas with beautiful coral reefs are valuable as resources for the tourist industry.[1]

In places with a large tidal range, such as Sea of Ariake (western Kyūshū) or the Seto Inland Sea, there are vast tidal flats consisting of mud. Around these tidal flats, observations can be made of various marine organisms such as crabs, shellfish, fish and migratory birds. Moreover, tidal flats that are very broad and shallow are ideal for dike construction and land reclamation. In fact in places such as these, paddy fields were opened up at an early stage in history. More recently, tidal flats have been reclaimed for urban and industrial development. As a result of reclamation ancient and modern, unspoiled tidal flats are these days becoming difficult to find.

Notes (P.12)
[1] Environmental damage caused by the construction of facilities to attract more tourists, such as hotels, is becoming a serious problem.

▲ ④ Currents around Japan

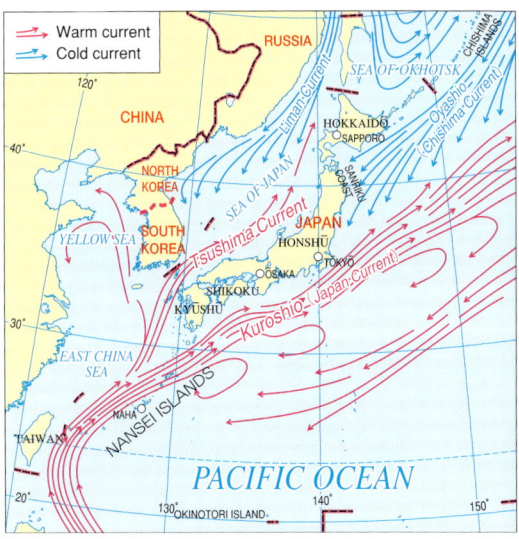

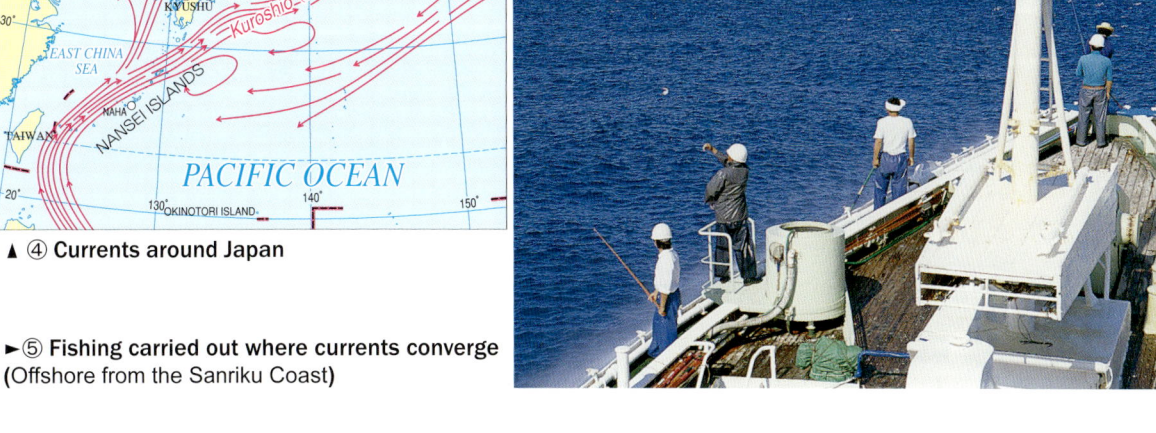

►⑤ Fishing carried out where currents converge (Offshore from the Sanriku Coast)

Japan's surrounding seas

The natural environment of Japan is influenced by the several ocean currents that flow around the nation's coasts. The warm Kuroshio flows from the south and heads north along the southern coast of the Japanese archipelago, then after running parallel with the Bōsō Peninsula, veers away from the land into the Pacific Ocean. The coasts where the Kuroshio flows close offshore are warmer than average even during the winter. Frost-free places such as the Bōsō Peninsula are suitable for early springtime flower cultivation.

A branch of the Kuroshio flows along the western side of Kyūshū, enters the Sea of Japan, and reaches Hokkaidō in the form of the Tsushima Current. When cold winter winds from Siberia cross the Tsushima Current, they take up evaporated water from the sea, and when the moisture-laden air rises on contact with the Japanese mountains, heavy snowfalls occur.

In contrast, the cold Oyashio (Chishima Current) flows southwards from the Chishima Islands chain, north of Japan, and runs parallel with the Sanriku Coast. When warm summer winds blow from the Pacific into Hokkaidō, they cross this cold current, and the air, rapidly cooled down by the cold current, becomes heavy with fog.

There are many different species of fish in the warm sea currents. In addition, since there is a large amount of plankton that fish feed on in the cold currents, many fish gather in the zone where the two currents meet (the *Shiozakai*). The northwest Pacific where these two currents meet is thus a world famous fishing ground. On the seabed, a flat area that is less than 200m deep is called a continental shelf. The Japanese archipelago is surrounded by these continental shelves. While around Honshū they can be 20-30km wide, in the East China Sea west of Kyūshū, the continental shelf is as wide as 500km or more. Neighboring countries are taking a keen interest in these continental shelves not only for their abundant fish resources, but also because of the possible existence below the shelf of valuable resources such as natural gas.

▲ ① **Four seasons in Kyōto (Kiyomizu-dera Temple)**　Cherry blossoms in spring, green leaves in summer, red leaves in autumn, and snow in winter: the beauty of nature in Japan changes with the season.

3 Climate of Japan

Japan, a country with four seasons

　Japan is a country where the seasons are very clearly defined. Although the timing of spring, summer, autumn and winter varies slightly depending on the year in question, the people of Japan can be certain that the four seasons will come round one after the other every year. One can enjoy the changes of the seasons since the same scenery takes on a quite different appearance in each season,[1] as shown in Figure 1.

The four seasons of Japan, from winter to summer

　A major factor that brings about the change of seasons in Japan is the seasonal wind (monsoon), which blows from opposite directions in the winter and summer. As winter arrives, a low-temperature Siberian anticyclone is formed above Mongolia and Russia in the Eastern part of the Eurasian continent. The cold air produced in this area becomes a Northwest wind that blows eastwards over Japan. This seasonal wind travels all the way to the Nansei Islands, bringing with it cold weather to all regions of Japan. As a result, temperatures in Asahikawa, Obihiro and other parts of Hokkaidō are even lower than in Helsinki in Finland or Oslo in Norway, even though these cities in Northern Europe are much more northerly than Hokkaidō in terms of latitude.

　With the arrival of spring, the Northwest wind becomes weaker, the temperature starts to rise, and animals that have been hibernating during winter revive while plants begin to grow again. Cherry blossoms begin to bloom in the south and the cherry flowering season moves northwards, indicating that spring on the Japanese archipelago is heading north. This is also the time when there is much work on the farm, with the land being prepared for rice transplanting and other kinds of cultivation.

　Before spring turns into summer, the rainy season (*baiu*) arrives. This is caused by a *baiu* front created over the Japanese archipelago when cold air from the Arctic and Siberia clashes with warm air from the equatorial regions. The result is about a month of ongoing drizzly rain. As the *baiu* front moves northwards and arround the time when the drizzle behind it

---

Notes (P.14)
[1] A pattern of four seasons, similar to that in Japan, is seen in many temperate areas around the world.

▶② **Process of seasonal change in precipitation** (Japan Climate Map, 1990) Seasonal winds from the ocean bring with them maritime air. When the air encounters the mountain ranges, it rises, and there are heavy falls of rain or snow. In summer the effect of the seasonal winds is smaller than in winter, and rain can come from various sources such as the *baiu* front and typhoons.

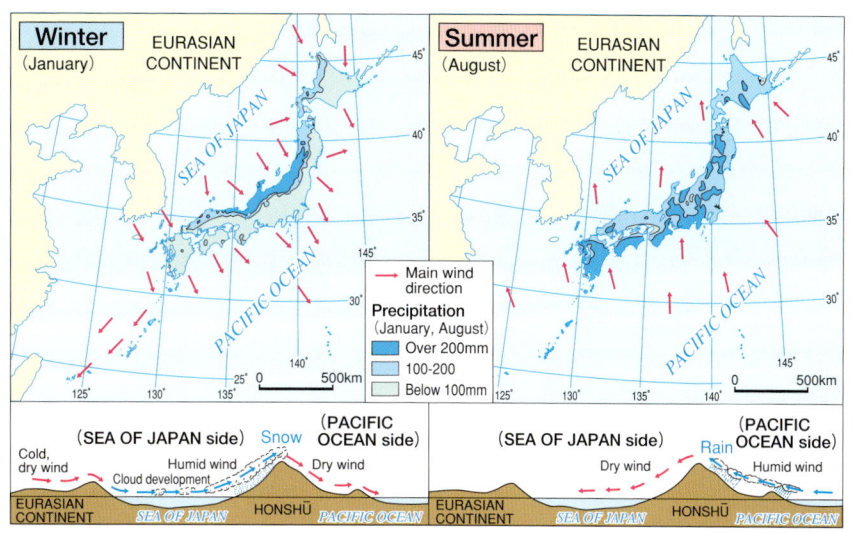

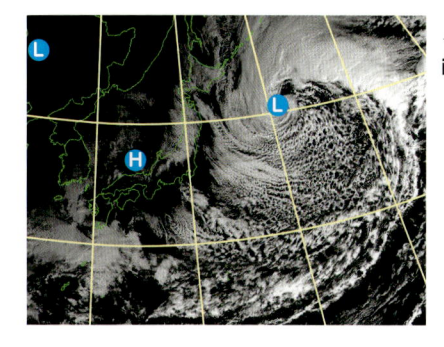

◀③ **Clouds when a typhoon is developing** (August)

▶④ **Rainy days are continuous during the *baiu* season** (Tōkyō, June)

clears up, torrential rain can fall in Kyūshū, Chūgoku and Shikoku Regions. However, while in some ways unwelcome, this type of rain provides an essential source of water for use in hydroelectricity generation and in farming, besides providing drinking water.

The four seasons of Japan, from summer to winter

Once the drizzly rain associated with the *baiu* front has cleared up, a high-temperature summer monsoon from Pacific high pressure becomes dominant, and summer truly gets under way in Japan. Sunny days become more frequent and the temperature rises quickly, sometime exceeding 35 degrees. Looking at the average temperature in August, we can see that summer in Ōsaka is even hotter than summer in Honolulu, Hawaii. Not surprisingly, summer is the season when the most number of people travel to the mountains or to the sea.

Towards the second half of August, Japan is visited by typhoons from the southern tropical seas. The violent winds and torrential rain brought by typhoons cause great damage to farm products, just at the time when they are about to be harvested, and cause floods and landslides that can result in loss of lives. Between August and September, in addition to typhoons there are also autumn rains similar to the drizzly rain *baiu* and as a result, the precipitation becomes quite high.

As autumn slips in, the wind changes back into the north wind and the weather turns cooler. Temperatures begin to fall as the summer heat subsides. In Hokkaidō and areas with high mountains the leaves start to change color. In contrast to cherry blossoms, autumn leaves first appear in the north and the change in color moves gradually southwards, indicating that cold weather is spreading from north to south.

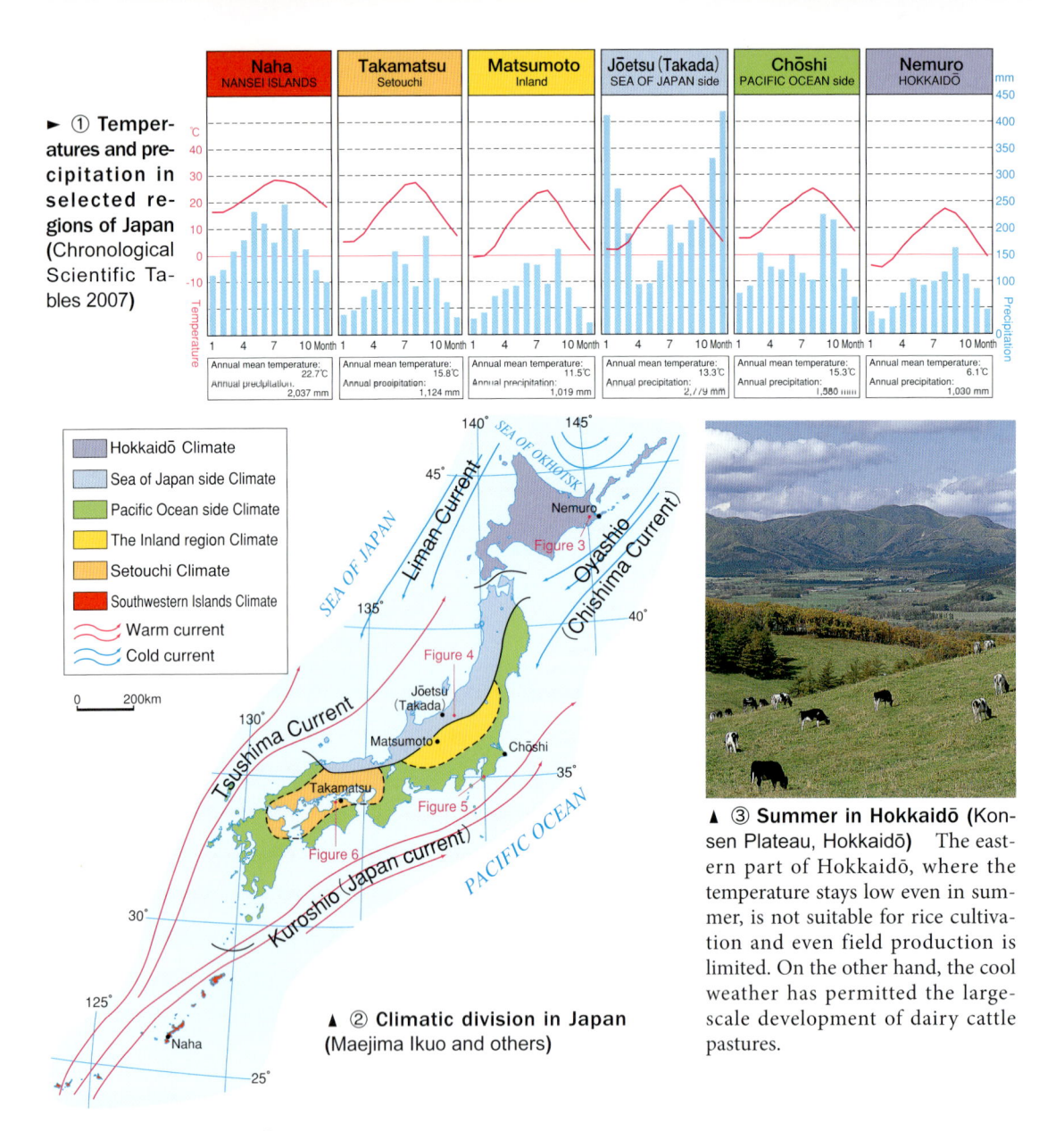

► ① Temperatures and precipitation in selected regions of Japan (Chronological Scientific Tables 2007)

Naha NANSEI ISLANDS	Takamatsu Setouchi	Matsumoto Inland	Jōetsu (Takada) SEA OF JAPAN side	Chōshi PACIFIC OCEAN side	Nemuro HOKKAIDŌ
Annual mean temperature: 22.7°C	Annual mean temperature: 15.8°C	Annual mean temperature: 11.5°C	Annual mean temperature: 13.3°C	Annual mean temperature: 15.3°C	Annual mean temperature: 6.1°C
Annual precipitation: 2,037 mm	Annual precipitation: 1,124 mm	Annual precipitation: 1,019 mm	Annual precipitation: 2,779 mm	Annual precipitation: 1,580 mm	Annual precipitation: 1,030 mm

▲ ② Climatic division in Japan (Maejima Ikuo and others)

▲ ③ **Summer in Hokkaidō (Konsen Plateau, Hokkaidō)** The eastern part of Hokkaidō, where the temperature stays low even in summer, is not suitable for rice cultivation and even field production is limited. On the other hand, the cool weather has permitted the large-scale development of dairy cattle pastures.

Climatic divisions of Japan

Since the Japanese archipelago covers a long latitudinal expanse from north to south, the climate differs between the northern regions and southern ones. As shown in Figure 1, the average January temperature in Naha, Okinawa, is over 15 degrees, whereas in Nemuro, Hokkaidō, it is lower than minus 4 degrees. Furthermore, the mountain ranges that run north-south along the length of the Archipelago act as a barrier, and this causes variations in the amount of rain and snow among the west side of Japan, the inland regions and the east side. Based on these features, Japan's climate can be divided into six categories as shown in Figure 2.

The "Hokkaidō climate" combines an extremely cold winter with a fairly hot summer (except for the eastern part of the island). The difference in temperature between summer and winter is therefore quite large. Because of the cold Oyashio (Chishima Current), which flows near the Pacific shore on the eastern side of Hokkaidō, temperatures in these areas do not rise much even in summer, and there are frequent dense fogs that block out sunlight. As a result, this area spends many cool summer days. In addition, Hokkaidō does not have a

▲④ **February in the Sea of Japan area** (Tōkamachi City, Niigata Prefecture) Snow is shoveled to the sides of the roads to allow cars to pass.

◄⑤ **February in the Pacific area** (Minamibōsō City, Chiba Prefecture) Thanks to a large number of sunny and warm days even in winter, flower and vegetable cultivation flourishes in this part of Japan.

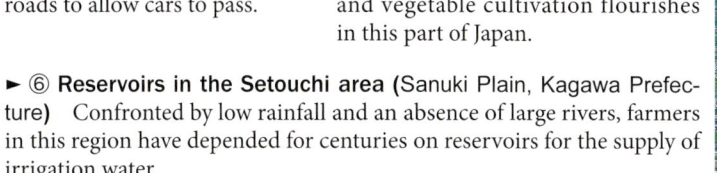

► ⑥ **Reservoirs in the Setouchi area** (Sanuki Plain, Kagawa Prefecture) Confronted by low rainfall and an absence of large rivers, farmers in this region have depended for centuries on reservoirs for the supply of irrigation water.

clear rainy season resulting in low precipitation throughout the year.

Taking the mountain ranges - the backbone of the Japanese archipelago - as a boundary, the climate in Honshū can be divided into four categories, namely the "Sea of Japan climate," the "Pacific climate," and the two climatic regions (Inland climate and Setouchi climate) in between. The "Sea of Japan climate" is remarkable for heavy snowfalls during winter. In winter, the Northwest seasonal wind rises on contact with the mountain ranges and produces a dense cloud layer with lots of snow, but the summer remains dry as the region is sheltered from the Southeast seasonal wind.

The "Pacific climate" winter has little snow and many sunny days. Because the Pacific area is shielded from the winter seasonal wind, it is enveloped in dry air from the mountains and enjoys sunny weather. Precipitation is high as a result of the rain that falls during the *baiu* and typhoon seasons in summer and autumn respectively.

The "Inland climate" has little snow and rain, but there is a large variation in temperatures between summer and winter and between night and day. Since this region is far from the sea, it is not much affected by seasonal winds and therefore has little rain all the year around.

The "Setouchi climate" is a mild climate with little rain throughout the year. This is because the cold winter seasonal wind is blocked by the Chūgoku Mountains, while the summer seasonal wind is blocked by the mountains of Shikoku. Consequently, this region consistently suffers from droughts, so much so that for hundreds of years, reservoirs have been constructed to store scarce water.

The "Nansei-Islands climate" has a warm winter with plentiful rain throughout the year. Thanks to the warm Kuroshio that flows along the shores of the Nansei Islands, winter does not feel so cold. Another characteristic of this climate is that the period of hot weather following the rainy season lasts longer here than in other regions. This is also a region where typhoons can develop most before traveling northwards.

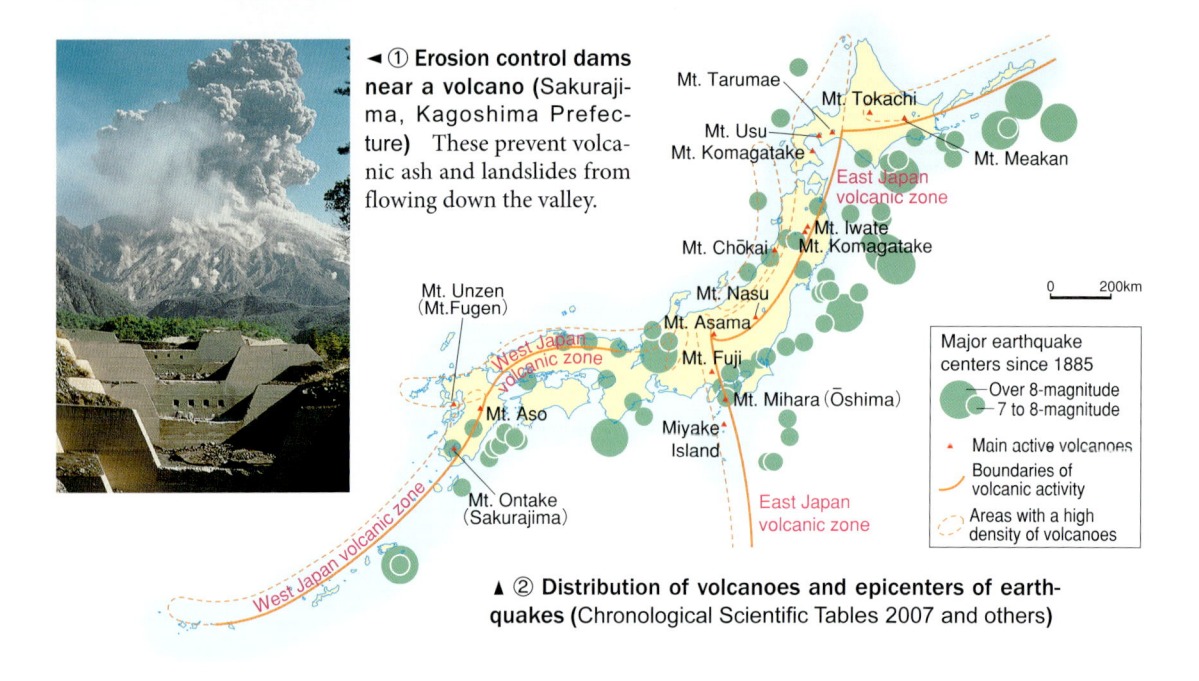

◀ ① **Erosion control dams near a volcano** (Sakurajima, Kagoshima Prefecture) These prevent volcanic ash and landslides from flowing down the valley.

▲ ② **Distribution of volcanoes and epicenters of earthquakes** (Chronological Scientific Tables 2007 and others)

4 Natural disasters and the endowments of nature

Living in a natural disaster-prone nation

As we have already seen, Japan is situated in a zone where there are several plate boundaries, and where the earth's crust is unstable. These plate boundaries are the source of many earthquakes and volcanoes. Japan, moreover, is also a country where extreme weather phenomena such as rainy-season cloudbursts and typhoons occur frequently. Japan is thus one of the countries with the highest number of natural disasters in the world.

Earthquakes and the resulting tsunami frequently cause injury and loss of life. In 1995, an earthquake in the south of Hyōgo Prefecture destroyed many buildings, and the fires that broke out after the earthquake killed over 6,400 people. The Tohōku-Pacific Offshore Earthquake of 2011 (also called the Great East Japan Earthquake) was accompanied by a tidal wave (tsunami) that claimed almost 20,000 lives. Around half of the Japanese population lives on low-lying land, where the ground is relatively soft. These lowlands are particularly prone to severe shocks during earthquakes and are vulnerable to tsunami. They are in other words quite prone to natural disasters.

When volcanoes erupt, they eject ashes and lava and threaten the lives of people in the areas that lie close to the volcanoes. The fine ashes that are carried far away by the wind block out sunlight and cause widespread abnormal weather. The eruption of Mt. Unzen (Mt. Fugen) in Kyūshū, in 1991 caused high-temperature volcanic gas and ash to rapidly flow down from the mountain, setting fire to the surrounding areas and killing many people. Later, the rain that followed the eruption caused large amounts of volcanic ash to slide down the slope of the volcano, causing problems for the towns at the foot of the mountain.

Japan is subject to many weather hazards. Floods resulting from cloudbursts during the *baiu* and typhoon seasons, and landslides from mountains with steep slopes and from volcanoes composed of soft friable rocks can create very considerable disruption. In addition, the strong winds and high tides that accompany typhoons can also cause widespread damage. Other kinds of weather hazard include the cold weather damage brought about by the *Yamase*, or cold winds, and droughts resulting from lack of rain.

◀ ③ **Farmland created from volcanic ash soils** (Okayama Prefecture) Land from volcanic ash becomes highly productive after the application of fertilizer.

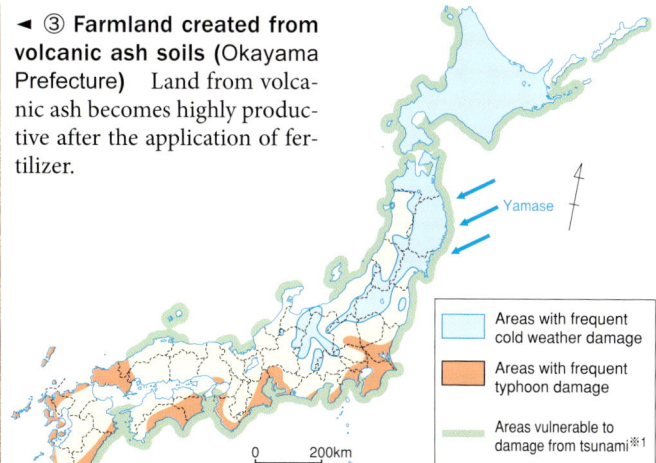

Yamase

Areas with frequent cold weather damage

Areas with frequent typhoon damage

Areas vulnerable to damage from tsunami ※1

※1 Areas that recorded tsunami of over 1metre since 1926

◀ ④ **Areas that frequently suffer damage from cold weather, typhoons and tsunami** (Chronological Scientific Tables, 2007 and other sources)

◀ ⑤ **Cleaning up accumulated volcanic ash** (Kagoshima City, Kagoshima Prefecture)

▶ ⑥ **Flooding in the city** (Fukuoka City, taken in 2003) Floods are caused by swollen rivers bursting their banks after heavy rain. At such times, river water spreads across the surrounding areas. As the paved ground in cities does not absorb water very well, flood water can accumulate quickly over roads and pavements.

Beneficial consequences of natural disasters, and the human response

Active volcanoes can cause injury to people, but they can also bring benefits such as beautiful volcanic scenery, hot spring resorts, and geothermal energy for power generation. Hot springs are created when underground water running through the cracks between rocks is heated by the magma[1] (molten rock) underneath the volcano. In regions with volcanoes, the accumulation of magma and mineral rich underground water below the volcanoes leads to the formation of a wide variety of useful mineral resources (including metals). Furthermore, the long-accumulated volcanic ashes turn into soil, which can be improved through the application of fertiliser and which now plays an important role in farming.

As we have learned on page 10, Japanese plains are created through a long process in which the materials produced by the erosion of the mountains are carried downstream by the river to the plain where gravel, sand and clays begin to accumulate as a result of repeated river flooding. This process still goes on even now, and can cause problems in plains that are densely inhabited. Japanese people have always tried to live with the threat of natural disasters. By understanding the kind of terrain that we live in and the kind of natural disasters that may happen, we can continue to live in harmony with nature.

Notes (P.19)
[1] Magma refers to the high temperature liquid rock material that exists beneath the surface of the earth.

Chapter 2
An Outline of Japanese History

When seen from the outside world, present-day Japan displays a number of characteristics that can be understood only with reference to its historical development, and in this chapter, we provide a brief history of the country, focussing on the main changes from prehistoric times to the present day.

▶ **Bronze bell** (134.7cm in height)   This is a type of bronze object that was made for use during the holding of prayers for good harvests, and is decorated with farming and hunting scenes.

1 Prehistoric Japan

The Jōmon period [1]

The presence of people in Japan dates back tens of thousands of years, to the height of the last glaciation when Japan was joined to the Eurasian landmass. This was the period of the Palaeolithic, or Old Stone Age. But the real history of Japan did not begin until about ten thousand years ago. At the end of the last glaciation, sea level rose, and Japan became an archipelago lying parallel with the continental land mass. People entered Japan mainly from the north, and the improvement of the climate enabled them to follow an economy based on hunting and gathering, and fishing. These people, who are known today as the Jōmon people, lived in villages, and inhabited Japan for several thousand years. The largest Jōmon site, at Sannai-maruyama, is located at the northern tip of Honshū.

2 Ancient Japan

The Yayoi period [2]

During the fourth century BC, a people different from the Jōmon hunter-gatherers entered Japan from China and from the Korean Peninsula, bringing with them knowledge of iron working and of irrigated rice cultivation. The adoption of a new rice-based economy led to an increase in productivity, and to the emergence of a more complicated society in which social class differences were apparent. The people who introduced these changes are referred to as the Yayoi people, and their arrival in Japan marked the beginning of the Yayoi period, and the start of the Ancient period of Japanese history. During the Yayoi period, western Honshū and Kyūshū began to assume more importance than hitherto, and this trend continued throughout the Ancient period. During the first and second centuries AD, internal warfar led to the emergence of a political entity known as the "Wa" which composed of many sub-units called "kuni". In very broad terms, these were the forerunners of the later provinces of Japan. The trend toward political organization gathered pace, and at the beginning of the third century, Chinese records refer to Himiko, the unmarried queen of "Yamatai-koku[3]", one of a hundred "countries" into which Japan was allegedly divided. Himiko, according to the Chinese records, enjoyed suzerainty over the "countries" of western Japan and acquired the title of Waō. By the end of the Yayoi period, the basic stratum of beliefs of the Japanese people had begun to emerge.

▼ **Keyhole-shaped tombs**   The largest of these ancient tombs, the Daisen tomb, is 830m long (the length of the actual mound, as distinct from the entire structure, is 480m) and 650m across at its broadest part. The base of the Shiō imperial tomb is 350m long, whereas that of the Pyramid of Cheops, in Egypt, is 230m long.

The Kofun, Asuka and Nara periods

Towards the end of the third century, there began a period of

---

Notes (P.20)
[1] **Jōmon period**   The name "Jōmon" comes from the cord pattern that was produced by a cord, or cords, being pressed into the surface of the clay of a pot before firing, pots decorated in this way being characteristic of the period. The Jōmon was a Neolithic or new stone age culture.
[2] **Yayoi period**   Until reecently, the Yayoi period was seen as a prehistoric period, but is now increasingly thought to be transitional.
[3] **Yamataikoku**   The location of this ancient state is a matter of dispute among scholars. Some maintain that it arose in Kyūshū, while other argue in support of the Yamato Basin as the hearth of Yamataikoku. Despite the seeming similarity of the names Yamato and Yamatai, the state of Yamatai infact arose in western Japan.

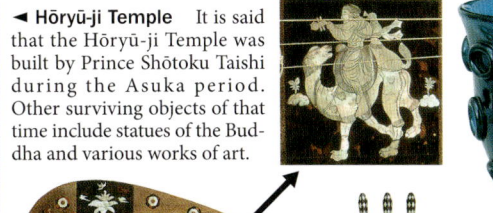

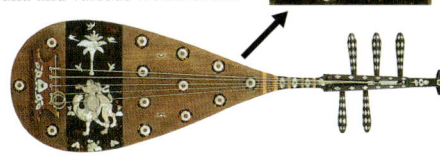

Hōryū-ji Temple It is said that the Hōryū-ji Temple was built by Prince Shōtoku Taishi during the Asuka period. Other surviving objects of that time include statues of the Buddha and various works of art.

A lute and lapis lazuli glass cup The lute made from Indian wood, is decorated with a picture of a camel. The beautiful glass vessel was also made in western Asia.

Japanese history that was characterized by the construction of large earthen burial mounds, and the Kofun or Tomb period, as this phase came to be known, lasted for about three hundred years. Huge tombs, many of them keyhole-shaped in plan, and of a design and size unparalleled elsewhere in the world, appeared first in the Yamato region, and then in many other parts of Japan. Gradually there emerged a society with the Yamato royal authority at its apex. This period is very important as the era when the Tennō or Emperor, first appeared, initially as Ōkimi (Daiō) or great king. Thus began an institution, that of the Emperor, which has been becoming unique feature of Japanese history as seen from the outside world.

The first capital of Japan was built at Asuka, in the southern part of the Yamato (Nara) Basin, at the end of the sixth century, and the Asuka period lasted until the early eighth century. During these times denizens from Korea and China brought Buddhism and Confucianism to Japan, while Japanese envoys to China during the Sui and Tang dynasties, on returning from China, introduced the Chinese system of government, together with important political reforms. As a result of these trends, Japan became equipped with a Chinese-style centralized government with the Emperor and the Imperial court at its apex. In this way, the early state of Yamato evolved into Japan, and for the first time, the term "Japan[4]" was used in preference to "Yamato" to describe the country. A network of straight roads, similar to those of the Roman Empire, radiated outwards from the Japanese capital. This period also saw the construction of the Hōryū-ji Temple, the world's oldest surviving wooden building, and a World Cultural Heritage Site.

In 710, the capital moved to Heijōkyō in the northern part of the Yamato basin, an event that marked the beginning of the Nara period. In this period Japan's legal codes, introduced from China were further refined, and untouched land was opened up for development. Moreover the newly emerging state set up a system of administration[5] that used the province as the basic unit of local government. This division of the national territory into provinces was to last for over a thousand years, and even today, echoes of it remain. Chinese thought and Buddhism continued to exert a strong influence on Japanese culture, and the impact of China may be seen in the treasures kept in the Shōsōin (the ancient treasury that belongs to the Tōdai-ji Temple). Some of these treasures show that in a certain sense, Nara, as Heijōkyō came to be known, was the eastern terminus of the trans-Asia Silk Road. Early Nara period historical documents such as the Kojiki and the Nihon Shoki, and the regional geographies of each of the provinces that appear in the Fudoki, compiled at the behest of the state authorities, are closely based on Chinese precedents. By contrast, the Man'yōshū, the oldest surviving collection of Japanese poetry, is entirely original, and indicates the strength of the indigenous elements of Japanese civilization. The publication of the Man'yōshū not only marked the beginning of Japanese poetry, but in linguistic terms is important in that it provides documentary evidence of the early use of Chinese characters to indicate Japanese sounds. This way of writing, known as Man'yōgana, continued to develop into the early Heian period, and gave rise to the distinction between the two types of Japanese syllabic script, hiragana and katakana. These scripts have become an essential part of modern written Japanese.

The Heian period

The Emperor Kanmu moved the capital to Nagaokakyō (Yamashiro province) in 784, and then ten years later, in 794, established the new capital of Heiankyō, at a site that lay to the northeast of Nagaokakyō. These moves were aimed at excluding the growing power of the Buddhist clergy and by reviving the legal codes, were intended to signify a reversion to the secular, Chinese-style central government of the early Nara period. It was hoped that by establishing a stronger and more efficient government, political control could be extended over the far north of Japan (Honshū), including territories inhabited by the Ainu people. However from the second half of the ninth century onwards, the aristocracy, and especially the powerful Fujiwara family, attempted to gain control of government, a trend that reached its peak in the first half of the eleventh century.

Notes (P.21)
[4] **Japan** Nihon or Nippon as the name of the country is derived from Chinese characters meaning of "Original of the Sun." The name "Japan" is believed to be derived from "Zipang", a term recorded by Marco Polo, and represents an attempt to copy pronunciation of the Chinese word for Japan.
[5] **Administrative divisions** See page 39.

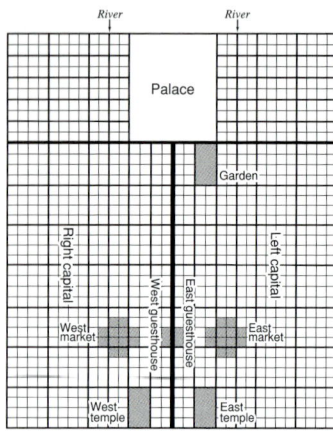

▲ **Heiankyō** The capital of Japan, founded in 794, and designed as a smaller and more orderly version of Changan, the capital of Tang dynasty China. The imperial palace was placed on the center of the north end of the city, and an 85m wide boulevard ran southwards from the palace to the main gate, bisecting Heiankyō (5.2×4.5km) into a "left" capital and a "right" capital. Most features of the original grid street plan can still be discerned today, although the central boulevard is much narrower than it was in the Heian period.

▲ **The Mongol invasions** The Mongols attempted two invasions of Japan, respectively in 1274 and 1281. The Kamakura bakufu pinned the invading forces to the coast of northern Kyūshū by constructing large defensive walls, while offshore, the small and highly maneuverable Japanese warships wreaked havoc amongst the large and lumbering troop-carrying vessels of the Mongols. The second of the two invasions was dispersed by a timely typhoon, which became known as the kamikaze, or divine wind.

Following the abolition of the practice of sending envoys (kentōshi) to China at the end of the ninth century, Japanese culture took on a progressively more Japanese character, and this trend was reflected in many artistic fields. In cultural achievement, it was the nobility who took the lead. A fusion of Buddhism and Shintōism also proceeded. Aristocratic women writers emerged, and created early masterpieces of literature such as the novel Genji Monogatari[1], and the essey Makuranosōshi of Seishōnagon. The Heian period came to an end in the late twelfth century, amid worsening disorder caused by conflict between reigning Emperors (Tennōs) and retired ones (Jōkōs[2]). In these increasingly lawless circumstances, armed warriors — the forerunners of the samurai — played an increasingly significant role. Heiankyō gradually became the city of Kyōto, and as such, and as the seat of the Emperor and the Imperial court, it remained the *de jure* capital of Japan until 1869, in other words for more than a thousand years. With the construction of Heiankyō, the frequent changes in the location of the capital that had occurred in previous centuries finally came to an end.

3 Medieval Japan

The medieval[3] period, that followed on from the 1,500-year period of ancient history in Japan, lasted for about four centuries, and may be divided into four phases or, as here, into two very broad ones, namely the Kamakura and Muromachi periods.

▼ **Kongō Rikishi statue** This statue represented a Buddhist deity, and was placed at the Tōdai-ji Temple gateway, to symbolically protect the temple compounds from the outside world. It is 8.4m high and is the biggest wooden statues in Japan. The statue fittingly represents the concept of brute force that was a characteristic aspect of Kamakura-period culture.

The Kamakura period

The earliest phase of Japanese medieval history was the Kamakura period, which lasted for about 150 years. While Kyōto remained the capital, the *de facto* seat of political power in Japan moved eastwards, to the town of Kamakura in eastern Japan. Here a government of warriors, known as a bakufu, or literally "camp office", was established under the military leader Minamoto no Yoritomo, who in 1192 took the title of Seii-tai-shōgun. From the historical point of view this period was of great significance as marking the beginning of samurai government. Although the political power returned to Kyōto 150 years later, government by military men was to last for the next for 700 years. What can be seen in the first half of the thirteenth century is a migration of the warriors of eastern Japan into the long-settled territories of western Japan. In the latter half of the thirteenth century, the attempted invasion of Japan by the Mongols was an unprecedented event in Japanese history, and amongst other things led to a waning in the power of the Kamakura bakufu. The rise of the samurai class exerted an important impact on religion and culture, and inspired the develop-

Notes (P.22)
[1] **Genji Monogatari** The Tale of Genji, as it is called in English, was written by lady Murasaki Shikibu early in the eleventh century, and is the world's earliest female novel.
[2] **Jōkō** This term means a retired Emperor. Some Emperors continued to wield considerable power and influence, even after their formal retirement.
[3] **Ancient and medieval periods** Japan was strongly influenced by the outside world during two periods of its history. In the Ancient period, Japan borrowed heavily from China, while in modern times, and especially after 1868, Japan imported ideas, institutions and technology from the West. By contrast, the medieval period was a time during which indigenous Japanese characteristics predominated.

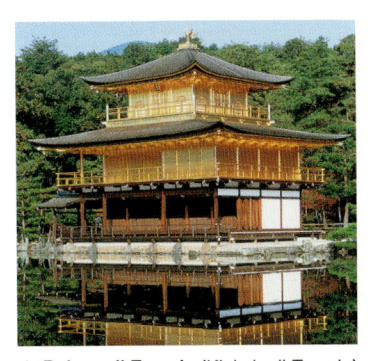

▲ **Rokuon-ji Temple** (Kinkaku-ji Temple) This famous and elegant temple was built in the Kitayama district of Kyōto in 1387, as a villa for the shōgun Ashikaga Yoshimitsu. The design of the grand floor is in the palace style of the Heian period, the first floor is the samurai house style and the top floor is laid out in the temple of the Zen sect of Buddhism.

▲ **Uesugi's Rakuchū-rakugaizu byōbu** Japanese paintings of this genre depict the vigor of everyday life throughout the four seasons, in the center of Kyōto (rakuchū) and in the city's suburbs (rakugai). They first appeared in the sixteenth century, and were done at a time when Kyōto was recovering its commercial prosperity. They depict amongst other things the lively festivals of Kyōto. Some of these, including the Gion festival, are still held in Kyōto today.

ment of new sects of Buddhism, such as Zenshū and Jōdo Shū, as well as new military genres of literature and scroll painting. Sculpture emerged as a vigorous art form during this period.

The Muromachi period

After the downfall of the Kamakura bakufu, strife broke out not only within the warrior class but also within the Imperial court, and Japan lapsed into a lengthy period of almost continuous unrest and civil warfare. (This, the Nanbokuchō period, ended in 1392). In 1378, Ashikaga Yoshimitsu set up a new bakufu in the Muromachi district of Kyōto, an event that marked the beginning of the Muromachi period. Violent unrest continued, however, and as a result of the Ōnin War (1467-77, between rival groups of Shugodaimyō, or feudal lords, accompanied by their samurai retainers) considerable parts of Kyōto were laid waste, and the Muromachi bakufu declined. The closing years of the Muromachi period are sometimes called the Sengoku period, also known as the "age of the overthrow of the higher by the lower" (Gekokujō), during which largely self-sufficient feudal fiefs appeared, controlled by hereditary lords known as daimyō or, in the case of the period in question, Sengoku daimyō, or provincial feudal lord. In broad terms, the Muromachi period can be seen as an age of violence and political instability with much civil turbulence and rioting. Yet at this time, substantial progress was made in agriculture and in commerce, the latter aided by the development of marine and overland communications. In Kyōto and Sakai, machishū, or communities of urban merchants, flourished and developed forms of self government. A similar movement could also be seen in the towns and villages of Japan. Meanwhile refined forms of artistic expression appeared in fields such as ikebana (flower arrangement) while performing arts such as nō and kyōgen became fashionable, making the Muromachi period an age of considerable cultural achievement and an era that helped to shape the way of life of future generations of Japanese people down to the present day. A notable development during this period was the fusion of cultures and customs of different social classes.

4 Feudal Japan[4]

Insofar as they were predominantly feudal ages, the Azuchi-Momoyama (1568-1600) and Edo (1603-1867) periods were much the same as the Kamakura and Muromachi periods. But the era that lasted from the middle of the sixteenth century to the middle of the nineteenth is distinctive enough to justify a four-fold division of Japanese history into four ages, namely ancient, medieval, feudal, and modern. In this regard, Japan departs from the conventional tripartite division of ancient, medieval and modern that characterizes the histories of many other countries.

The Azuchi-Momoyama period[5]

After the overthrow of the Muromachi bakufu and suppression of the Ikkō-ikki[6] riots, Oda Nobunaga, a

---

Notes (P.23)
[4] **Feudal period** This period of Japanese history differed from the medieval period in that its main theme was the unification of Japan under feudal rule. But we must not forget that it was also a time when many Japanese people became aware of Europe and its culture, and when Japan became involved, albeit marginally, in the emerging world-wide European sphere of influence.
[5] **Azuchi-Momoyama** Azuchi was a base of the powerful feudal lord Oda Nobunaga, while Momoyama, also known as Fushimi, was constructed as a capital of Japan by Toyotomi Hideyoshi. Fushimi was linked by canal and river to central Kyōto and Ōsaka as well as by roads.
[6] **Ikkō-ikki** This term refers to the rebellious, monks priests and farmers of the Ikkō (Shinshū) sect. They launched uprisings against daimyō rule in the fifteenth and sixteenth centuries.

▲ **Nanbanbyōbu** These are screen paintings that depict the coming of the "barbarian ships" (**nambansen**) and their captains, who were supposed to transport tigers and other strange cargo from exotic, far-off parts of the world. The paintings depict children who have come to see the ships, and women sightseers with their servants, hoping to catch a glimpse of the captains and their crew. They also show priests, crucifixes, and other religious subjects.

◀ **The lively atmosphere of Nihonbashi** This beautiful painting, which dates from the early Edo period, depicts the bustling and crowded life at the center of Edo, the most important city in Japan and, with a population of about a million people in the 1720s, the largest city in the world. Edo was a major commercial center, and a city of prosperous merchants and artisans. Nihonbashi was the starting point of five of Japan's major highways, which radiated outwards from Edo.

Sengoku daimyō, established political and regius control over most of the country. But his dream of bringing the whole of Japan under his control collapsed with his assassination. Nobunaga's attempt to unify Japan was carried through by his successor, Toyotomi Hideyoshi, who assumed power as *de facto* national leader in 1590. By means of a through survey of the countryside (the kenchi, as it was called) in 1582, Hideyoshi carried out a "sword hunt"(katana-gari) of the commoners throughout Japan (1588) removing weapons from those who were not samurai, and thereby consolidating a rigid and strictly controlled social structure. This enabled Hideyoshi to unify the country for the first time in centuries, peace and stability returned to Japan. Whereas Nobunaga had been tolerant of Christianity (which arrived in Japan in the 1549), Hideyoshi tried to ban it, but the coming of Christianity and of matchlock guns (first imported in 1543) formed part of a wave of contact with Europe and its culture, and European influences began to exert a strong impact on Japanese society and culture. At the same time, developments in Japanese artistic expression, from the tea ceremony to painting and the performing arts, made the Azuchi-Momoyama period a time of diverse artistic accomplishment.

The Edo period

In 1600, Tokugawa Ieyasu defeated his rivals at the Battle of Sekigahara and in 1603 appointed himself shōgun. He set up a bakufu — the Tokugawa bakufu as it came to be called — in the castle town of Edo and in 1615 he destroyed the Toyotomi family and brought Japan under his control. Thus began the Edo period, which apart from a few easily suppressed minor uprisings, held sway continuously until 1867, a period of over 250 years. During this period, at a time when much of the rest of the world was embroiled in warfare, Japan remained at peace. Edo-period Japan was characterized by a blend of centralized authority and local autonomy. On the one hand, the shōgun and the bakufu, based in Edo, exerted virtually unchallenged authority throughout the country; on the other, Japan was divided into approximately 250 han or feudal fiefs, with about a third of the country under the direct control of the bakufu. Each fief was ruled by a daimyō who enjoyed considerable freedom of action in the way he governed his fief and exploited its resources. This bakuhan (bakufu and han) system was held in place by a number of devices, including the practice of sankin kōtai whereby each daimyō was required to visit Edo and spend a fixed period of time there, paying court to the shōgun. The shōgun established control not just over the daimyō and the samurai class, but over foreign influences as well. Christianity was banned in 1612, and thereafter the Tokugawa shōguns deliberately isolated their country[1] from the rest of the world, making it illegal for Japanese to travel overseas and for foreigners (with the exception of licensed Dutch traders) to visit and reside in Japan. From the early seventeenth century onwards, the economy developed swiftly, helped by the bakufu and the fief governments, which introduced reforms that benefited and encouraged economic activity. Marine communications along the coasts of Japan were improved substantially, and a national market gradually emerged. Urban growth was an important feature of the first half of the period. Edo, Ōsaka and Kyōto became nodes in an urban network that included many castle

▼ **Ukiyoe and the painting of Vincent Van Gogh** The ukiyoe woodblock paintings of the Edo period exerted a major influence on European art, and on artists such as V.V Gogh (1853-90). The right painting of Gogh is a copy of the print of ukiyoe of Utagawa (Andō) Hiroshige (1797-1858).

Notes (P.24)
[1] **Edo-period isolationism** From 1639, the Tokugawa bakufu prohibited all trade and other contact with foreign countries, and foreigners were banned from visiting and settling in Japan. Exceptions were made in respect of some Chinese and Koreans, and Dutch merchants were allowed to trade and reside under strict supervision in Dejima, an island in Nagasaki harbor. During the eighteenth century in particular, the Dutch merchants in Nagasaki played an important role in transmitting European thought and technology to Japan, and it was through them that many Japanese learned about developments in Europe, and about European culture in general.

▲ The procession of the Meiji Emperor arriving in Edo Here we see the procession of the closely guarded Meiji Emperor, who had set out from his residence in Kyōto, arriving at what used to be the shōgun's castle in Edo, shortly before the city's change of name to Tōkyō.

▶ The Tomioka silk reeling mill The new Japanese state played a significant role in early industrialization, and here we see the state-owned Tomioka silk reeling mill, a "model factory" of its time. The mill incorporated machinery imported from France, and French technicians gave advice on the running of the factory. Over half of the workers were daughters of former samurai and wore Japanese traditional dress, kimono rather than western dress.

towns and port towns, and an increasingly commercialized economy, that rested on the sustained development of agriculture, transformed the countryside and brought about a rise in rural living standards. Many areas began to specialize in the production of particular products for a national market, a trend that continues to the present day. Economic growth led to the emergence of a diverse and lively merchant-class culture, which was taken up by the elite in Edo and then spread throughout the country. Elementary school education, became very widely established throughout Japan in this period. Meanwhile the centuries-old supremacy of Chinese-derived thought (including Confucianism) was challenged by the thinkers of the National Learning or Kokugaku school, who by stressing the importance of indigenous Japanese philosophy laid the foundations for the rise of Japanese nationalism that became a highly important force after the Meiji Restoration of 1868, and that lent strength to Western political ideas there were infiltrating Japan via the Dutch trading colony in Nagasaki (Japan was not quite as isolated from the rest of the world as is sometimes suggested). New forms of artistic expression, including the picaresque stories of the writer Ihara Saikaku and the woodblock printings of Utamaro, Hokusai and Hiroshige, also appeared during this period.

5 Modern Japan

Modern Japan

In 1853, Commodore Perry of the United States Navy sailed to Uraga, just outside of Edo (Tōkyō) Bay and forced the bakufu to open the doors of Japan to trade with the West. Unable to meet the challenge, and gravely weakened by internal dissent, the bakufu soon became discredited and quickly lost its authority. The bakufu finally fell in 1867, and the Emperor was restored to power. His transfer from Kyōto to Tōkyō (the new name given to Edo) in 1868 is referred to as the Meiji Restoration. Unusually by modern standards, the transfer of power from the bakufu to the new, modernizing imperial government, went ahead smoothly and without interruption, save for some uprisings in Kyūshū (the most important of these, the so-called Seinan War, was quickly suppressed). From the 1870s onwards, Japan selectively imported ideas, institutions and technology from the West, while preserving its own traditional culture and society largely intact, though with the potential for considerable change in the future. Contact with the rest of the world broadened and deepened, and the impact of the West, which accelerated swiftly, was strongly felt in politics, the economy, society, military matters, law, medicine, and learning and education generally. Industrialization proceeded apace, and was at the forefront of economic growth. Thus it was that Japan emerged as Asia's first modern capitalist state. The process involved the creation of an overseas empire. Taiwan became a Japanese colony following the 1894-95 war with China (The Sino-Japanese War), and Japan's victory in the Russo-Japanese War of 1904-05 was in due course followed by the annexation of Korea. From a geographical viewpoint it is important to note that various elements of the modern infrastructure of Japan, including for example, the road network and the settlement system are essentially continuities from pre-modern times. In 1869, following the transfer of the Emperor from Kyōto, Tōkyō became the capital of Japan and the shōgun's former castle (Edo castle), somewhat symbolically, became the Imperial Palace.

Present Japan

The Japanese people count years according to the reign of the Emperor (the year 2009 is referred to in Japan as Heisei 21). Since 1912 there have been three imperial reigns: Taishō, Shōwa, and Heisei. These reigns have encompassed a period of unparalleled change in Japan, including war with China in 1938, and the Pacific War which ended in Japan's defeat in 1945. The year 1945 marked as important a watershed in Japanese history as the year 1868, and heralded the emergence of a new democratic Japan, and the spectacularly rapid growth of Japan's modern industrial economy. A country employing the strengths of its centuries-old tradition while opening up an exciting and innovatory future — that is the essential feature of Japan.

Chapter 3
Various perspectives of Japan

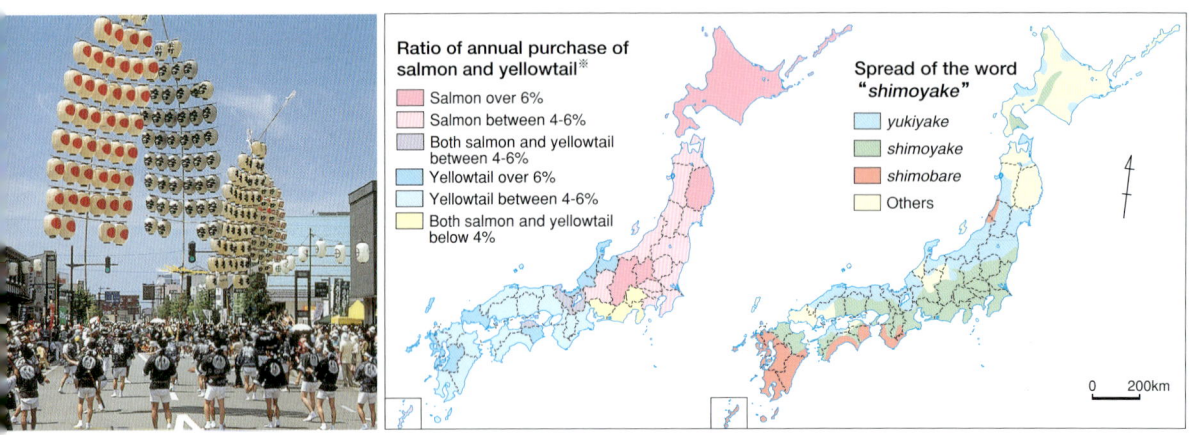

▲ ① *Kantō* festival (Akita City)   This is a festival to pray for a good harvest. The entire *kantō* represents an ear of rice, and each lantern symbolizes the straw bags for rice. A large *kantō* can weigh up to 50 kg.

▲ ② **Regional differences in food and dialects** <Geographic diagram of dialects, and others>   ※Ratio of salmon and yellowtail in one household's fish purchase in one year.

1 Life-style and culture of Japan

Differences in life and culture by region

The traditional culture of Japan has been created along with nature, economy and the everyday lives of the people. For example, some festivals such as the *Kantō* Festival of Akita have pre-modern agricultural significance. Moreover, annual events, such as the *hatsumōde* (first shrine visit of the New Year), the *bon* festival (in honor of the departed spirits) and the *shichi-go-san* (festivals for children aged seven, five, and three) have their links to the four seasons, and have been passed down from early times to people living today.

The different traditional life-styles and cultures that developed in the various regions of Japan still remain intact and serve to typify those regions. For instance, to ensure that they can escape the weight of the snow, the *gasshō*-style houses of Shirakawagō in Gifu Prefecture are built with steep-sloped roofs so that the snow slides off. In Okinawa Prefecture, where extensive damage is caused by typhoon, houses are built with roofs that are low and made out of concrete so as to avoid damage from the strong winds. In terms of the diet, salmon is consumed more in Eastern Japan, while Western Japan eats more yellowtale. This can be seen in Figure 2. Important regional differences exist in dialects, too. Thus, the word used in the regions along the Pacific Ocean, "*shimoyake*," (forstbite) translates as "*yukiyake*" (to get tanned by snow) in regions of the Sea of Japan. In these ways, depending on whether regions are broadly divided into eastern and western, or whether they face the Pacific Ocean or the Sea of Japan, geographical differences in culture and lifestyle can easily be observed.

▲ ③ **Japanese *anime* that are popular overseas (Los Angeles, United States)** In some overseas DVD and video game rental shops, Japanese *anime* have their own shelves.

▲ ④ ***Kaiten-zushi*** (rotating *sushi*)(Hawaii, United States) In countries that have no tradition of eating raw fish, *sushi* is becoming popular. This shop has a very similar menu to that offered by a typical *sushi* restaurant in Japan.

Initiatives to protect traditional cultures

With the modern prevalence of bread and meat in the Japanese diet, and with the importance of western-style clothes in contemporary fashion, the Japanese way of life in some ways has been substantially westernized since the Second World War. Since the 1960s, a mainly American-style way of life and culture has spread among the Japanese population, and the signs of this way of life include supermarkets, fast food restaurants, and convenience stores, all of which have become indispensable elements of everyday life in Japan. In one way, this transformation has served as a unifying influence among the various regions of the country, but in another way, it has also led to the disappearance of the traditional cultures that used to distinguish the Japanese regions one from the other.

On the other hand, strenuous efforts are being made to preserve especially rare traditional cultures. As we have seen, laws have been established to protect the historical heritage of Kyōto, Nara and Kamakura. Furthermore, steps are being taken to ensure that traditional handicrafts such as Kyōto's *nishijin-ori* (*nishijin* textile) and Iwate's *nanbu-tekki* (*nanbu* ironware) are passed on to future generations as industries that make excellent use of human skills.

Japanese culture in the global world

Japan has adopted aspects of various overseas cultures, such as *kanji* (Chinese characters) and Buddhism, but there are examples in which aspects of Japanese culture have been adopted elsewhere in the world. Japanese *anime* (animation) and computer games are popular worldwide. In Europe, the U. S. and Asian countries, Japanese *anime* appear on television and in cinemas, and bookstores across the world sell translated *manga* (cartoons) in different languages.

Japanese food is becoming popular overseas because it is considered healthy. Supermarkets across the world now sell essential seasonings for Japanese food including *miso* (soybean paste) and *shōyu* (soy sauce). Besides food, the following are world-famous elements of Japanese culture: *karaoke*; sports such as *jūdo* and *sumō*; and traditional forms of drama such as *kabuki* and *noh*.

In this way, Japanese culture has pervaded the world, and plays a role in the establishment of international friendship and mutual understanding. It is worthwhile for Japanese to work to transmit the culture of their country to the rest of the world.

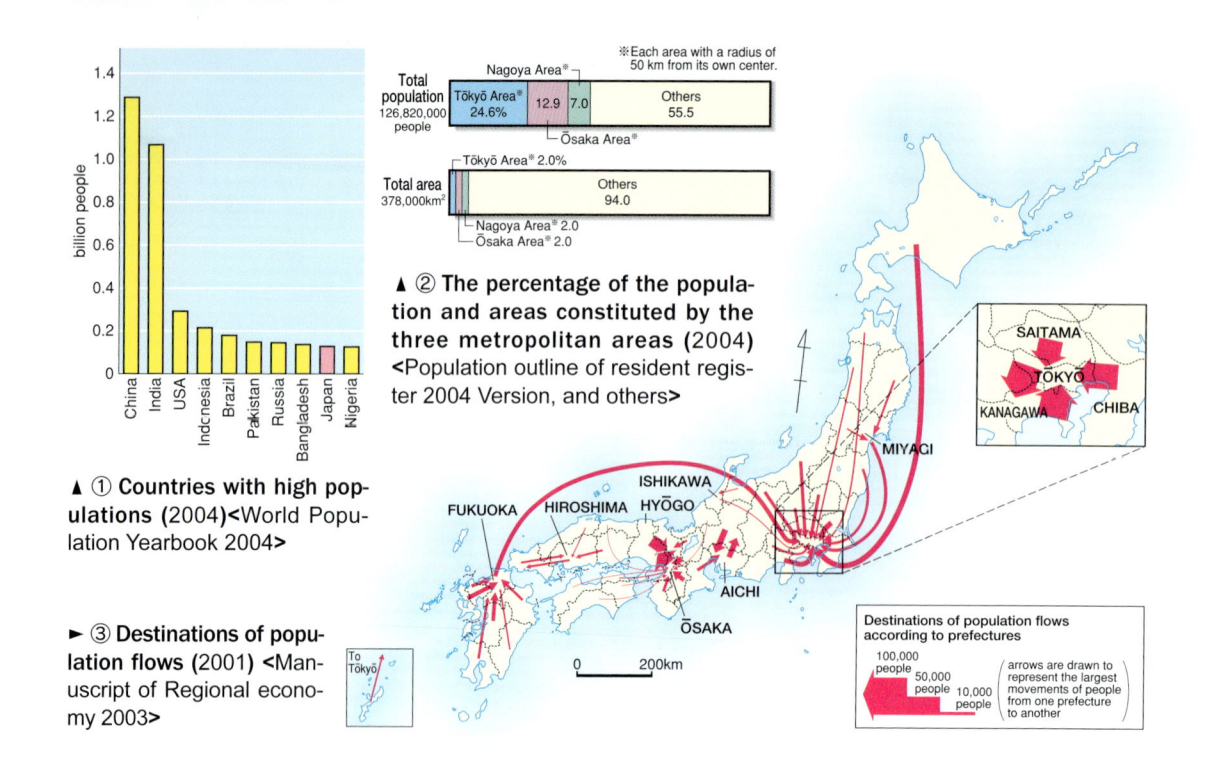

▲ ① Countries with high populations (2004) <World Population Yearbook 2004>

▲ ② The percentage of the population and areas constituted by the three metropolitan areas (2004) <Population outline of resident register 2004 Version, and others>

► ③ Destinations of population flows (2001) <Manuscript of Regional economy 2003>

2 Population distribution and population change of Japan

Population distribution of Japan

With a population of 127,060,000 people (2006), Japan ranks ninth in the world in terms of population size. Its population density is 336 people (2006) per square kilometer, or seven times more than the world average.

Japan is a mountainous country, and the population is concentrated in plains and basins which constitute less than 30% of the country's surface area. Moreover approximately 45% of the Japanese population lives and works in the three metropolitan areas of Tōkyō, Ōsaka and Nagoya. Along with their increasing industrial diversity, these areas are linked to other areas by *shinkansen*, expressways and domestic air services. Companies have tended to concentrate in these areas, attracted to them because of the labor market that they represent, and because of the presence in them of great numbers of affluent consumers. Beyond the main metropolitan areas, people also continue to crowd into the central cities of the Japanese provinces. These include Sapporo, Sendai, Hiroshima and Fukuoka. In contrast, there are regions of rural villages and isolated islands with extremely small populations.

Overpopulation and depopulation

Rapid movement of people out of villages and isolated islands into metropolitan areas got under way in the 1950s and continued into the period of high economic growth. As a result, the centers of the metropolitan areas became overpopulated, and high urban population densities caused many problems, with traffic congestion, noise and air pollution, and difficulties of garbage disposal being among the most conspicuous. Due to rising land prices, many people moved out to live in the suburbs, attracted also by a comfortable

▲ ④ **Trend of percentage of elderly population, by country** <2004 Trends of population, and other sources>

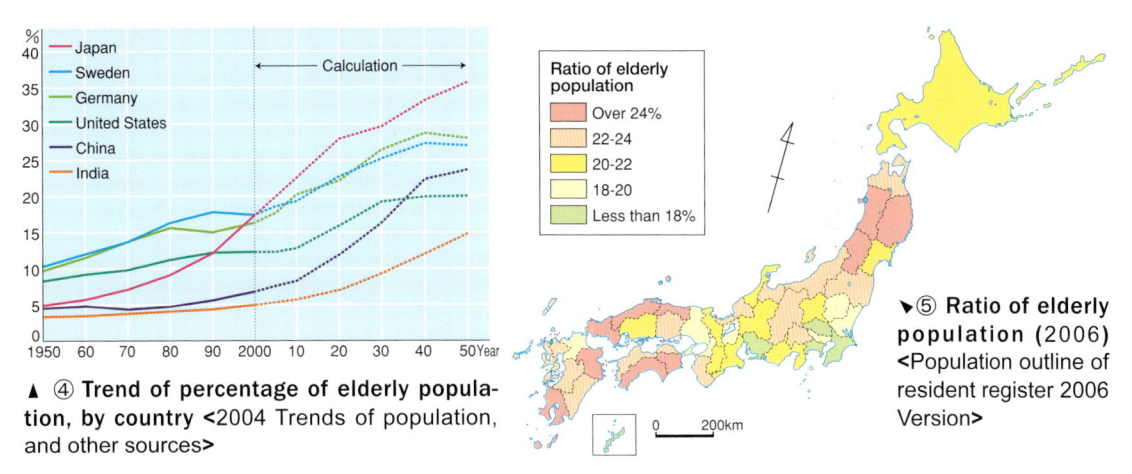

▼⑤ **Ratio of elderly population (2006)** <Population outline of resident register 2006 Version>

◀ ⑥ **Past and future changes in Japan's population pyramid** <2007 Trends of population> Those below the age of 14 are called the youth population, and those over the age of 65 are called the elderly population. The population between the age of 15 and 64 is called the productive population because it corresponds to the time in which people are most likely to be engaged in productive activities.

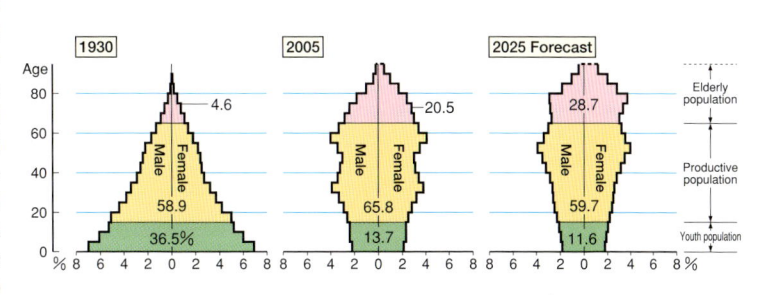

natural (living) environment. However, since the latter half of the 1990s, the vacant sites of former factories that relocated to the suburbs have been used for urban redevelopment projects, and city-center apartments have begun to appear. Thus redevelopment is drawing people back into the central urban areas and city-center populations are beginning to grow again.

On the other hand, agricultural districts have experienced outflows of young people who have moved to the cities for education and employment and who have not returned. With the fall in the village population and the increasing aging of the people who remain in the countryside, Japan's rural areas have increasingly lagged behind the main urban areas. In rural areas, maintaining local society is becoming harder as schools, shops and hospitals close down, while means of transport such as buses and railroads disappear. However, some regions that suffer from depopulation have engaged in community development initiatives involving tourism and the promotion of local specialties, and some, albeit in a minority, have achieved good results.

The progress of population aging

The population of Japan has been increasing at a favorable rate since the later half of the nineteenth century, and grew rapidly during the period immediately following the Second World War, a surge in population called the baby boom. However, the birth rate has been falling in recent years. While children are becoming fewer, the elderly population is increasing at a fast pace. Young people constituted 40% of the Japanese population in the 1930s, but the elderly now account for 20% and this figure is expected to rise. As a result of this trend, Japan is now having to confront the issue of an aging population. Among the problems associated with aging are possible labor shortages, rising expenditure on medical and nursing facilities, and increasing demands on the pension systems.

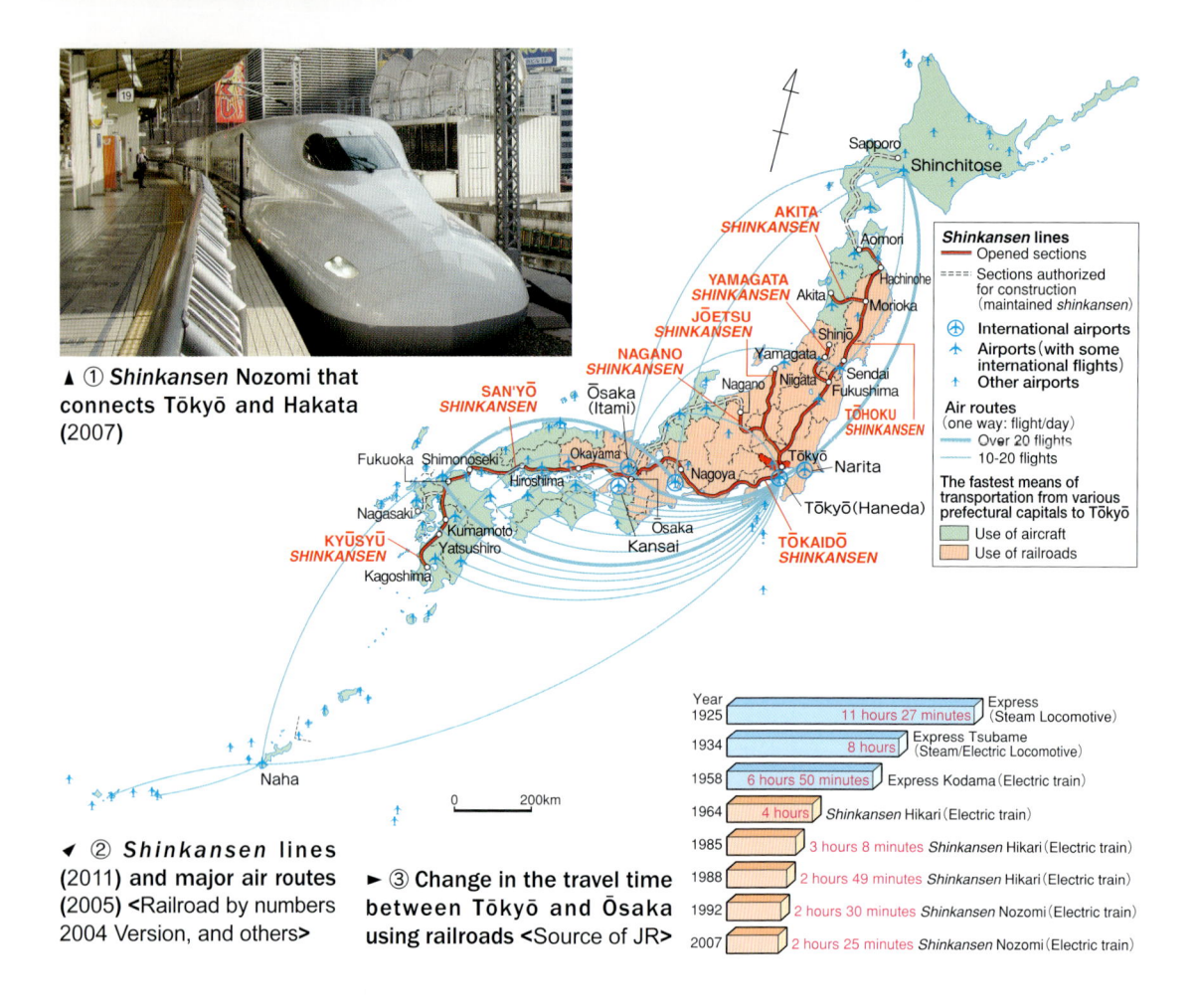

▲ ① *Shinkansen* Nozomi that connects Tōkyō and Hakata (2007)

◀ ② *Shinkansen* lines (2011) and major air routes (2005) <Railroad by numbers 2004 Version, and others>

▶ ③ Change in the travel time between Tōkyō and Ōsaka using railroads <Source of JR>

Year	Time	Service
1925	11 hours 27 minutes	Express (Steam Locomotive)
1934	8 hours	Express Tsubame (Steam/Electric Locomotive)
1958	6 hours 50 minutes	Express Kodama (Electric train)
1964	4 hours	Shinkansen Hikari (Electric train)
1985	3 hours 8 minutes	Shinkansen Hikari (Electric train)
1988	2 hours 49 minutes	Shinkansen Hikari (Electric train)
1992	2 hours 30 minutes	Shinkansen Nozomi (Electric train)
2007	2 hours 25 minutes	Shinkansen Nozomi (Electric train)

3 Increasing ties within the Japanese Archipelago

The development of transportation and our lives

Transportation plays a crucial role in the development of industries and in the lives of people. During the period of high economic growth in Japan, new rapid-transit roads and railways were built. These included the Tōmei and Meishin Expressway, as well as the Tōkaidō *shinkansen*, and thanks to these developments, the transport network improved at a fast pace. Provincial airports were also constructed in various regions across Japan and these are now engaging in intense competition with the *shinkansen* to capture passengers for long-distance travel. The improved rapidity of the transportation system has radically cut traveling times within Japan.

On the other hand, in depopulating regions, such as the mountainous areas of Chūgoku and Shikoku, some rail and bus services have been either sharply curtailed or abolished altogether. For the inhabitants of these regions, commuting to school and work, as well as getting to hospitals, has become increasingly difficult.

Automobile transportation and regional transformation

The predominant means of transportation in Japan is the car. As a result of the improvement of the transportation network, more people use cars, and this trend has had a great influence on the development of industries and on people's ways of life.

Along the expressways and railway lines in the suburbs, shopping malls with many

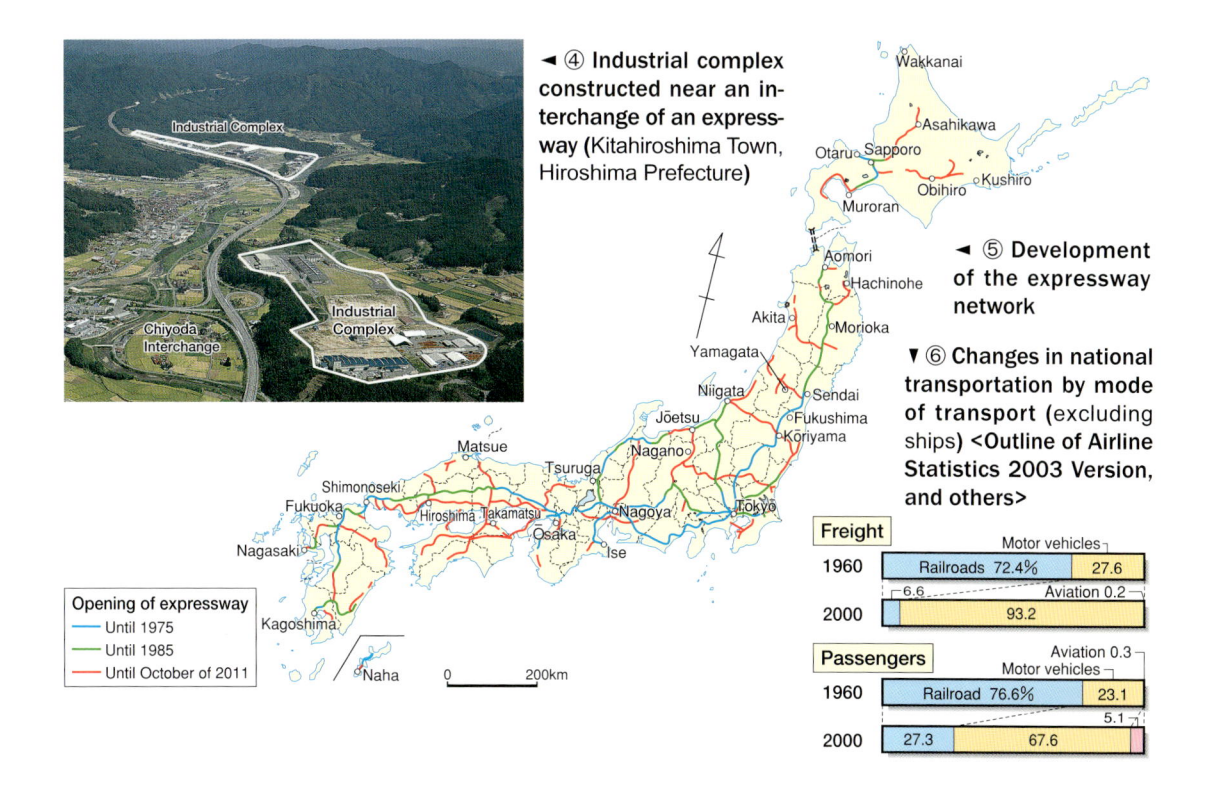

◄ ④ Industrial complex constructed near an interchange of an expressway (Kitahiroshima Town, Hiroshima Prefecture)

◄ ⑤ Development of the expressway network

▼ ⑥ Changes in national transportation by mode of transport (excluding ships) <Outline of Airline Statistics 2003 Version, and others>

Freight		Motor vehicles
1960	Railroads 72.4%	27.6
2000	6.6	93.2 / Aviation 0.2

Passengers		Motor vehicles / Aviation 0.3
1960	Railroad 76.6%	23.1
2000	27.3	67.6 / 5.1

Opening of expressway
— Until 1975
— Until 1985
— Until October of 2011

parking spaces have been constructed and these nowadays attract many customers. Conversely, many downtown areas in cities have deteriorated as they have become less populated. Close to road interchanges, where transportation is convenient and land is cheap, industrial complexes and distribution centers have been constructed. Because of better road and rail provision, some areas have experienced population increase as the presence of new factories has boosted the number of local job opportunities.

▲ ⑦ Cut flowers delivered by aircraft (Narita International Airport, Chiba Prefecture) Some 70% of the cut flowers imported into Japan are transported by aircraft.

The world and Japan tied together through transportation

As an island country, Japan relies greatly on aircraft and ships for the movement of goods and people. Improvements in the shipping that allow for cheap bulk cargo transport have made it much easier to move raw materials, including fuels and iron ore, crude oil and coal, and heavy items such as automobiles. In addition, air cargo is increasingly used as a means of transportation so as to maintain freshness of food and flowers, and to transport lighter goods like expensive precious metals, and electric machinery.

There has been a dramatic increase in the number of international air flights and routes that connect Japan with the rest of the world, and as a result, more people are becoming caught up in the large world-wide movement of individuals for overseas travel, employment and study abroad. More and more airports in Japan have international routes that connect with cities in Europe, the U. S. and Asia. However, in recent years they are competing against other large-scale international airports in Asia which are striving to become airline hubs.

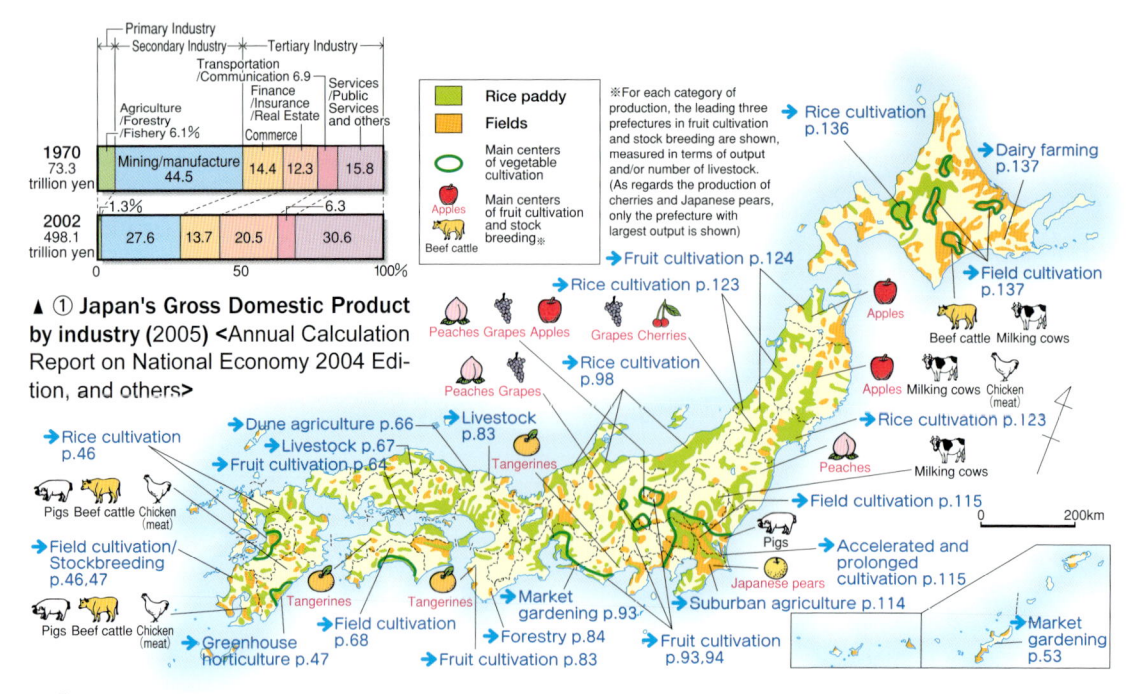

▲ ① **Japan's Gross Domestic Product by industry (2005)** <Annual Calculation Report on National Economy 2004 Edition, and others>

▲ ② **Agricultural areas and land use of Japan (2005)** <Stock Raising Distribution Statistics 2005, and others>

4 Industrial perspective of Japan

Industrial population of Japan by sector

Industry in Japan can be divided into three sectors: primary industries which include agriculture, forestry and fisheries, secondary industries which include occupations such as mining, manufacture and construction, and tertiary industries which include all other industries such as retail and wholesale trade and a wide range of services. By examining the composition of the working population of Japan according to industry, it becomes apparent that tertiary industries account for two-thirds of economic activity.

Characteristics of the agriculture of Japan

Rice-cropping is carried out throughout the country and is the heart of Japanese agriculture. As shown in Figure 2, more than half of the arable land in Japan is occupied by rice paddies. However, the diversification of the Japanese diet after the Second World War led to a surplus of rice. The government then endorsed a policy of reducing rice acreage[1] starting from 1969. Since the authorization of free rice production and sales[2], various areas have engaged in creating tasty brand-name rice, and this has led to fierce competition among localities where rice is produced.

As regards vegetable cultivation, the development of suburban agriculture in areas

---

Notes (P.32)
[1] Even in prosperous rice-cropping areas such as the Tōhoku and Hokuriku Regions, an increasing number of farmers are switching out of rice paddy production and into the cultivation of other crops such as soybeans and barley.
[2] Until then, under the Staple Food Control Act that was enforced in 1942, the government bought up rice from farmers and sold it to the Japanese population at set prices.

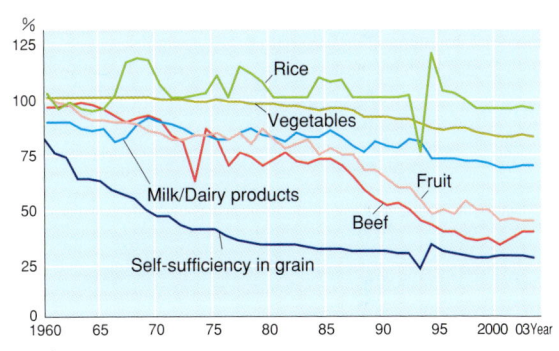

▲ ③ Change in the Japanese self-sufficiency rate, by selected agricultural products <Table of food supply and demand 2003>

close to metropolitan areas takes advantage of the proximity of large markets. By contrast, in regions distant from areas of mass consumption, farmers adjust shipping times and destinations according to market supply conditions and price. Similar strategies are followed by farmers engaged in greenhouse farming in Miyazaki and Kōchi Prefectures. While competing against cheap imported goods, the livestock industry in Japan has taken initiatives to improve its position with respect to the market by concentrating on the management of large-scale farm holdings, and by introducing new brands designed to appeal to the consumer. These strategies can be seen at work in areas distant from the metropolitan areas, in localities such as eastern Hokkaidō and southern Kyūshū.

The agricultural agenda and new initiatives

Agriculture in Japan has been modernized and its output raised by using large amounts of fertilizer on cultivated land of limited extent. Because of this, Japan is one of the world's leading countries in terms of crop yield per unit area. On the other hand, due to the high production costs of small-scale farming, Japan produces relatively expensive agricultural products, and is therefore at a disadvantage in the international market. Food self-sufficiency has declined for many years, and Japan has now become the world's biggest importer of agricultural products. The farm population is falling, and many regions are facing up to the twin issues of an aging population and a lack of successors willing to run farms in the future.

Farmers are adjusting to changing circumstances by switching to the output of tasty and appealing products that meet the demands of the consumers, and by using smaller quantities of pesticides and chemical fertilizer.

Standing at a turning point - the forestry and fishery industries

Generously endowed with forests where rare woods such as *Yoshino* cedars and *Kiso* cypresses grow, Japan has a logging industry which was once a thriving occupation. However, harsh working conditions on steep slopes, and an increasing inflow of cheap imported woods, have deterred young people from joining the industry.

For very many centuries, Japan benefited from the abundant marine resources of its surrounding seas, and coastal fishing developed on the basis of favorable natural conditions such as the convergence offshore of cold and warm sea currents. In more recent times, deep-sea fishing of salmon and trout was also a profitable occupation. However, because of the restrictions on fishing activity that arose after the introduction of Exclusive Economic Zones off the coasts of other countries, the Japanese fish catch is in decline. In recent years, there has been a shift from "fishing" to "aquafarming," and various areas are nowadays involved in fish and marine product cultivation and culture.

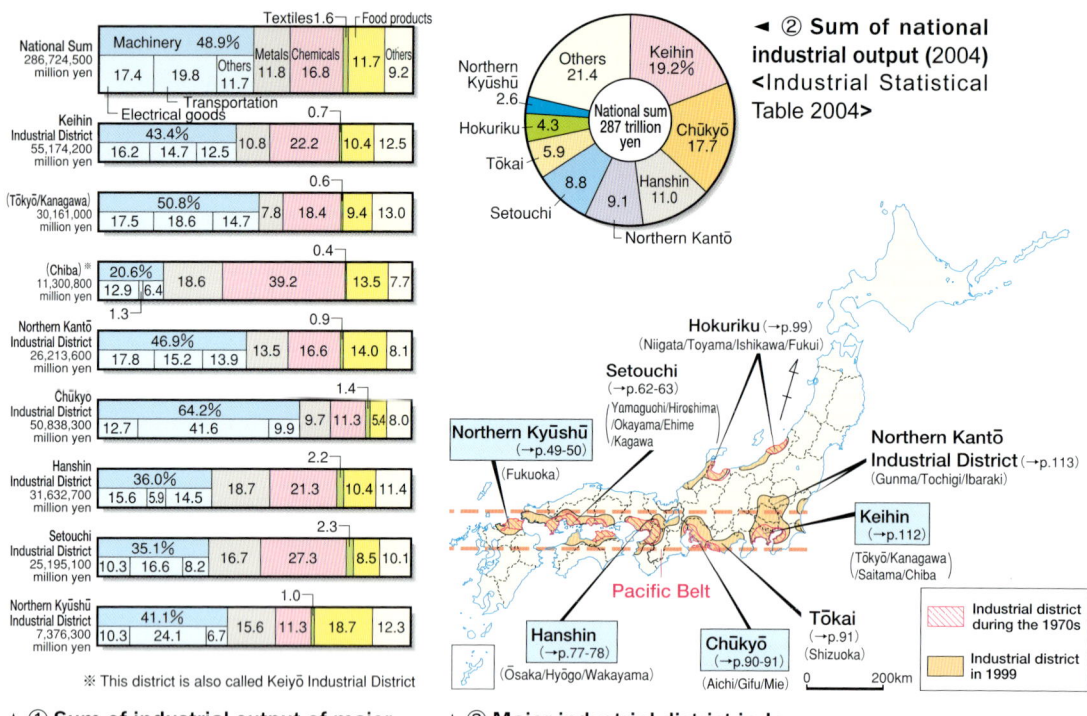

▲ ① Sum of industrial output of major industrial districts (2004) <Industrial Statistical Table 2004>

◀ ② Sum of national industrial output (2004) <Industrial Statistical Table 2004>

▲ ③ Major industrial district in Japan

The development and characteristics of Japanese industries

After the 1880s, textile industries, including silk-reeling and cotton textiles, grew rapidly. In the early twentieth century, the construction of the Yahata Steel Works in Fukuoka Prefecture marked the beginning of the growth of the iron and steel industry. After the First World War, four major industrial districts began to take shape. After the Second World War, the creation of large areas of reclaimed land along the Seto Inland Sea and Pacific coasts, and especially at coastal locations around Tōkyō Bay, was prepared the way for the emergence of a petrochemical industry that used imported raw materials. The result was the emergence of an axial region called the Pacific Belt, which contained the main centers of Japanese manufacturing. However, the oil crisis of 1973-74 caused the price of oil to rise drastically, and the relative importance of energy-hungry heavy industries began to decline. Meanwhile, there was a rapid development of the automobile industry as well as technology-intensive industries such as precision machinery. From the 1980s, there emerged a new generation of industries manufacturing ICs, electronic equipment and computer-related products, a category that is often referred to as high-technology industry. In parallel with this transformation, factories are dispersing away from the coast where transportation of raw materials used to be important, to inland areas where land and manpower are available.

The transformation of industry of Japan

Scarce in domestic resources, Japanese industries have developed through the processing of traded products, whereby Japan processes imported raw materials to make goods that are then exported. However, in the 1980s, a dramatic increase in the exports of Japanese industrial products led to trade friction between Japan and her main European

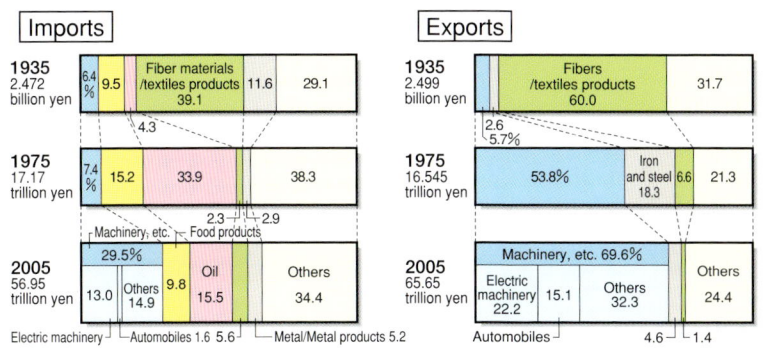

▲ ④ **Changes in Japan's foreign trade, by commodities** <Commerce White Paper, 2006, and other sources>

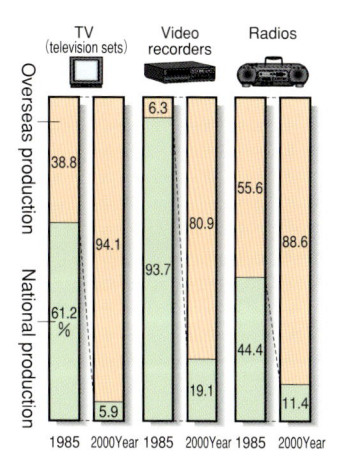

▲ ⑤ **Ratio of national and overseas production of major electric machinery made by Japanese companies** <Data of public welfare electric machinery 2001>

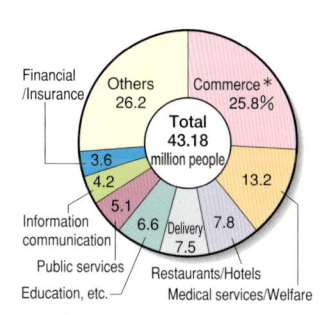

▲ ⑥ **Tertiary Industries in 2006** <Annual Report of Labor, 2006>
*Total of wholesale and retail sales

and American trading partners. In response, Japanese corporations began to build factories overseas at locations where goods could be produced and sold locally. In this way, Japan ceased to be a direct exporter of these products. The overseas relocation of factories was also encouraged by an abrupt rise in the value of the yen after 1985, and the latter half of the 1980s saw another surge in the construction of Japanese-owned factories transferring to other Asian countries. Soon, only headquarters and research laboratories of companies were left behind in Japan. This trend led to an increase in imports and also caused a hollowing-out of the industry with decreases in industrial production within Japan, and a rise in unemployment. To counteract this problem, Japanese companies are engaged in the invention of high-technology products that can be made in Japan itself, but that can compete in the international market. Such initiatives often involve close cooperation among manufacturers, universities, and local institutions. An example is Sharp Corporation's Liquid Crystal TV factory in Mie Prefecture which employs state-of-the-art equipment and techniques to manufacture highly complicated products.

Characteristics of Tertiary Industries

Tertiary industries are important in densely populated metropolitan areas and in the areas surrounding these regions. As an integral part of the process of modern urban development, department stores and speciality stores become concentrated at the heart of metropolitan areas, and city centers became crowded with people shopping. Moreover there are two other kinds of change. In Japan, the ratio of tertiary industries is growing in areas in which tourism, a type of service, is the major industry. More people than ever before nowadays work in the fields of information communication, medical services and welfare provision, and education.

Along with the diversification of people's lifestyle, and the development of transport and communications, Japan's commerce has undergone a substantial transformation. Following the emergence of new forms of commerce, including the introduction of 24-hour convenience stores and Internet and TV shopping, door-to-door delivery services have also assumed a new importance.

Chapter 4
The regional geography of Japan

Geographical perspectives and regional divisions

We have learned so far about the regional differences in the landforms and climates of Japan. These differences are what bring about both natural disasters and the benefits of nature. By now, we also know a little about regional differences in life-styles, industries and cultures.

Dividing Japan into several distinct regions helps us to understand precisely what kind of nation Japan is and illustrates the way in which people live, since it allows for the characteristics of each region to be seen from different viewpoints. Not only will this approach reveal how each region is correlated to others, but it will show what Japan and the lives of its people are made up of.

Dividing the entire area into several different divisions is called regionalization. Regionalization is a crucial process in mastering geography.

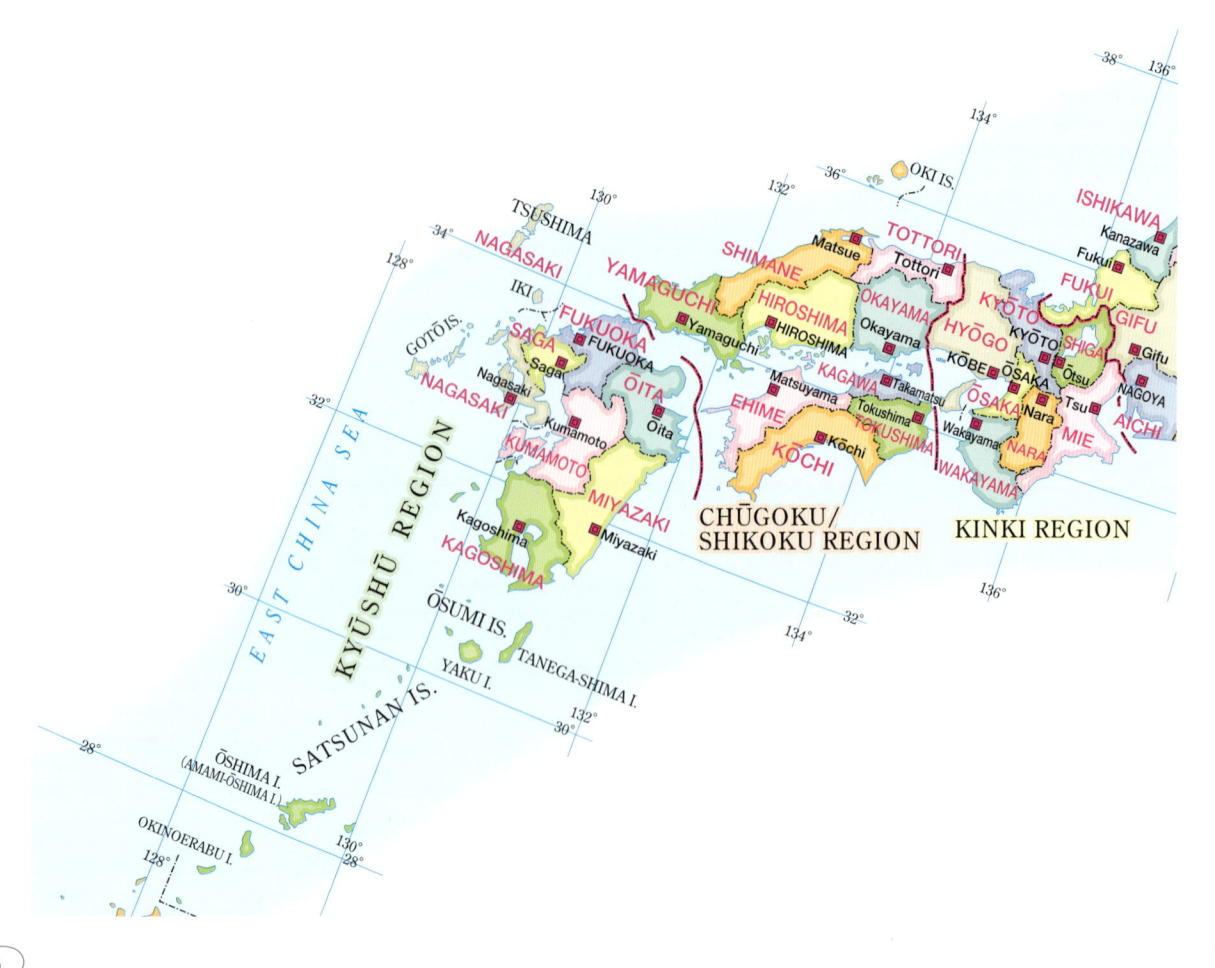

Regions and Prefectures

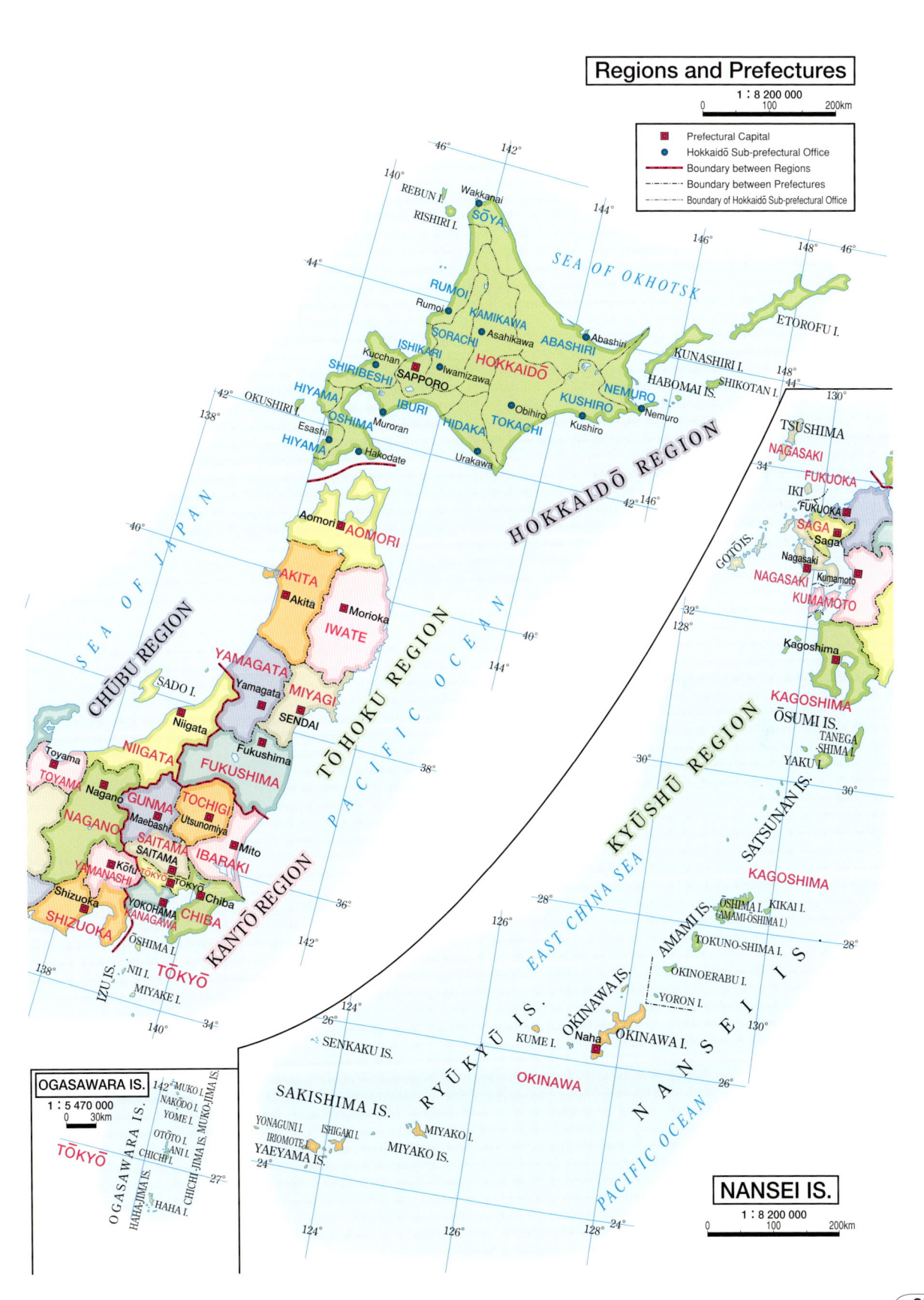

1 : 8 200 000

- ■ Prefectural Capital
- ● Hokkaidō Sub-prefectural Office
- —— Boundary between Regions
- ---- Boundary between Prefectures
- -·-· Boundary of Hokkaidō Sub-prefectural Office

HOKKAIDŌ REGION

Sub-prefectures: SŌYA, RUMOI, KAMIKAWA, ABASHIRI, SORACHI, ISHIKARI, NEMURO, KUSHIRO, SHIRIBESHI, IBURI, HIDAKA, TOKACHI, OSHIMA, HIYAMA

Cities: Wakkanai, Rumoi, Asahikawa, Abashiri, Kucchan, Iwamizawa, Sapporo, Obihiro, Nemuro, Kushiro, Esashi, Muroran, Urakawa, Hakodate

Islands: REBUN I., RISHIRI I., OKUSHIRI I., ETOROFU I., KUNASHIRI I., SHIKOTAN I., HABOMAI IS.

TŌHOKU REGION

Prefectures: AOMORI, AKITA, IWATE, YAMAGATA, MIYAGI, NIIGATA, FUKUSHIMA

Cities: Aomori, Akita, Morioka, Yamagata, Sendai, Niigata, Fukushima

SADO I.

CHŪBU REGION

Prefectures: TOYAMA, NAGANO, YAMANASHI, SHIZUOKA

Cities: Toyama, Nagano, Kōfu, Shizuoka

KANTŌ REGION

Prefectures: GUNMA, TOCHIGI, SAITAMA, IBARAKI, TOKYO, KANAGAWA, CHIBA

Cities: Maebashi, Utsunomiya, Mito, Saitama, TOKYO, Yokohama, Chiba

IZU IS., ŌSHIMA I., NII I., MIYAKE I.

KYŪSHŪ REGION

Prefectures: NAGASAKI, FUKUOKA, SAGA, KUMAMOTO, KAGOSHIMA, OKINAWA

Cities: Fukuoka, Saga, Nagasaki, Kumamoto, Kagoshima, Naha

Islands: TSUSHIMA, IKI, GOTŌ IS., ŌSUMI IS., TANEGA-SHIMA, YAKU I., SATSUNAN IS.

NANSEI IS.

1 : 8 200 000

AMAMI IS., ŌSHIMA I. (AMAMI-ŌSHIMA I.), KIKAI I., TOKUNO-SHIMA I., OKINOERABU I., YORON I., RYŪKYŪ IS., OKINAWA IS., KUME I., OKINAWA I., SENKAKU IS., SAKISHIMA IS., YONAGUNI I., IRIOMOTE I., ISHIGAKI I., YAEYAMA IS., MIYAKO I., MIYAKO IS.

OGASAWARA IS.

1 : 5 470 000

TOKYO, MUKO I., NAKŌDO I., YOME I., OTŌTO I., ANI I., CHICHI-JIMA, MUKO-JIMA IS., HAHA-JIMA, HAHAJIMA IS.

SEA OF OKHOTSK, SEA OF JAPAN, PACIFIC OCEAN, EAST CHINA SEA

① The seven regional divisions based on prefectures

Why seven regions?

Japan is made up of 47 prefectures. But the prefecture is too small a unit to use as a basis for dividing the nation into regions. We must therefore use units consisting of several prefectures grouped together. Each grouping of prefectures will be called a Region, and each Region will be studied as a unit. The seven Regions are: Kyūshū, Chūgoku/Shikoku, Kinki, Chūbu, Kantō, Tōhoku, and Hokkaidō. We will study the Regions in turn, beginning in the southwest and proceeding to the northeast of the arch-like Japanese archipelago.[1]

There are several other ways of dividing Japan into major regions. However, as will become apparent in the following sections, for studying the characteristics of Japan in terms of the perspectives of nature, society and culture, the divisions as shown in Figure 1 are the most appropriate.

These divisions have been used ever since the end of the Second World War, and the

---

Notes (P.38)
[1] Depending on the level of cohesiveness of the region, we may study these as being divided into 2 or 3 sub-regions.

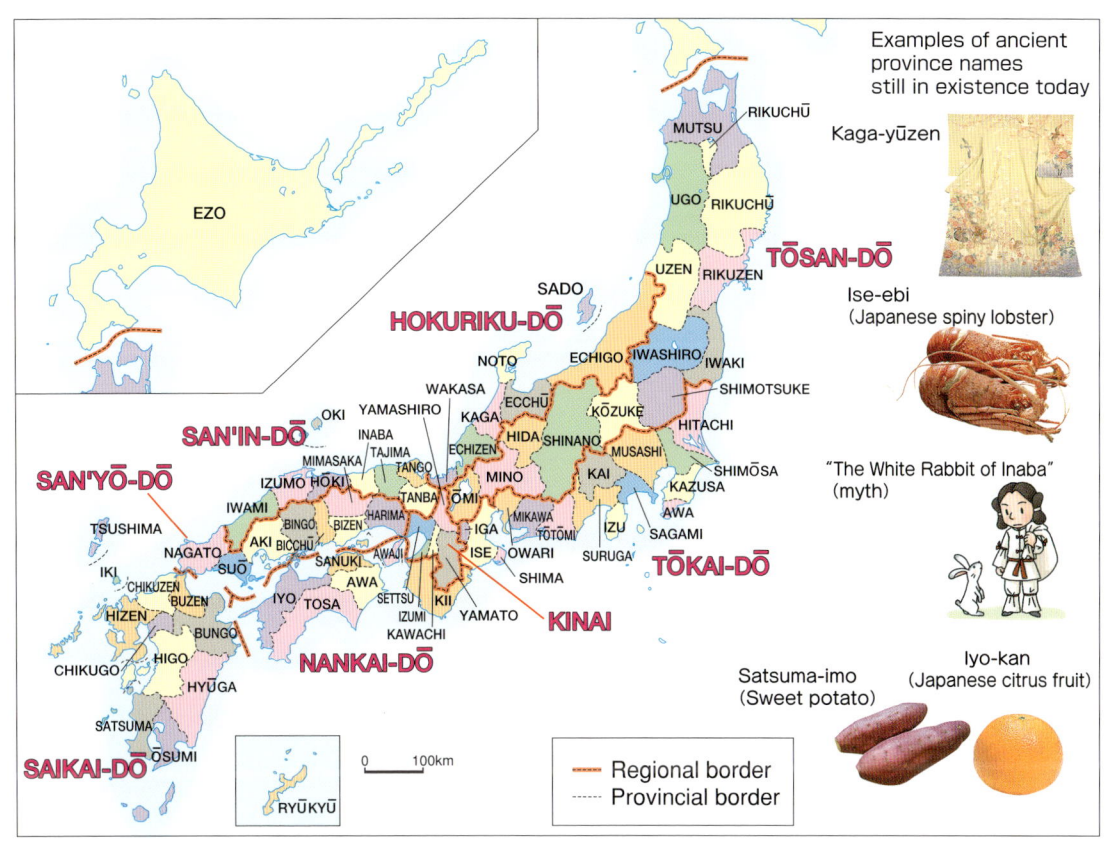

▲ ② **The old divisions based on provinces**　This map shows the regional divisions as of 1868. In 1871, *han* (feudal fiefs) were abolished and replaced by prefectures. *Do* (circuit) were divisions equivalent to today's regions.

basic regional pattern dealt with here is the same as the one that was studied in 1940s. The regions that will be discussed form a pattern that has become firmly established within Japanese society.

Historical divisions and provinces

　Regions were not used as a basis for studying the geography of Japan until 30 years after the establishment of prefectures in 1871. Up to that time, the basic region was the *dō* (circuit), and this term was collectively used throughout the nation. Figure 2 shows the pattern of the *dō*, and of the provinces that made up each *dō*. These divisions were created during the Nara Period (AD 710-784), Hokkaidō being added much later, in 1869. The *dō* continued to be used even after the capital moved from Kyōto to Tōkyō in 1869, though their use made it look as though Kyōto were still the nation's capital city.

　Why were these divisions, that had been used for such a long period of time, revised during latter half of the Meiji Period (1868-1912)? Interesting though this question may be, it is also worth paying attention to the names of the provinces that existed within the *dō* divisions, for these names are still used in the daily lives of the Japanese people today.

39

PART 2

Chapter 1
Kyūshū Region

Kyūshū Region

The Kyūshū Region, which is located in the southwest of Japan, consists of eight prefectures: Fukuoka, Saga, Nagasaki, Kumamoto, Ōita, Miyazaki, Kagoshima, and Okinawa. As we can see from Figure 2 on page 39, Kyūshū has roughly the same area as the Saikaidō, which is made up of 12 provinces. Why, then, is it called the Kyūshū (nine provinces) Region?

The term shū (province) when applied to Kyūshū refers to provinces (kuni) such as Satsuma no kuni, but can also mean island. Kyūshū means "the island of nine provinces." From Figure 2 of page 39, we can see that in former times there were nine provinces in this, the third largest island of Japan, and the name Kyūshū was used originally to describe the island.

In the tenth century, the islands of Iki and Tsushima were promoted from the status of "island" to that of "province." The Ryūkyū archipelago was not absorbed into Japan until the beginning of the seventeenth century. At the end of the twelfth century, the Ryūkyū Kingdom was established. The kingdom maintained relations with Japan, China and various Southeast Asian nations, and developed its own unique culture. It was taken over by the Satsuma han (the Satsuma feudal fief) at the beginning of the seventeenth century. The kingdom was abolished in 1872, and was replaced by Okinawa prefecture in 1879.

As mentioned above, Kyūshū is an old name that dates from the Nara period (710 - 784). When Japan came to be divided into "districts" based on prefectural areas, this name, which until that point had referred to the island of Kyūshū alone, was applied to the entire area of the Saikaidō. In 1900, its name was changed to the Kyūshū Region.

The Kyūshū Region accounts for only a little more than 10 percent of the area of Japan, but it contains an area with an extent of over 1,000km both in direction from east to west and from north to south. This distance is almost equal to that between Tokyo and the northern tip of Hokkaidō.

Reflecting its proximity to the Eurasian continent, the Kyūshū Region since ancient times has shared close links not only with China and the Korean peninsula, but also with various European countries. In the middle of the sixteenth century, Kyūshū became Japan's gateway for the entry of ideas, information and traded products from Europe. The existence of strong ties with Asia remains a conspicuous feature of the Kyūshū Region to this day.

◀ ① **Restored Shuri Castle (**Okinawa Prefecture**)** Shuri Castle, built in the capital of the Ryūkyū Kingdom, was burned down during the Pacific War, but was restored in 1992. Shuri Castle was registered as part of the World Heritage Site "Gusuku Sites and Related Properties of the Kingdom of Ryūkyū" in 2000.

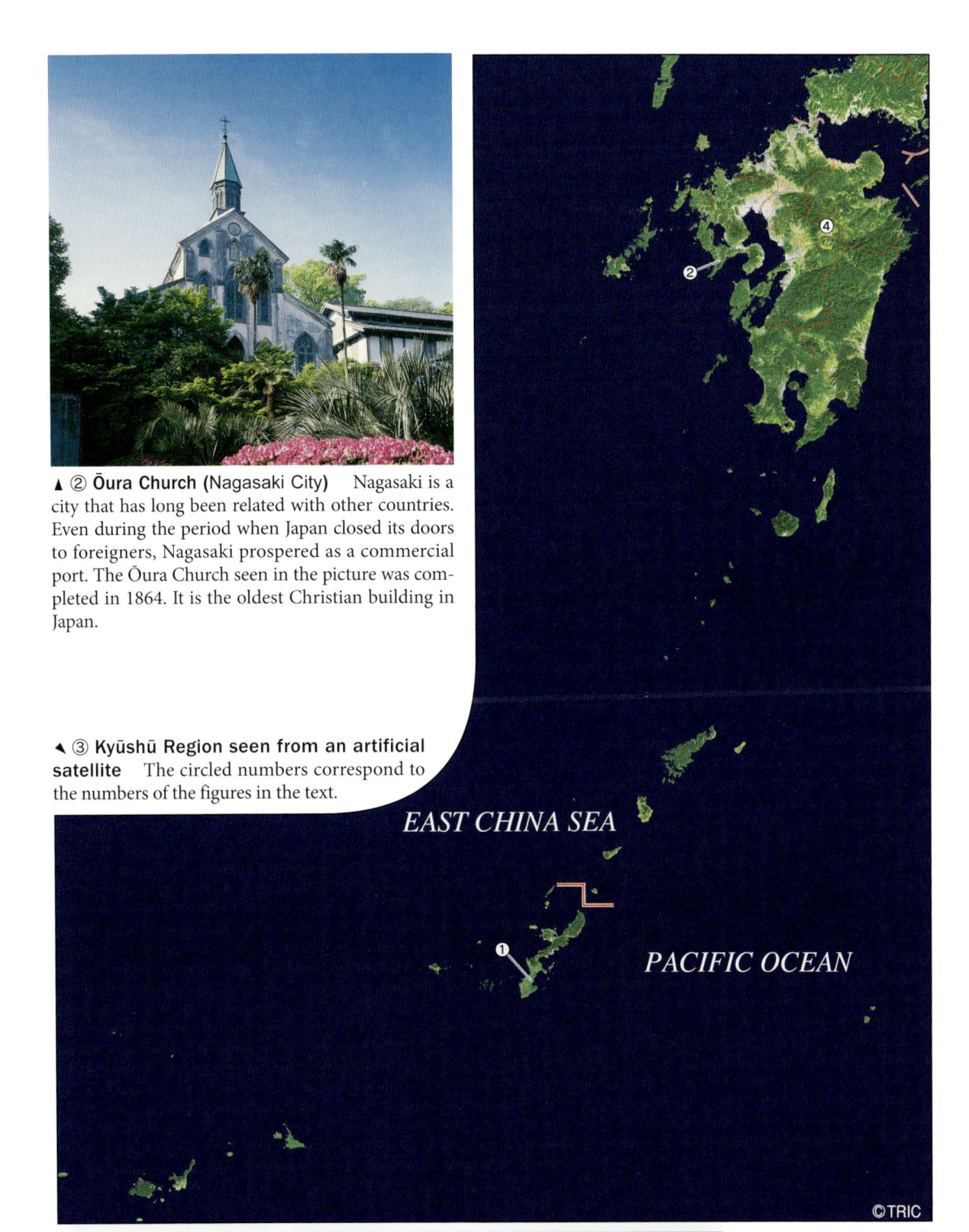

▲ ② **Ōura Church (Nagasaki City)** Nagasaki is a city that has long been related with other countries. Even during the period when Japan closed its doors to foreigners, Nagasaki prospered as a commercial port. The Ōura Church seen in the picture was completed in 1864. It is the oldest Christian building in Japan.

◂ ③ **Kyūshū Region seen from an artificial satellite** The circled numbers correspond to the numbers of the figures in the text.

◂ ④ **Mt. Aso (Kumamoto Prefecture)** A volcano with the world's largest caldera. About 50,000 people reside in the wide caldera that surrounds the central volcano, and the floor of the caldera is nowadays given over largely to agriculture and livestock husbandry.

41

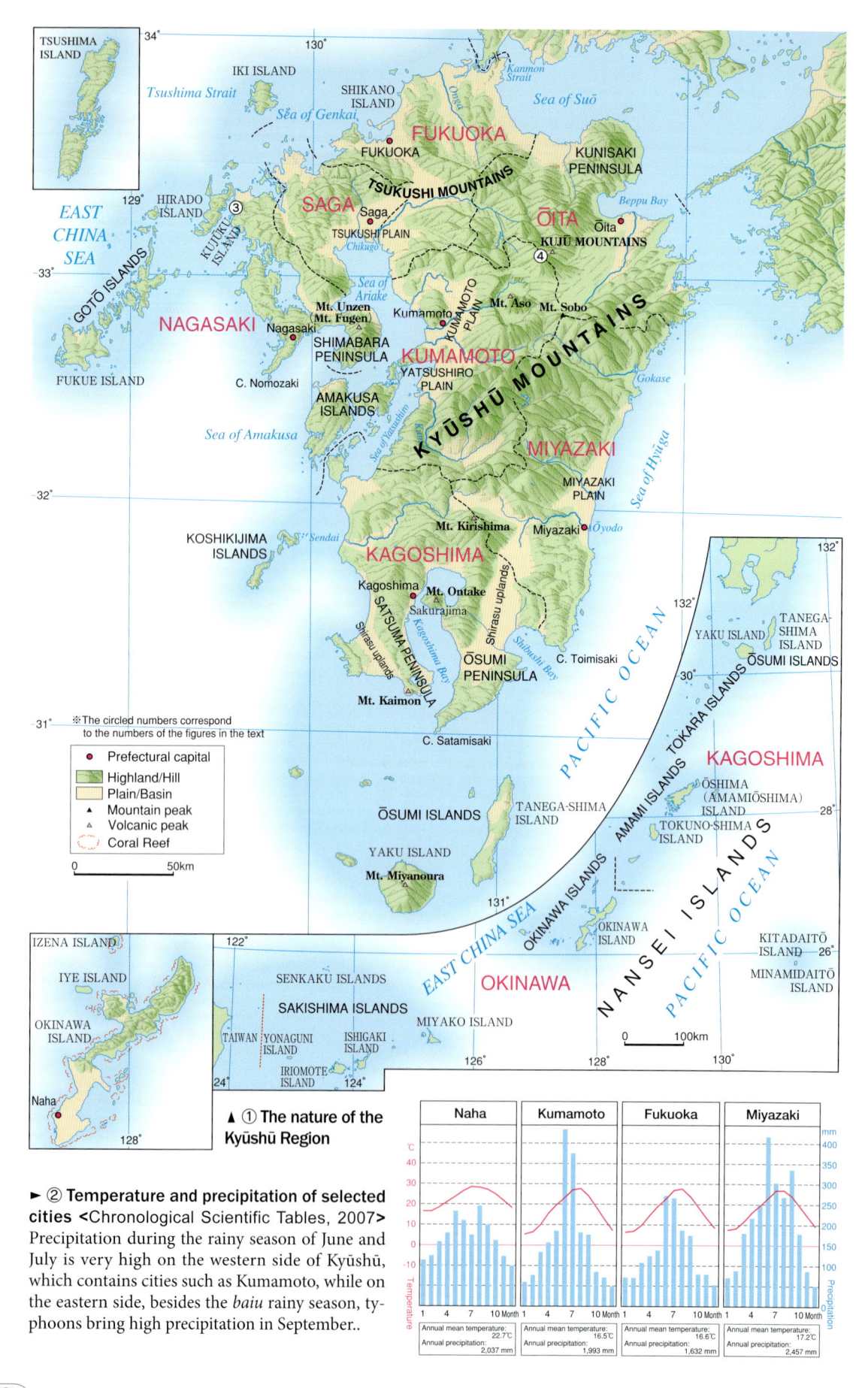

▲ ① The nature of the Kyūshū Region

► ② Temperature and precipitation of selected cities <Chronological Scientific Tables, 2007> Precipitation during the rainy season of June and July is very high on the western side of Kyūshū, which contains cities such as Kumamoto, while on the eastern side, besides the *baiu* rainy season, typhoons bring high precipitation in September..

	Naha	Kumamoto	Fukuoka	Miyazaki
Annual mean temperature:	22.7℃	16.5℃	16.6℃	17.2℃
Annual precipitation:	2,037 mm	1,993 mm	1,632 mm	2,457 mm

▲ ③ **An intricate ria coast** (Kujūku Island, Nagasaki Prefecture) Along the ria coast, aquaculture flourishes, taking advantage of the intricate and sheltered inlets.

▶ ④ **Kyūshū Electric Power Hacchōbaru geothermal Power Plant** (Kokonoe Town, Ōita Prefecture) One of the benefits of volcanic activity is the possibility for generating geothermal power, an eco-friendly source of energy.

1 Looking at the map

Volcanic Kyūshū and coralline Okinawa

Looking at the Kyūshū Region from an artificial satellite in space, the first thing that comes into view is the enormous navel-like caldera in the middle of the island. This was created through the eruptions of Mt. Aso. To the south, the mountains of the Kyūshū Mountains continue like a backbone. Further south still lies Sakurajima. The Mt. Ontake of Sakurajima is another of the volcanoes of Kyūshū, and its surrounding bay was created by sea water entering the volcano's caldera. With its numerous volcanoes, Kyūshū is sometimes called the "island of fire." In 1991, Mt. Unzen (Mt. Fugen) erupted, causing widespread damage, and burning down the surrounding areas. Then again, the vast open landscapes of Kyūshū, the numerous hot springs, the plentiful groundwater, and even geothermal energy can all be regarded not as disadvantages, but as local benefits of nature.

Headlands and bays, and many small islands, make up the beautiful ria coast that stretches from Saga Prefecture into Nagasaki Prefecture, in the northwestern part of the Kyūshū Region. In addition, within the Nansei archipelago, there are also islands surrounded by coral reefs.

A warm and rainy climate

The Kyūshū Region is warm even during winter, for the warm Kuroshio and Tsushima Currents, flow close to its eastern and western coasts respectively. While the monthly average temperature during the summer in the Kyūshū Region does not differ much from the Kantō Region, the monthly average temperature during the winter is higher than that of Kantō by 3 to 4 degrees Celsius. Moreover, the seasonal winds blowing from the northwest during the winter often bring cloudy weather to the northern parts that face the Sea of Japan, while the southeastern parts beyond the Kyūshū Mountains enjoy many sunny days. The winters of the Nansei Islands are much warmer.

In summer, humid seasonal winds coming in from the south bring heavy rainfall. Rainfall is especially heavy during the *baiu* season (rainy season) in the months of June and July, when cloudbursts can cause large-scale mudslides. Landslides and mudslides, caused by heavy rain, are particularly common around the end of the *baiu* season. What is more, the eastern side of the Kyūshū as well as the Nansei Islands serve as paths for typhoons, and experience a second period of heavy rainfall during autumn. In the northern parts of Kyūshū, where there are few large rivers, water shortages and droughts can occur in years when rainfall is lower than average.

▲ ① **A high-speed ferry leaving Hakata for Korea** (Port of Hakata, Fukuoka Prefecture)　Ferries such as this one (high-speed-ferry) take three hours to cover the 200 km between Hakata and Pusan, in South Korea.

▲ ② **Location of Fukuoka Prefecture, and the destinations of international flights from Fukuoka Airport** (2007) <JTB Timetable, October 2007>

◀ ③ **A Fukuoka subway sign written in Japanese, Hangul (Korean), English and Chinese**

▶ ④ **Visitors to Japan by the country or area of origin, arriving at Fukuoka Airport and Narita International Airport** (2003) <Annual Report of Statistics on Legal Migrants, 2004, percentages>

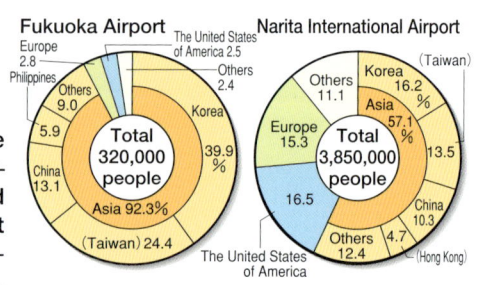

2 The Kyūshū Region's strong ties with other Asian nations

Close links with other Asian nations

　Of all the major regions of Japan, Kyūshū lies closest to the Asian mainland, and in particular lies closest to the Korean Peninsula and to China. As Figure 2 shows, if we were to center ourselves in Fukuoka, the distance to Seoul (Korea) and to Ōsaka, or the distance to Shanghai (China) and to Tōkyō, would be almost the same respectively. It follows that the Kyūshū Region has relatively strong links with Asian nations, and in fact the Kyūshū and the Ryūkyū Islands have traditionally been Japan's gateway to the cultures of China and the Korean Peninsula. For example, Nagasaki was the only Japanese port given permission to conduct foreign trade during the Edo Period when Japan's links with the outside world were otherwise cut by government decree. In addition, during the Ryūkyū Kingdom Period (from the fifteenth to the nineteenth centuries), there was a flourishing trade among the Ryūkyū Islands, China and Southeast Asia.

　Even to this day, there are very many exchanges between Kyūshū and the Asian nations. Fukuoka Airport is connected to more than 10 Asian cities and caters for over 15 international airline companies. Many of the routes connect Kyūshū with cities in South

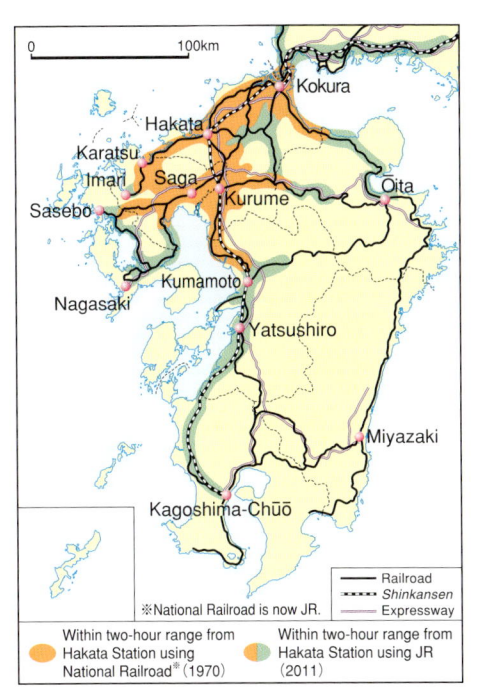

▲ ⑤ **Places reachable within two hours by train from Hakata Station** <JTB Timetable, October 2011, other sources>

▲ ⑥ **Central Fukuoka from the air** The administrative unit of Fukuoka City was created through the merger of Fukuoka, which originated as a medieval castle town, and Hakata, a merchant town that grew into a major center for trade.

Korea and China; travelers frequently use these routes to go back and forth for tourism, work and study. As a result, Fukuoka is the first big city in Japan whose subway system carries signs written in Hangul, the language used in the Korean Peninsula, as well as in Chinese. In addition, Fukuoka hosts many Asian-related cultural events, such as annual film and music festivals. Added to the exchange of people is the exchange of merchandise. Many cargo ships and ferries ply between the ports of Pusan (Korea), Hakata, and Kitakyūshū.

Fukuoka, Kyūshū's central city

The central city of Kyūshū is Fukuoka. Many workers and students commute daily into Fukuoka from the surrounding towns, and over the years an extensive metropolitan area has thus emerged, with Fukuoka at its center. While the population of Fukuoka City alone is 1.35 million, the population of the Fukuoka Metropolitan Area has reached 2.7 million, nearly double that of the central city (2006). Because of the concentration in the region of numerous universities and colleges, an unusually large number of young people live within the Fukuoka Metropolitan Area. The population growth rate is also much higher than the national average. The Kyūshū regional branch offices of the central government ministries are all located in Fukuoka's central business district, as are many banks, the Kyūshū branches of big national corporations, and the headquarters of large Kyūshū-based companies, as well as large shopping malls, theaters, and music halls. Every weekend, many shoppers and tourists visit the area by rail and bus, most of them coming from northern part of Kyūshū. As a result of all these activities, goods, people, and information have become concentrated in the Fukuoka Metropolitan Area, especially since the 1990s.

▲ ① **The Tsukushi Plain in summer (left) and winter (right)** Double-cropping, in which a summer crop is followed by a winter one, is carried out in the Tsukushi Plain, which lies between Fukuoka and Saga Prefectures.

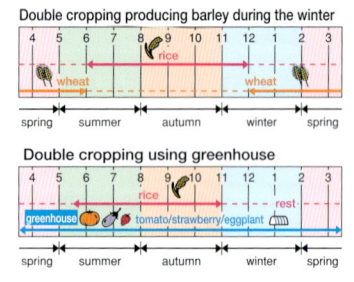

◄ ② **How double cropping works** Double cropping is a system that changes the crops according to the season, with for example rice being grown in the summer, and strawberries and barley for beer during the winter.

► ③ **Value of agricultural production, area, and population by region, 2005.** <Statistics of Agri-cultural Production Income 2005, and other sources> It can be seen that the value of agricultural production of the Kyūshū Region is higher than in any other major region of Japan, compared with the share of area and population.

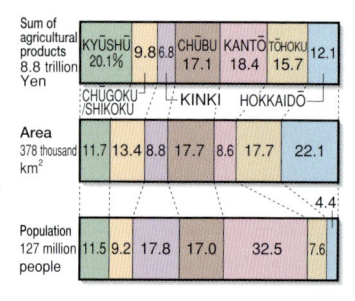

	KYŪSHŪ	CHŪGOKU/SHIKOKU	CHŪBU	KINKI	KANTŌ	TŌHOKU	HOKKAIDŌ
Sum of agricultural products 8.8 trillion Yen	20.1%	9.8	6.8	17.1	18.4	15.7	12.1
Area 378 thousand km²	11.7	13.4	8.8	17.7	8.6	17.7	22.1
Population 127 million people	11.5	9.2	17.8	17.0	32.5	7.6	4.4

3 North and South Kyūshū: Contrasts in agriculture and in life-styles

Northern Kyūshū, a region centered on rice production

The Kyūshū Region makes a major contribution to Japanese food supply, and accounts for 20 percent of the value of national agricultural output. The main contrast in the island's agricultural geography is between the north, which is mainly involved in rice production, and the south, where the main emphases are on the raising of livestock and farming.

The Tsukushi Plain and the Kumamoto Plain are typical of the rice production centers of Kyūshū. The Tsukushi Plain looks out on Ariake Bay, which has an unusually wide tidal flats. At low tide, extensive mudflats are revealed. Ever since the Edo Period (1603-1867), people have been extending the cultivated area by reclaiming these tidal flats for agricultural use. Furthermore, taking advantage of the warm winters, farmers are able to grow two crops a year. In the past, this meant that another crop was grown in the paddy fields after the rice was harvested, but in recent years, the government has been encouraging farmers throughout Japan to take land out of rice cultivation, and in northern Kyūshū, vegetables and fruit varieties are grown, as well as barley for beer production, using greenhouses. Some of the farmers who produce specialties such as strawberries or tea can earn relatively high incomes from agriculture. By contrast, other, older farmers are giving up agriculture because they can no longer work the land on account of old age, and cannot

▲④ Breeding of "Kagoshima black pork" (top) and a sticker that provides a Certificate of Origin (right)

▲⑤ Harvesting greenhouse-grown bell peppers (Saito City, Miyazaki Prefecture).

find a successor. Some farmers run efficient farms by paying rent for the land that is made available in this way, or by carrying out agricultural work on behalf of the farmers who can no longer work the land.

Southern Kyūshū: a region centered on farming and stock-breeding

In the southern part of Kyūshū, there are extensive plateaus that consist of a friable white sand, the product of old volcanic ash. In Japanese, this material is called *shirasu*. While *shirasu* plateaus can be suitable for sweet potato or tea cultivation, they do not retain surface water, and are prone to be dried up during in droughts. In Kasanohara, which forms part of the *shirasu* plateaus that cover much of Kagoshima Prefecture, production of various crops such as vegetables, forage crops and flowers has been made possible by drawing water from a large artificial reservoir.

Southern Kyūshū, moreover, is Japan's leading region for the breeding of beef cattle, pigs, and chickens. Since the 1970s the Japanese consumption of meat has risen because of the westernization of the diet, and consequently livestock farming became a profitable activity. Livestock rearing is not only carried out only by individual farmers but is sometimes run as a business by big companies which process meat products, or import fodder from abroad. Japanese supermarket companies are also involved in livestock farming in Kyūshū, either directly or through contracts with individual local livestock farmers. In Kyūshū, cheap meat is produced by efficient management operations that are based on the raising of large numbers of livestock in one location.

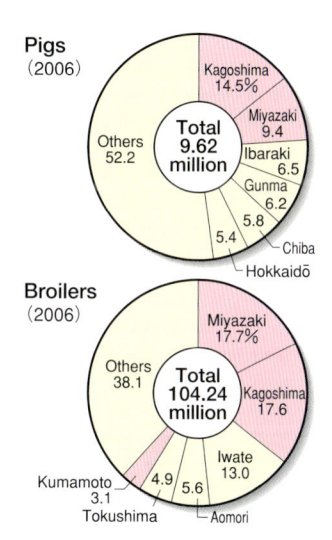

Pigs (2006)
Total 9.62 million
- Kagoshima 14.5%
- Miyazaki 9.4
- Ibaraki 6.5
- Gunma 6.2
- Chiba 5.8
- Hokkaidō 5.4
- Others 52.2

Broilers (2006)
Total 104.24 million
- Miyazaki 17.7%
- Kagoshima 17.6
- Iwate 13.0
- Aomori 5.6
- Tokushima 4.9
- Kumamoto 3.1
- Others 38.1

▲⑥ Leading prefectures for pig and broiler production (a broiler is a type of chicken raised specifically for meat) <Statistical Report of Agriculture, Forestry, and Fishery, other sources>

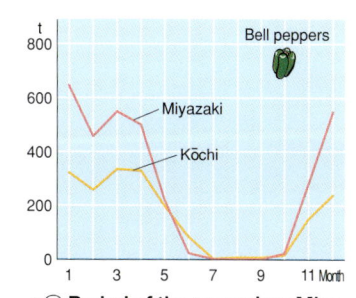

▲⑦ Period of the year when Miyazaki bell peppers are shipped to Tōkyō (2005) <Annual Report of Metropolitan Central Wholesale Market 2005>

▲ ① **Aquaculture beds for breeding Yellowtail** (Nagasaki Prefecture)

Nowadays, however, even cheaper meat is being imported from overseas and to compete with these imports, some farmers have opted for the production of high quality varieties of meat such as "Miyazaki beef" or "Kagoshima black pork", products with a guaranteed taste and quality.

In the Miyazaki Plain, greenhouse horticulture flourishes, based on the cultivation of cucumbers and bell peppers. This is a type of agriculture where winter shipments can fetch high prices, and involves the use of facilities such as greenhouses to bring forward the time of harvesting. The early vegetables are transported to the Tōkyō and Ōsaka markets by truck. In recent years, however, progress in transport and in perishable food preservation has enabled foreign producers to compete with their Japanese counterparts. Imports of cheap vegetables from neighboring Asian nations such as China and Korea have risen, putting Miyazaki producers under considerable pressure. In response, local farmers are attempting to increase their revenues by producing safe and high-quality vegetables by decreasing the use of pesticides, as well as by selling vegetables directly to consumers.

From fishing to aquafarming

In the sea to the west of Kyūshū, there is a vast continental shelf that extends to the Eurasian continent, and this serves as an important fishing ground. While coastal nations such as Japan, South Korea, and China observe strict fishery regulations to protect their respective marine resources, many fishing boats come from various places to catch shoals of carangidae, mackerel, sardine, flatfish, and so on. In terms of the quantity of fish caught, Nagasaki Prefecture ranks as one of Japan's leading prefectures for fishing. However in recent years, making a living solely out of fishing has become increasingly difficult given the decrease in fish stocks, as well as the decrease in fish prices. As a result, there has been large-scale movement of people from fishing to aquafarming. Yellowtails, sea breams, prawns, and eels are among the species raised on local fish farms.

Many people who live along the shores of Ariake Bay raise *nori* (laver-a type of seaweed), making use of the opportunities offered by the shallow inshore waters. This area boasts one of the highest levels of *nori* production in Japan. Since 1989, a large-scale land reclamation project has been going on along the Isahaya shoreline, on the western edge of Ariake Bay. The construction of a closed dike separating the sea from the area to be reclaimed has caused much concern as regards possible negative impacts on both the environment and the local fishing industry.

▲ ② **Sea dike across Isahaya Bay, completed in 1999.**

▲ ① **View of area around Dōkai Bay in 1963 (left) and 2004 (right)** (Kitakyūshū City, Fukuoka Prefecture)
By 1960s, the water quality was so bad that Dōkai Bay was called the "Sea of Death." This was the result of heavy pollution of the water by effluent from the steel works. However, the regulations that were later implemented brought about a dramatic improvement in the Bay's water quality.

4 From steel manufacture to automobile and IC production

Changes in the Kitakyūshū Industrial District

Industrial development in Kitakyūshū began in 1901, when the Japanese government built an iron and steel works in the former village of Yahata, close to the shore of Dōkai Bay. This steel works was the ancestor of the present-day plant that is operated by the Nippon Steel Corporation. The site was chosen partly because of its proximity to the coal and limestone resources of the Chikuhō area, and partly because it was easy to import iron ore and coal required for iron manufacturing from China, across the East China Sea. From around 1930 onwards, there was a sharp increase in the production of iron and steel, and the area began to be called the Kitakyūshū Industrial District, and thus became one of the four major industrial districts of Japan together with the Keihin (Tōkyō and Yokohama), Hanshin (Ōsaka and Kōbe) and Chūkyō (Nagoya).

The Kitakyūshū Industrial District developed on the basis of heavy industries such as steel and cement manufacturing, and by the 1960s, when industrial output was at a peak, water and air pollution had become serious problems. With the cooperation of local governments, citizens and corporations, strenuous efforts for environmental improvement began to be made.

From around 1970, steel production in Kitakyūshū entered a period of decline. The new steel plants that had been constructed near the Keihin and Hanshin Industrial Districts were closer to the main urban markets than the Kitakyūshū works, and were able to import cheap iron ore and good quality coal from overseas. More recently, the Japanese iron and steel industry as a whole is not as prosperous as it used to be. This is partly due to keen competition from low-cost foreign steel producers, and partly because the demand for steel has been reduced due to the growing popularity of new substitutes for iron and steel. Because of this, many Japanese steel works have reduced the scale of their operations and some have even closed down, their former sites being partly converted into theme parks.

Today, Kitakyūshū's success in overcoming environmental problems has encouraged research into better methods of waste and ash disposal, and has led to research into the recycling of waste to provide industrial materials. In addition, efforts are being made in collaboration with international bodies for the improvement of measures against pollution in developing countries.

▲ ① Toyota Motor's Kyūshū plant, built on a vast site (right), and part of the interior (left) (Miyawaka City, Fukuoka Prefecture)

◄ ② An IC plant owned by NEC (Kumamoto City, Kumamoto Prefecture) Many of Kyūshū's IC plants use advanced technology introduced during the 1990s.

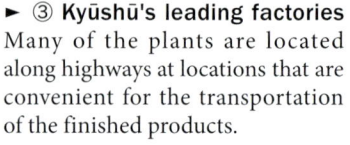

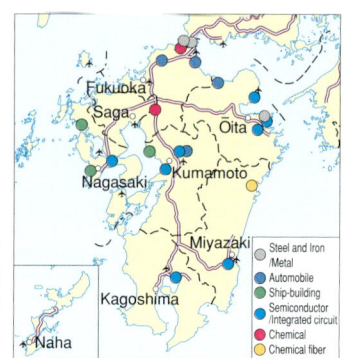

► ③ Kyūshū's leading factories Many of the plants are located along highways at locations that are convenient for the transportation of the finished products.

The rise of IC assembly and automobile manufacturing

During the last 30 years, Kyūshū's industrial base has gradually shifted from the production of steel to the manufacture of newer products. Since the 1970s, electronics, in particular the manufacturing of integrated circuits (IC) have developed in various localities in Kyūshū. In fact Kyūshū is often called the "Silicon Island," since it constitutes Japan's biggest concentration of IC manufacturing and since ICs are made from silicon. Reflecting their need to draw on local supplies of labor, the IC plants of various corporations were built at different places in the island, as opposed to being concentrated all in one zone. The ICs that are assembled in these places are transported by air to various regions in Asia, where they are installed into electrical appliances such as computers and cameras. These completed products are not only sold throughout the world, but are also often re-imported into Japan. Within the IC industry, although labor shortages in Japan have recently impelled Japanese manufacturers to assemble ICs at Asian locations, many of the Kyūshū plants have been keeping a position of leadership in technological guidance.

Until the 1950s, the Chikuhō area of Fukuoka Prefecture was one of the major coal mining regions of Japan. With the replacement of coal by petroleum as a major source of energy, the demand for coal decreased, and many mines closed down. To stave off high unemployment, large automobile plants belonging to Nissan and Toyota were constructed in places such as Kanda Town (in Fukuoka Prefecture), and Miyawaka City, in the Chikuhō area. Up to that point, most of Japan's automobile factories had been concentrated in the heavily industrialized Tōkai and Kantō regions, and the companies running the newly constructed automobile plants in Kyūshū found it easier to secure local labor than they would have done if they had built new factories in the existing industrial regions. In addition, compared to the existing industrial regions of Japan, Kyūshū offered locations from which completed vehicles could be more easily exported directly to China, where

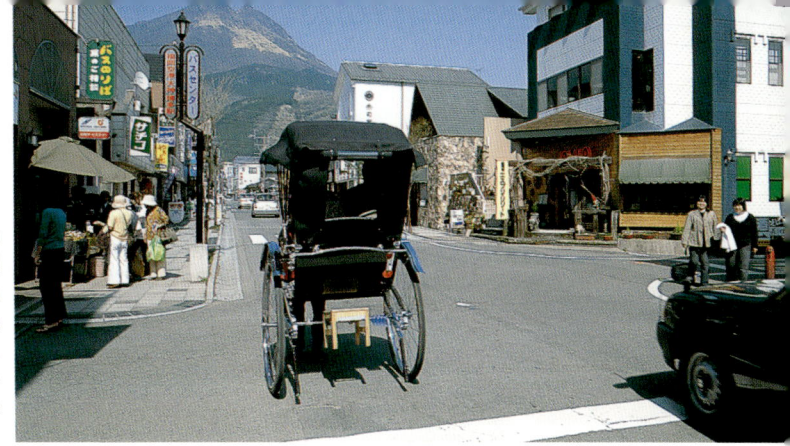

▶ ① **Yufuin Hot Springs Resort** (Yufu City, Ōita Prefecture)　Rustic, beautiful resort of Yufuin is located in the basin near Mt. Yufudake, a live volcano. It has been popular, especially since the 1980s. The success resulted from the town building in harmony with nature and culture since the late 1960s.

demand was rapidly increasing. Since an automobile is assembled out of a combination of approximately 30,000 parts, around the automobile plants are clustered numerous plants that produce automobile components. Kyūshū, including the Chikuhō area, thus changed into a region in which automobile-related industries began to congregate.

5 Gifts of nature and the development of tourism

Onsen (hot springs) and theme parks

　Hot springs, gifts of a volcanic environment, abound in the Kyūshū Region. Many tourists visit the old-established hot springs sites of Beppu (Ōita Prefecture), Unzen Hot Springs (Nagasaki Prefecture), and Ibusuki Hot Springs (Kagoshima Prefecture), as well as newer resorts such as Yufuin Hot Springs (Ōita Prefecture) and Kurokawa Hot Springs (Kumamoto Prefecture). In recent decades, longer holidays and higher incomes have made it possible for an increasing number of Japanese people to enjoy visits to tourist resorts, and hot springs have flourished as a result. While the majority of the tourists come mainly from Fukuoka Prefecture, others come from different regions of Japan and also from Asia. For example recently, there has been an increase in the number of tourists visiting Kyūshū from South Korea, China and other Asian countries. As the tourism industry is associated with various businesses such as restaurants and hotels, theme parks, and souvenir shops, it serves an important role in regions with limited job opportunities.

　In Kyūshū, theme parks opened one after the other throughout the 1990s. Examples include Huis Ten Bosch outside Nagasaki, that models itself on a fictional port town in the Netherlands, as well as Miyazaki Prefecture's Seagaia that re-creates the attractions of a resort in the tropics[1].

　In Yaku Island, located in the southern part of Kagoshima Prefecture, abundant rain and warm temperatures have allowed the growth of an ancient natural forest of Cryptomeria trees that are thousands of years old. Since being registered as a Natural World Heritage site, Yaku Island has seen a substantial increase in tourists, and agendas have been drawn up concerning the protection of this valuable natural environment.

Notes (P.51)
[1] These theme parks failed to raise their profits despite the enormous amount of money that has been spent in their construction. Efforts such as cutting back on facilities and building learning zones for devising systems to protect the environment are being made in an attempt to raise profit levels.

▲ ② **Eisā** (Okinawa Prefecture)   The *Eisā* is a type of dance performed at the late summer Bon festival, in which drums and *sanshin* are used.

◀ ③ Okinawan cuisine

▲ ① **Location of Okinawa** <JTB Timetable, October 2007>   It is interesting to identify foreign cities and Japanese cities that are approximately the same distance away from Naha, Okinawa's capital city. Kagoshima and Taipei are both approximately 650km away in distance, Fukuoka and Shanghai are 850km from Naha, and Tōkyō and Manila both lie at a distance of approximately 1500km from Okinawa's capital.

6 The southern islands, Okinawa

The history and distinct culture of Okinawa

As a result of its location, Okinawa has a long history of exchanges with China and Southeast Asian nations, and its contacts with Asia have been even closer than in the case of Kyūshū. In early times, exchanges with the Asian mainland were made by ships that used the Kuroshio (the Japan Current) and the seasonal winds. Moreover, because Okinawa was occupied by the United States after 1945, it was strongly influenced by American culture. In this way, a distinctive culture, displaying several non-Japanese elements, has emerged in Okinawa. Even to this day, including the restored Shuri Castle, there are many sites that reflect the unique history of Okinawa. Okinawa is known for its distinct life-style and for its unique cultural features, and is known for *Karate*, its cuisine, and its dialects, in addition to traditional handicrafts such as textiles, dyed goods, and ceramics. In the performing arts, there are songs and dances based on distinctive musical scales. Some of famous examples are the Okinawan folk song *Shima-uta* (Island Song), an instrument made from snakeskin called the *Sanshin*, and the Okinawan folk dance *Eisā*. It is perhaps not surprising, given this cultural background, that many popular singers and TV personalities are from Okinawa.

Warm climate: a boon for agriculture

Okinawa has a warm climate even during the winter, so much so that tropical plants such as mangroves and hibiscuses can grow. Cherry blossoms start blooming around the end of January, and on the beaches between March and April the swimming season begins. Close, humid weather predominates from May onwards, and from summer into fall, many typhoons arrive in the Islands.

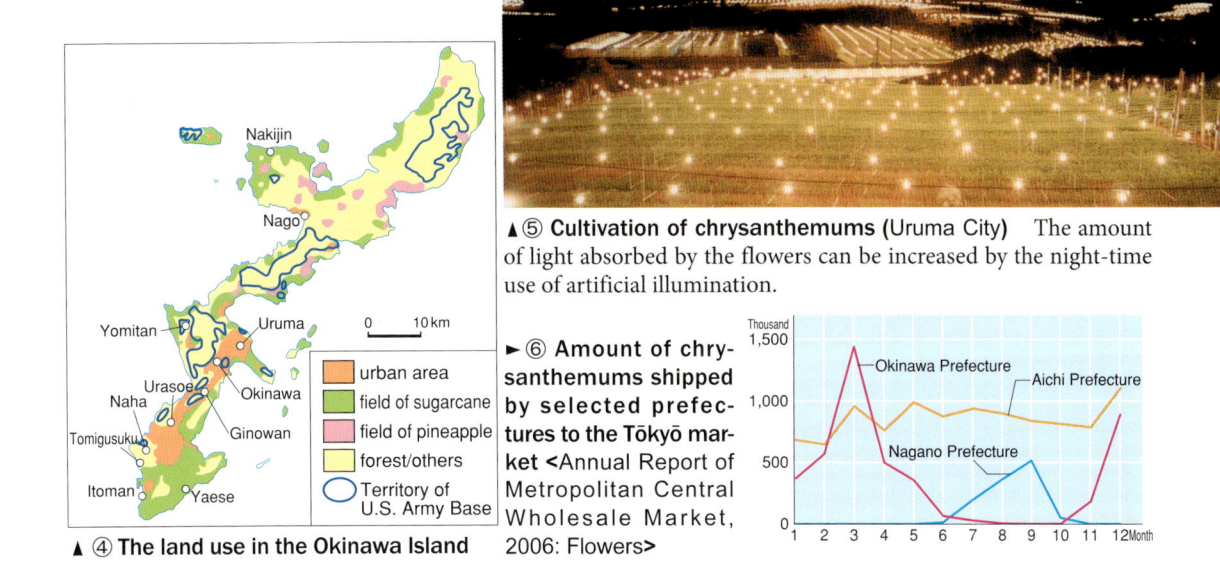

▲⑤ **Cultivation of chrysanthemums** (Uruma City)   The amount of light absorbed by the flowers can be increased by the night-time use of artificial illumination.

▶⑥ **Amount of chrysanthemums shipped by selected prefectures to the Tōkyō market** <Annual Report of Metropolitan Central Wholesale Market, 2006: Flowers>

▲④ **The land use in the Okinawa Island**

Okinawa was previously an important center for the cultivation of sugar cane and pineapples, crops that grew well in the warm climate. However as elsewhere in Japan, cheap imports caused difficulties for Okinawa's sugar and pineapple growers. In response, farmers turned to market gardening, and began to grow profitable early vegetables and flowers. The raising of chrysanthemums under artificial lighting is especially popular. Many local farmers specialize in the production and shipping of early-season products during the winter and early spring when cultivation in other prefectures is not yet advanced enough to meet demand. In particular, large volumes of watermelons and haricot beans are transported to destinations elsewhere in Japan, using ferries and aircraft. In recent years, there has been an increase in the production and shipping to other prefectures of bitter melons, called *gōyā*.

Living next door to military bases

During the Second World War, Okinawa became a battlefield on which many residents lost their lives or got injured. Following that tragic war, Okinawa was occupied by the military forces of the United States. Although Okinawa was returned to Japanese control in 1972 after a long campaign, the island, being close to Asia, remains of considerable strategic significance to the United States, and American military installations still occupy 20 percent of the island's surface area. These bases interfere with the lives of the local people, and also retard the economic development of the region. A majority of the people of Okinawa hope for the return of the American military installations to Japan.

Many of those who are currently living around the American military installations are in jobs related to the bases. In order to reduce Okinawa's economic dependence on the American presence and to abolish economic differences with the rest of Japan, the government has funded the construction and improvement of roads, seaports and airports in Okinawa. However, there are few employment opportunities other than those related to the bases or in the construction industry, and every year, many Okinawans leave their prefecture in search of work elsewhere in Japan. Contrary to the overall picture of economic stagnation, some large companies based in other parts of Japan have begun to locate their telephone call centers in Okinawa.

▲ ① **People enjoying diving around the coral reefs** (Okinawa Prefecture)

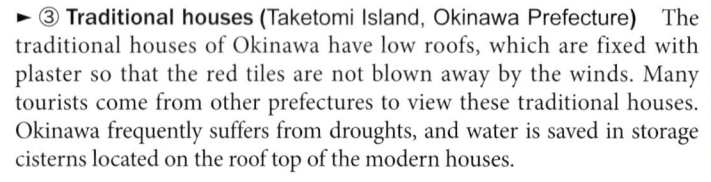

▲ ② **Mangroves** (Iriomote Island, Okinawa Prefecture)

► ③ **Traditional houses** (Taketomi Island, Okinawa Prefecture) The traditional houses of Okinawa have low roofs, which are fixed with plaster so that the red tiles are not blown away by the winds. Many tourists come from other prefectures to view these traditional houses. Okinawa frequently suffers from droughts, and water is saved in storage cisterns located on the roof top of the modern houses.

Development of the tourist industry and environmental protection

Beautiful coral reefs can be found around the islands of Okinawa. The coral reefs not only protect the land from the sea, but they are an important asset for the tourist industry. Marine sports, such as sub-aqua diving, can be enjoyed in many places around the coral-line coasts. Attracted by its beautiful natural environment and by its distinctive culture, large numbers of tourists come to visit Okinawa every year. Furthermore, there has been an increase in the number of people who come from other prefectures to live in Okinawa recently. After the mid 1980s, the annual number of tourists increased by more than 2.5 times, from around 2 million people in 1985 to 5.5 million in 2005. The money spent by these tourists goes a long way toward supporting the economy of Okinawa. However, the boom in tourism has created many environmental problems. These include the removal of large amounts of earth and sand for hotel and resort-related construction sites as well as for new golf courses, and also the contamination of the offshore waters, a problem that is causing the gradual disappearance of the coral reefs.

The island of Iriomote is covered with primeval forests that resemble tropical forests. Rare and interesting fauna are found in these old-established forests, including the Iriomote cat (*Mayailurus iriomotensis*) which is designated by the Japanese government as an endangered species. Mangroves flourish at river mouths where fresh water and sea water meet. It is essential that future plans for the construction of hotels and other tourist facilities take into account the need to conserve the natural habitat. The same holds true in the island of Ishigaki Island, where there are plans to construct a new airport. In recent years in Okinawa, an increasing emphasis has been put on ecotourism, which enables one to enjoy tourism while protecting the natural environment simultaneously.

Japan seen through its regions
History of Minamata disease and Ecotown intiatives

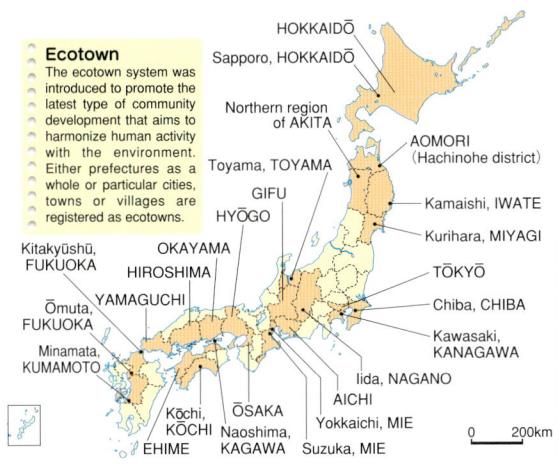

Ecotown
The ecotown system was introduced to promote the latest type of community development that aims to harmonize human activity with the environment. Either prefectures as a whole or particular cities, towns or villages are registered as ecotowns.

▲ ① Regions registered as Ecotowns (2007)
<Source: Ministry of Economy, Trade and Industry>

► ② Regions that have experienced outbreaks of Minamata Disease <Minamata Data>

▲ ③ Garbage sorted according to type of material in Minamata (Minamata City, Kumamoto Prefecture)

During the 1950s and the 1960s, along the coast of Sea of Yatsushiro, in western Kyūshū, there appeared a disease that caused severe neurological and muscular disorders. Although unidentified for some time, the source of the disease was later discovered to be the fish that lived in water polluted by organic mercury that had been dumped into the bay area in the waste water discharged by neighboring chemical factories. The disease became known as Minamata Disease, and those who were officially diagnosed with it had to be paid medical fees by the companies that had caused the pollution. In fact, however, many victims have still not yet received adequate compensation.

Following the outbreak of Minamata Disease, from the 1970s, initiatives were taken to clean the polluted sea. First, nets were used to get rid of the contaminated fish. In addition, sludge at the bottom of the sea was removed and land reclamation was carried out along the coastal area that had been affected. These efforts paid off and in due course, it was confirmed that fish in the bay area were safe to eat, and commercial fishing in the area was resumed in the 1990s. The area is now returning to its previous state as the stretch of clean sea that it once was.

Another issue that arose from Minamata Disease was the surfacing of discrimination and prejudice among the population. Victims and their families suffered a great deal because of this. In order to bring an end to discrimination, the Municipal Museum of Minamata Disease and other facilities for residential interaction were established. Furthermore, through agreeing to accept an environmentally sensitive system of sorted household garbage disposal (households place different kinds of waste in different containers), local people have begun to interact with one another once more.

In the context of these and similar initiatives, Minamata was designated as an ecotown by the Japanese government. An ecotown is a region that aims to completely eliminate waste and to create a community that harmonizes with the environment. Once a place is designated as an ecotown by the government, the region qualifies for the receipt of subsidies for the construction of garbage recycling facilities and waste disposal factories. Many regions have been designated as ecotowns following efforts they have made to overcome local pollution problems and re-establish environmental quality. Examples of ecotowns other than Minamata are Kitakyūshū, Kawasaki, and Yokkaichi.

Chapter 2
Chūgoku/Shikoku Region

Chūgoku/Shikoku Region

The Chūgoku/Shikoku Region is the combined area of Chūgoku, which occupies the western end of Honshū, Japan's largest island, and the island of Shikoku. In terms of administrative units, the region consists of the five prefectures of Chūgoku (Yamaguchi, Hiroshima, Okayama, Shimane, and Tottori), and the four prefectures of Shikoku (Tokushima, Kagawa, Ehime and Kōchi) making a total of 9 prefectures in all.

As we can see from Figure 2 on page 39, the Chūgoku/Shikoku Region used to straddle the three dō (circuits) of San'indō, San'yōdō, and Nankaidō. In 1903, most of the San'indō and the San'yōdō was grouped into the Chūgoku Region and most of the Nankaidō formed the Shikoku Region. Since the 1960s, the two regions have come to be widely perceived as one, and for this reason the Chūgoku and Shikoku Regions are now generally grouped together into one unit.

The names Chūgoku and Shikoku date back as far as the fourteenth century. At first, the term Chūgoku applied to a relatively small region, and it was not until the beginning of the seventeenth century that it was used in its present sense, to apply to that part of Honshū that lies to the north of the Seto Inland Sea.

The name Chūgoku comes from the abbreviation of chūkan no kuniguni, the "middle provinces" that lay between Kyūshū and Kinai. The name Shikoku comes from the fact that in ancient times, the island was divided into four provinces.

The mountain ranges of the Chūgoku Mountains and the Shikoku Mountains run in an east-west direction, and the island-studded Seto Inland Sea lies like a belt between them. Since ancient times, this sea has been used as an important transport route. In recent years, north-south links within the region have been strengthened through the opening of three great bridges across the Seto Inland Sea, connecting Honshū and Shikoku.

Despite this recent development, the Chugoku/Shikoku Region remains separated into three distinct sub-regions, namely Setouchi, consisting of the Seto Inland Sea and its coastlands; San'in, which includes the Chūgoku Mountains and the adjacent Sea of Japan coastlands; and southern Shikoku, which lies to the south of the Shikoku Mountains. Each of these sub-regions has its own distinctive characteristics resulting from differences in relief, climate, industry and culture.

◀ ① **Ōnaruto Bridge and Naruto Whirlpool (**Tokushima Prefecture**)** The Naruto Strait is a narrow strait located between Shikoku and Awaji Island. Large whirlpools form with the ebb and flow of the tides. After the opening of the Ōnaruto and Akashi-kaikyū Bridges that connect Honshū with Shikoku, highway buses replaced ships as the main means of transportation between Tokushima and the Ōsaka-Kōbe Area.

▲ ② **Regional division of the Chūgoku/Shikoku Region**

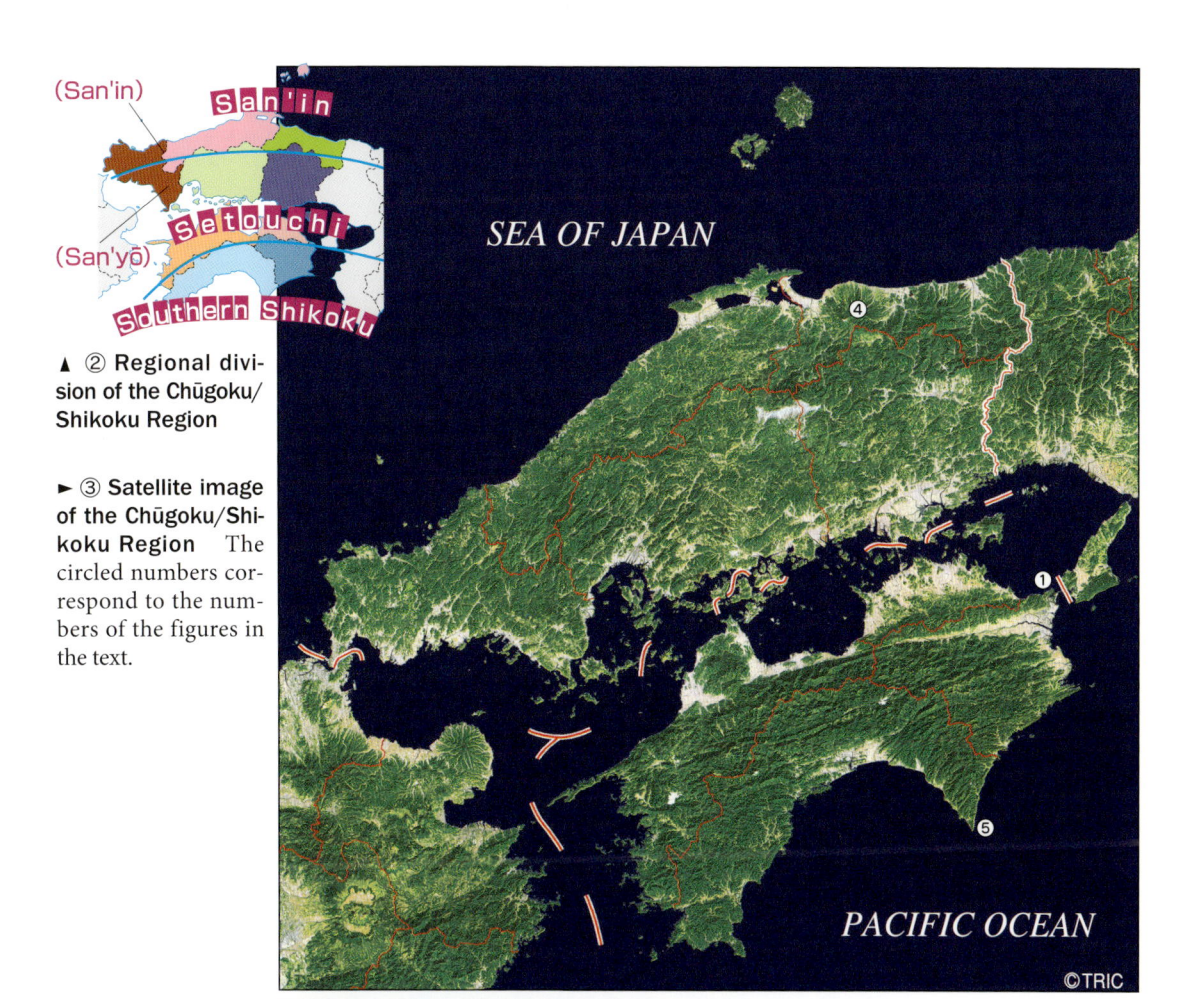

► ③ **Satellite image of the Chūgoku/Shikoku Region** The circled numbers correspond to the numbers of the figures in the text.

► ④ **Mt. Daisen during the winter (Tottori Prefecture)** The coastlands of Tottori Prefecture experience heavy snowfall during the winter due to the prevalence of the northwesterly seasonal wind from the continent. During the winter, the slopes of Mt. Daisen become crowded with people skiing.

◄ ⑤ **C. Murotozaki (Kōchi Prefecture)** The cape of Murotozaki faces the Pacific Ocean, and strong waves break along the shore. There are only a few plains in this part of Japan, and plateau surfaces are used for fields and paddy land. Southern Shikoku lies in the path of typhoons.

57

▲ ① Nature of the Chūgoku/Shikoku Region

▼ ② Temperature and precipitation of selected cities

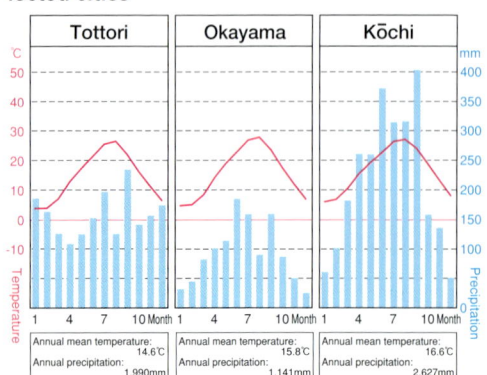

Tottori
Annual mean temperature: 14.6℃
Annual precipitation: 1,990mm

Okayama
Annual mean temperature: 15.8℃
Annual precipitation: 1,141mm

Kōchi
Annual mean temperature: 16.6℃
Annual precipitation: 2,627mm

▼ ③ Seto Inland Sea and Kurushima-kaikyo Bridge (Ehime Prefecture)

▲ ④ **The gentle slopes of the Chūgoku Mountains** (near Pass Ningyō, Okayama Prefecture)

▲ ⑤ **Steep slopes of the Shikoku Mountains** (Mt. Ishizuchi, Ehime Prefecture)

1 Looking at the map

Three seas and two highlands areas

The temperate Seto Inland Sea occupies the center of the Chūgoku/Shikoku Region, and is bounded by Honshū, Shikoku and Kyūshū. The Chūgoku/Shikoku Region as a whole is characterized by a pattern of alternating seas and mountains. From north to south, these comprise the Sea of Japan coast, the Chūgoku Mountains, the Seto Inland Sea, the Shikoku Mountains, and the Pacific coast of southern Shikoku. Excluding active volcanoes such as Mt. Daisen, mountains with gentle slopes stretch across interior Chūgoku, with small valleys located between highlands blocs such as the Kibi Highlands and the Iwami Highlands. In contrast to this pattern, the terrain of the Shikoku Mountains are characterized by its bumpiness and its steep slopes. Located as it is between these two highlands, the Seto Inland Sea has many islands, and its beautiful landscapes are famous throughout the world. So far as land use is concerned, a major problem of the Seto Inland Sea is acute shortage of flat land, since highlands often continue right up to the edge of the shore. Throughout history, a response to land scarcity has been land reclamation, a process that has taken advantage of the large difference between high and low tides in the Seto Inland Sea.

Three types of climates made by two highlands and seasonal winds

The northern part of the Chūgoku/Shikoku Region looks out on to the Sea of Japan. In winter, affected by the northwesterly seasonal wind, the eastern part of the region experiences heavy precipitation. By contrast, facing the Pacific Ocean, the southern side receives heavy rainfall in summer, brought by the southeasterly seasonal wind. Setouchi has relatively little precipitation all year round. This is because the mountains that lie to the north and the south tend to shut out moisture-carrying winds. Water shortage is made worse by the absence of large rivers. Throughout Setouchi, and from early historical times, reservoirs have been used in an attempt to overcome water scarcity. The warm and dry climate has made it possible for salt farm[1] to be developed throughout the Setouchi area.

Notes (P.59)

[1] This refers to pan used to make salt by evaporating saltwater. After the Edo period (1603-1867), many salt evaporation pans were developed along the coasts of the Seto Inland Sea. However, after the Second World War, these pans disappeared with the introduction of modern methods of salt manufacturing. Some of the major salt evaporation pans were at Akō, Naruto, Sakaide and Mitajiri (presentday Hōfu).

▲ ① Central Hiroshima seen from the air

2 Industries and life in Setouchi

Setouchi's cities

The map shows that many cities of this region are located along the coastline of the Seto Inland Sea. Compared to other regions, large-scale plains are few and far between.[1] Many of the region's cities first developed as castle towns that were built in small-scale plains near the mouths of rivers. Okayama, Hiroshima, Takamatsu and Matsuyama are examples of this type of city. Some cities, such as Shimonoseki and Onomichi, grew as harbor settlements that depended on the maritime transport of the Seto Inland Sea. At the same time, other cities, such as Kurashiki, Fukuyama, Kure, Innoshima and Niihama, depended on industry which at first flourished and later went into decline.

Hiroshima, the city of international peace

Located on the Ōta River delta, Hiroshima played an important role as a military base for infantry after the Meiji period (1868-1912). During the Second World War, on August 6, 1945, an atomic bomb[2] was dropped on Hiroshima from an aircraft belonging to the United States Army Air Force. This was the first atomic bombing in the history of mankind, and the city suffered tremendous damage, including the death and injury of many civilians who became the victims[3] of the bomb. Following the end of the war, Hiroshima saw rapid reconstruction, and at present, it is the largest city in the Chūgoku/Shikoku Region with a population of over a million people. Furthermore, as a peace memorial city, Hiroshima continues to educate the rest of the world about the horrors of nuclear weapons.

Highway provision, and the Honshū-Shikoku Bridges

For many years, coastal maritime transport flourished in the sheltered waters of the Seto Inland Sea. From early times, ships were preferable to land transport, for they made

---

Notes (P.60)
[1] There are no plains in Setouchi comparable in size to the Kantō or Nōbi Plains.
[2] On August 9, 1945, a second atomic bomb was dropped on Nagasaki.
[3] Approximately 140,000 people died as a result of the intense heat of the blast and the nuclear radiation. Including those who later died of their injuries ("*hibakusha*" patients), more than 200,000 lives were lost.

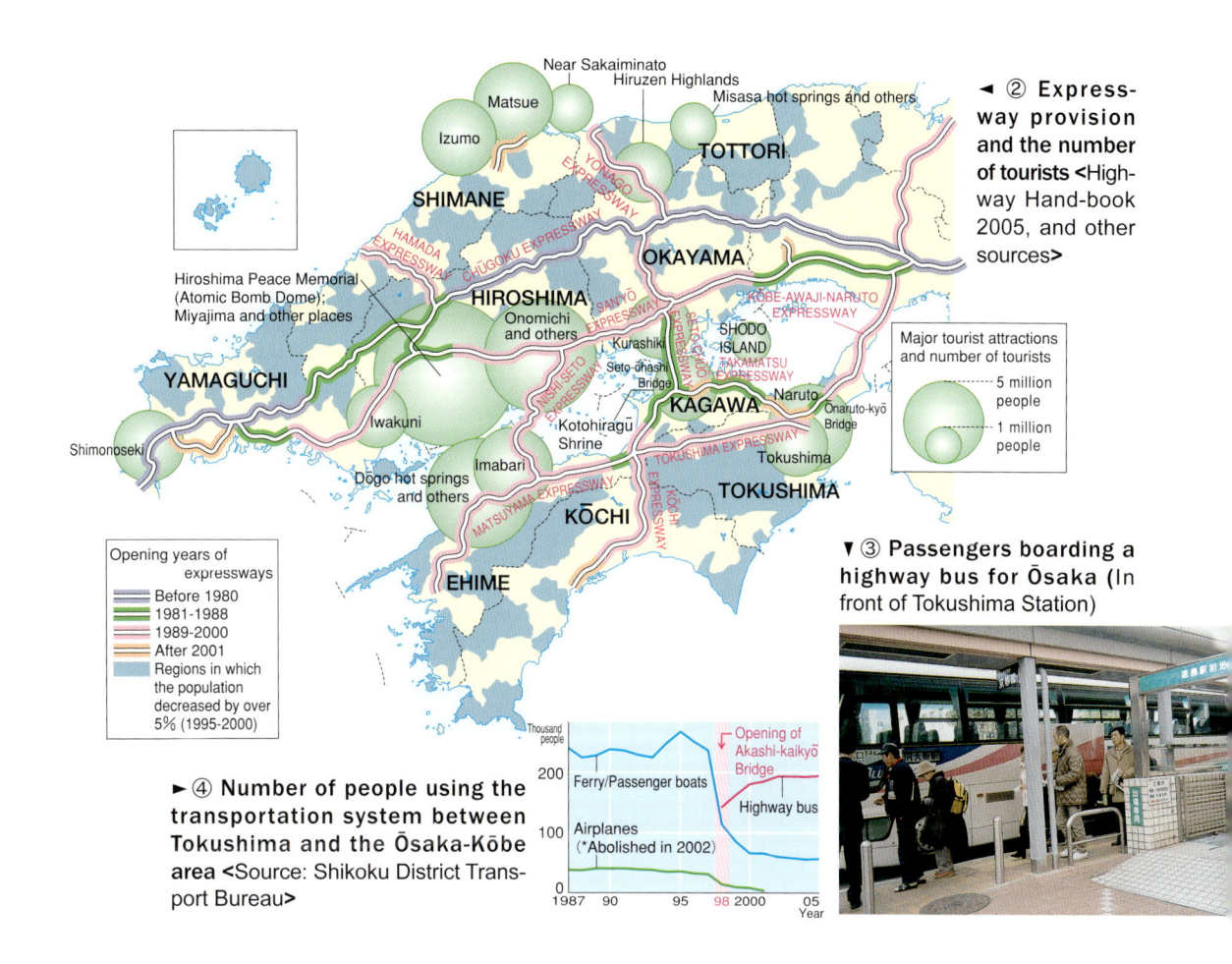

◄ ② Expressway provision and the number of tourists <Highway Hand-book 2005, and other sources>

Major tourist attractions and number of tourists
— 5 million people
— 1 million people

Opening years of expressways
— Before 1980
— 1981-1988
— 1989-2000
— After 2001
— Regions in which the population decreased by over 5% (1995-2000)

▼ ③ Passengers boarding a highway bus for Ōsaka (In front of Tokushima Station)

► ④ Number of people using the transportation system between Tokushima and the Ōsaka-Kōbe area <Source: Shikoku District Transport Bureau>

it possible to transport a large amount of goods in one sailing. However, shipping in the Seto Inland Sea began to decline in importance when railroads developed, from the late nineteenth century onwards, and after the Second World War, land transport developed rapidly. In short, the decline in shipping is due to changes in the modes of transportation that reflect the ever-increasing demand for faster shipments of goods.

Within the region, land transport developed mainly in an east-west direction. A rapid-transport railroad and several new roads have become the principal routes for land transport, namely the San'yō *Shinkansen* railroad and the San'yō Expressway, both of which run along the coast, and the Chūgoku Expressway that weaves across the Chūgoku Mountains. In recent years, in addition to these east-west links, new north-south connections are being constructed. Besides the provision of highway networks connecting San'in and San'yō, transport between Honshū and Shikoku became far easier with the opening of the Honshū-Shikoku Bridge Expressways, which include the three spectacular trans-Seto Inland Sea bridges of Kōbe-Naruto, Kojima-Sakaide and Onomichi-Imabari. These bridges have brought about an increase in the number of people crossing the sea for shopping, schools and work.

Changes in the transport network have strongly influenced industrial growth in Setouchi. Maritime transport is still the preferred mode for carrying heavy and voluminous goods, and harbor facilities remain very important for industries that use bulky raw materials. Moreover, the development of modern roads in recent years has led to the emergence of zones of factories and of freight and parcel delivery facilities close to highway interchanges.

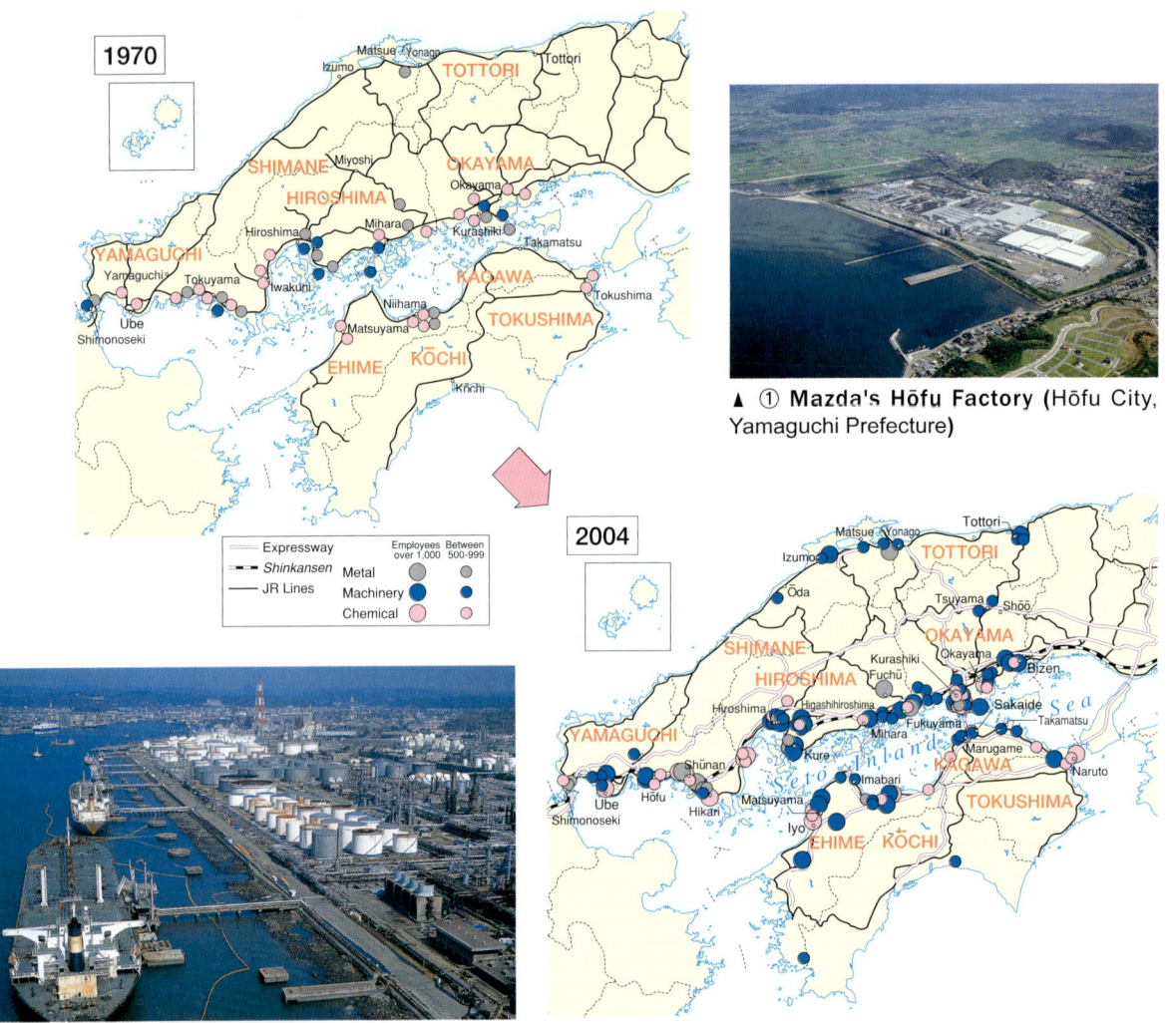

▲ ① **Mazda's Hōfu Factory** (Hōfu City, Yamaguchi Prefecture)

▲ ② **Mizushima Coastal Industrial Complex** (Kurashiki City, Okayama Prefecture)

▲ ③ **Changes in the Setouchi Industrial District** <National Factory Survey 1996-1997, other sources>

Setouchi's varied industries

While there are various industries in each region of Setouchi, the plains along the coasts of the Seto Inland Sea have been particularly important as regards industrial development. Transport is relatively easy when factories are constructed along the coastline. For example, a coastal location allows an iron and steel works to import heavy raw materials and to ship finished products to the market. Petrochemical plants can also reduce their transportation expenses by opting for coastal locations. Flat land is scarce along the coastline of the Seto Inland Sea, and many factories have had to be built on land reclaimed from the sea. Land reclamation has made possible the establishment of a large number of factories along the coast. Examples include the Bridgestone and Mazda factories at Hōfu, and at Bannosu in the northern part of Sakaide. The remaining sites of former salt evaporation pans and of old land reclamation projects completed in the Edo period (1603-1867) have been frequently selected as places for reclaiming land on which to build large factories.

▲ ④ **Changes in products: Teijin textiles and Hitachi shipbuilding**　Previously, Teijin produced textiles, and Hitachi Shipbuilding assembled ships. At present, utilizing their old-established industrial techniques and existing facilities, both firms are engaged in research and development into new products, and the production of these products.

　These industrial developments have brought into being distinctive landscapes of crowded factory zones with their backs to the mountains. Furthermore, since old reclaimed land and salt evaporation pans were largely scattered here and there, the factories that have been constructed on these sites are also scattered throughout the Setouchi Area. The result is that industrial clusters have arisen here and there between beautiful natural coastlines and in the midst of zones of fishing and agricultural villages.

　The following are examples of such cities: Mizushima in Kurashiki and Iwakuni with their petrochemical complexes, Shūnan, Ōtake, and Fukuyama, with large-scale iron and steel works, Kure, Innoshima and Onomichi with shipyards, and Hiroshima, Kurashiki, and Hōfu with motor vehicle assembly plants. These heavy and chemical industry bases played an important role especially during the 1960s and 1970s when the Japanese economy was growing very rapidly.

　However, after the 1980s, the development of cities reliant on heavy industries that faced the Seto Inland Sea came to a halt as the relative importance of these types of industry declined, while there was rapid growth in industries with a high level of processing[1] and that depended on the use of high technology. Inland, factory construction continued, especially on industrial estates close to highways. An example is Shōō, Okayama Prefecture, located in the Tsuyama Basin. Being only two hours away from Ōsaka and three hours away from Hiroshima, Shōō has successfully attracted factories with high levels of processing. The city is also attempting to create new types of industry by marrying scientific research with the industrial technique development that is being carried out at Higashihiroshima, in Hiroshima Prefecture.

Notes (P.63)
[1] The products of steel works and those of the petrochemical plants are processed many times before they are converted into products that we use for our daily lives, such as cars, clothes and medicines. When several processes are involved, it is said that "the level of processing is high."

Cultivation raft

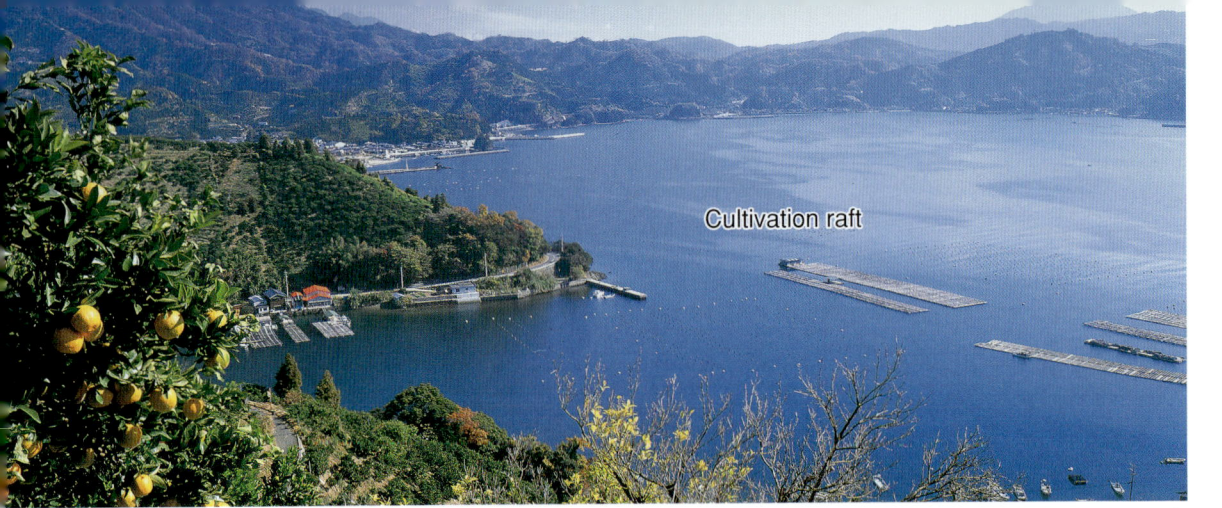

▲ ① **Cultivation and culture of citrus fruits** (Ehime Prefecture). Setouchi provides a favorable environment for the cultivation of citrus fruits (left). The photograph shows the calm waters of a bay under a serene sky. This kind of gentle landscape is typical of the region.

◄ ② **Rice-cropping on reclaimed land** (Okayama Prefecture)

Links between nature and Setouchi's agriculture and fisheries

Natural conditions have always presented a major challenge for farming in Setouchi, and finding ways of coming to terms with nature has become a characteristic feature of the region's agriculture.

First, in order to expand the limited amount of cultivated land, farmers often resorted to land reclamation. Reclaimed land, some of it dating from the Edo period can be seen in various regions of Setouchi, but perhaps the most famous example is the broad extent of reclaimed land around the shores of Kojima Bay. Moreover, reservoirs were constructed in many locations for the purpose of securing water for agriculture. In no other region of Japan have so many measures been taken to improve the natural environment for farming. Fruit cultivation in hilly areas is another characteristic of agriculture in Setouchi, a region where flat land is scarce. Ehime Prefecture is famous in Japan for its citrus fruit production, and Okayama Prefecture is a leading national producer of peaches and grapes.

The Seto Inland Sea is surrounded by mountains on all sides. The sea is studded with many islands, large and small, whose people make their living by fishing, agriculture, the stone industry, maritime trade, and tourism. The complex and long coastline is well endowed with small-scale, but good harbors that are mainly involved in the coastal fishing industry.

Moreover, a sheltered environment of bays and islands has been a favorable environment for aquaculture. In Setouchi, the marine farming of oysters and seaweed continues to flourish even today.

▶ ① **Unloading crabs at Port of Sakai** (Sakaiminato City, Tottori Prefecture)

3 Industries and life in San'in

A region with a long history

Known throughout Japan for the famous Shintō shrine of Izumo-taisha, San'in is a historically important region and a birthplace of myths. Although not a major region in present times, and although none of its cities has a population of 300,000 or over, San'in contains a variety of small cities including old-established commercial centers such as Yonago, and former castle towns such as Tottori, Matsue and Hagi. In feudal times, these cities were centers of trade and commerce. Today, cities such as Matsue are taking initiatives to attract tourists by marketing traditional goods and by promoting services for tourists, such as the sight-seeing boats that go around castle moats. Traditional Japanese-style confectionery is sold as part of the tourist drive, and publicity is given to local hot springs. Registered as a World Cultural Heritage Site in 2007, the fifteenth-century silver mine of Iwami Ginzan[1] is also becoming a tourist attraction.

Traditional industries and fishing industry

With its shortage of cultivable land, San'in is not endowed with favorable conditions for agricultural production. However, the region has succeeded in switching labor and technical expertise to the production of new crafts and agricultural products with a high value in relation to weight. Examples include the production of Japanese paper (*washi*) at various places in the Chūgoku Mountains, abacus manufacturing in the Izumo Area (the eastern part of Shimane Prefecture), and the production of Sekishū tiles in the Iwami Area (western part of Shimane Prefecture).

▲ ② **A sight-seeing boat sailing in the moat of Matsue Castle** (Matsue City, Shimane Prefecture)

Notes (P.65)

[1] Mining began at the beginning of the sixteenth century and yielded large quantities of silver. At present, the remains of the mine are conserved, and evidence of the mining techniques used in those days can be seen.

▲ ① **Shallot agriculture on the Tottori sand dunes** (Tottori Prefecture)

▲ ② **Cattle raised in Hiruzen Highlands** (Okayama Prefecture)

Along the coast of the Sea of Japan, fisheries continue to flourish. Sakaiminato is San'in's largest fishing port. The processing of marine products is still prevalent in Nagato, where whale fishing thrived during the Edo period. In some fishing grounds offshore from the coast of San'in, fishermen use the very bright, *isaribi*, at night, to attract shoals of cuttlefish. This light of these fishing boats can be seen on satellite images.

Dune agriculture and the contribution of measures against desertification

Along with the rest of the Setouchi Area, San'in has always suffered from a scarcity of cultivable land, and crops have had to be grown wherever circumstances permit. From early times, farmers have endeavoured to grow crops on the extensive sand dunes that lie along the Sea of Japan coast. Artificial irrigation, has made it possible to use the dune zone for vegetable cultivation, and watermelon production, in particular, has become a flourishing business. San'in is also one of western Japan's leading areas for shallot cultivation.

Local expertise in converting unpromising sand dunes into agricultural land has recently taken on world-wide significance. Results of research carried out by the Arid Land Research Center at Tottori University are being widely applied around the world for the development of afforestation projects. The Center has also pioneered new methods of agriculture in arid lands as well as measures to prevent desertification.

The pasture lands of the Chūgoku Mountains

Farmers in the Chūgoku Mountains have for centuries utilized the gentle slopes of the highlands areas, and the raising of Japanese cattle, in particular, has a long history. From the seventeenth century through to the 1920s, the Chūgoku Mountains zone was one of the country's leading regions for raising Japanese cattle. These cattle were originally used as draft animals, but an improvement in breeding techniques made it possible to raise cattle for beef production. Japan's famous brands of beef, such as Kōbe and Matsusaka beef, have their origins in the Tajima beef produced in the Chūgoku Mountains. In the mountains, in former times pastures and hayfields used to stretch far and wide across the mountain slopes, but many of the old grasslands are now gradually disappearing as a result of the decline in the rearing of Japanese cattle.

▲ ① **Tosashimizu Harbor** (Kōchi Prefecture)

▲ ② **Beds for the farming of sea bream** (Ehime Prefecture)

4 Industries and life in Southern Shikoku

Pacific Ocean fisheries

Apart from the Kōchi Plain, steep slopes predominate in southern Shikoku, and in most parts of the region, the slopes of the Shikoku Mountains come right down to the coastline. Rapid rivers and many beautiful ravines can be seen throughout the area. An example is the Shimanto River, a river known for its clearness and *ayu* (smelt) fishing.

The Kii Channel in the east and the Bungo Channel in the west function as borders separating the open sea (the Pacific Ocean) from the Seto Inland Sea. One of the characteristics of Southern Shikoku is the presence of various fisheries that make good use of the natural marine environment of the Pacific. In former times, sardine and whale fishing were carried out, but at present, the emphasis is on fishing for tuna and bonito.

Muroto, which looks out on to the Pacific Ocean, is an important harbor for deep-sea fishing, and the large ocean-going fishing boats that it accommodates are used mainly to catch tuna. Along the Muroto Coast and in other places off southern Shikoku, since the prohibition of commercial whale-fishing, whale-watching has become a tourist activity. In addition, Tosashimizu is famous for the *ippon-zuri* (pole-and-line fishing) of bonito in inshore waters. Many factories for the production of *katsuo-bushi* (dried bonito flakes) and of fish paste and other processed marine products, are located in the small coastal cities of southern Shikoku, where they function as traditional enterprises.

However, in recent years, the aging of the fishermen, and the decline in the local fish catch both have cast a shadow over the future of southern Shikoku's fishing industry. By contrast, aquaculture is flourishing. The products include cultivated pearls and fish varieties such as sea bream, yellowtail, and young yellowtail, and the main centers for fish farming are in Ehime and Kōchi Prefectures.

▲ ③ *Ayu* (smelt) **fishing using traditional techniques on the Shimanto River** (Kōchi Prefecture)

▲ ① **Greenhouses in the Kōchi Plain** (Kōchi Prefecture)

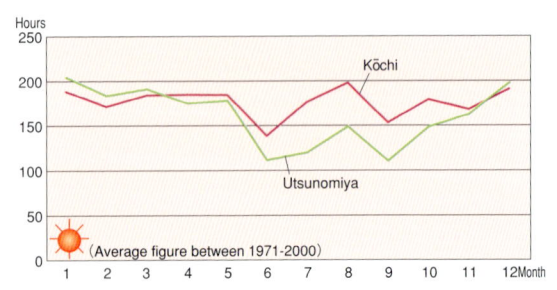

▲ ② **Differences in daylight hours** <Chronological Scientific Tables 2005>

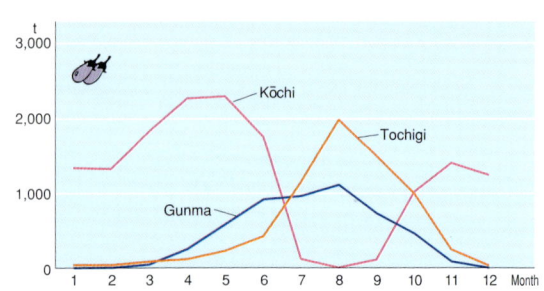

▲ ③ **Arrival times of eggplants on the Tōkyō Market (2005)** <Metropolitan Wholesale Market Annual Report, 2007>

Long-distance transportation of vegetables from the Kōchi Plain

For many years, vegetables have been grown on the Kōchi Plain of southern Shikoku and have been shipped to distant markets, such as those in the Kantō and Kinki Regions. Kōchi's warm climate allows the cultivation of early vegetables, such as eggplants and bell peppers, that can command a high price on the main urban markets of Japan, especially if such shipments can be sent to market early in the year when there are few supplies arriving from elsewhere. Even including the costs of shipment, early crop cultivation in the Kōchi Plain can be a highly profitable business, and Kōchi farmers have perfected the art of meeting demand in distant areas of mass consumption. This is a kind of agricultural development that depends on mass production and mass consumption.

Brand-name agriculture in Shikoku

Since early times, Umaji, a village located in the mountains of Kōchi Prefecture has been known for its production of *yuzu*, a variety of Japanese citrus fruit that looks rather like a shrunken grapefruit. Umaji *yuzu* producers have successfully developed a brand name that is known throughout Japan and as a result, Umaji-made products that have been processed from *yuzu*, are sold nationwide. Agriculture in Umaji is highly profitable, even though the village is located within the Shikoku Mountains and is in area that suffers from rural depopulation and aging of the population.

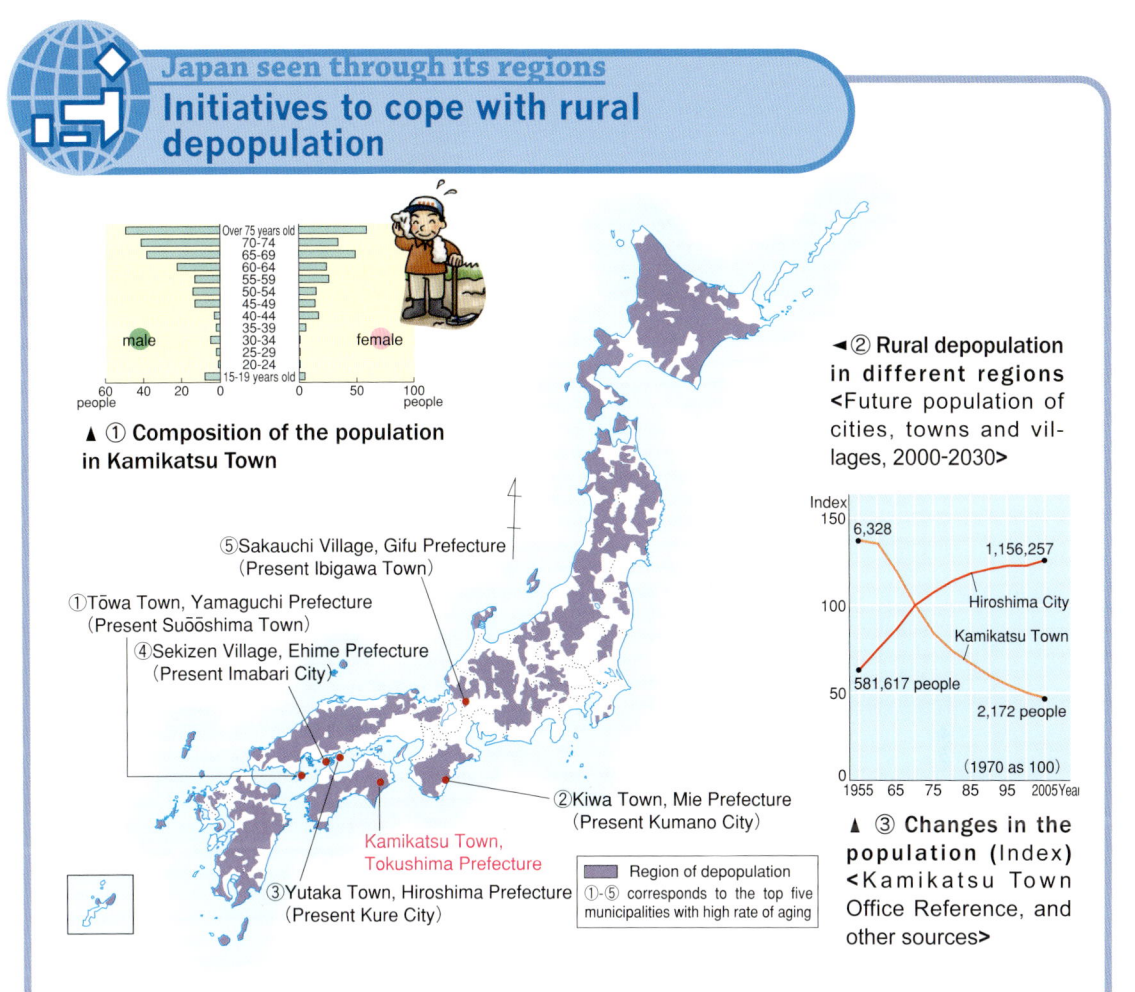

Japan seen through its regions
Initiatives to cope with rural depopulation

▲ ① Composition of the population in Kamikatsu Town

◄ ② Rural depopulation in different regions
<Future population of cities, towns and villages, 2000-2030>

⑤ Sakauchi Village, Gifu Prefecture (Present Ibigawa Town)
① Tōwa Town, Yamaguchi Prefecture (Present Suōōshima Town)
④ Sekizen Village, Ehime Prefecture (Present Imabari City)
Kamikatsu Town, Tokushima Prefecture
③ Yutaka Town, Hiroshima Prefecture (Present Kure City)
② Kiwa Town, Mie Prefecture (Present Kumano City)

Region of depopulation
①-⑤ corresponds to the top five municipalities with high rate of aging

▲ ③ Changes in the population (Index)
<Kamikatsu Town Office Reference, and other sources>

When rural depopulation occurs, village life is made difficult by an outflow of young people, who leave the village to seek work in towns and cities. The Chūgoku Mountains zone is said to have been the first zone in Japan to have suffered from rural depopulation. During the period of fast economic growth, from the early 1960s to the early 1970s, there was a rapid outflow of population from villages in the mountains. The outflow of young people resulted in the aging of the populations of rural areas, and in consequence, created today's twin problem of an aging population and a low and falling birth rate. Furthermore, due to the decline in the number of local people capable of maintaining and supporting social life in remote villages, a variety of features such as old-established customs, local industries and traditional historical festivals have been lost. The same has been true of the elaborate systems of terracing for cultivation, that had been developed on mountain slopes over a period of centuries.

Many initiatives have been taken to counter the process of rural depopulation. For example, of Kamikatsu, in Tokushima Prefecture, set up a local information system which enabled women and older people to assist with the local production of *tsuma* (the decorative leaves and flowers that adorn plates of food at Japanese restaurants). Learning from this example, agriculture that uses information systems to produce and market high-value products can bring back much-needed vitality to remote mountain villages. Relatively close to major cities, mountain villages in Hiroshima Prefecture have developed an exchange project aimed at maintaining local agricultural production. The project involves volunteers from cities participating in one-day trips to villages to help farmers who are unable to maintain their former levels of production. The term "rural depopulation," does not make clear the different conditions faced by each region of Japan. Thus, it is important to take measures against rural depopulation that fully take into account each region's particular circumstances.

Chapter 3
Kinki Region

Kinki Region

The Kinki Region consists of the two fu (special prefectures) and five ken (ordinary prefectures) that lie to the east of the Chūgoku/Shikoku Region: Hyōgo, Wakayama, Ōsaka, Kyōto, Nara, Shiga, and Mie.

As is shown in Figure 2 on page 39, the area formerly consisted of 10 provinces, including five in Kinai, and five dō. Kinai was referred to as the central region of the country in ancient times and was distinct from the surrounding dō. The term Kinki Region first appeared in geography textbooks in 1899. Although the capital was transferred from Kyōto to Tōkyō in 1869, Kinki, which had contained the residence of the Emperor for over a thousand years, was still designated as Japan's central area. Mie is thought to have been included in the Kinki Region for this reason and also because of the existence in the prefecture of the important Ise-jingū Shintō shrine. Ōsaka and Kyōto were designated as fu, or special prefectures, because they were considered to be more important than ken, or ordinary prefectures.

The name Kinki does not refer to the capital, that is, the central city of the country, but rather a capital "district." In fact, Kinki was the only part of Japan referred to as such in geography textbooks.

As Figure 2 shows, the Kinki Region exhibits a clear pattern of mountain ranges extending along the southern and northern sides, and a lowland zone that occupies the center. This division is not a hard and fast matter, but nevertheless each of the three sub-regions of Kinki has its own characteristics, in respect of relief, climate, society, economy, history, culture and various other aspects, and in studying the geography of the Kinki Region, it is advisable to keep the threefold division in mind.

Of the seven regions of Japan, the Kinki Region is the second smallest after the Kantō, but the population is the highest after the Kantō Region. Even though Kinki accounts for a little less than 9 percent of the surface area of Japan, it contains 18 percent of the Japanese population. This reflects the presence of the Keihanshin urban and industrial zone, Japan's second largest metropolitan area, which encompasses Ōsaka, Kyōto and Kōbe. This zone is an old-established urban region and contains thriving industries. The differences between the Keihanshin and the Kantō Regions provide an interesting theme for study.

◀ ① **Yakushi-ji Temple and Mt. Wakakusa (Nara City)** Nara was built as the city of Heijō-kyō (capital of Japan) and flourished for 74 years starting in AD 710. The Yakushi-ji Temple, shown in the picture, was registered as a World Cultural Heritage Site "Cultural Asset of Ancient Nara" in 1998. In 2010, the city will celebrate the 1,300[th] anniversary of the establishment of the capital.

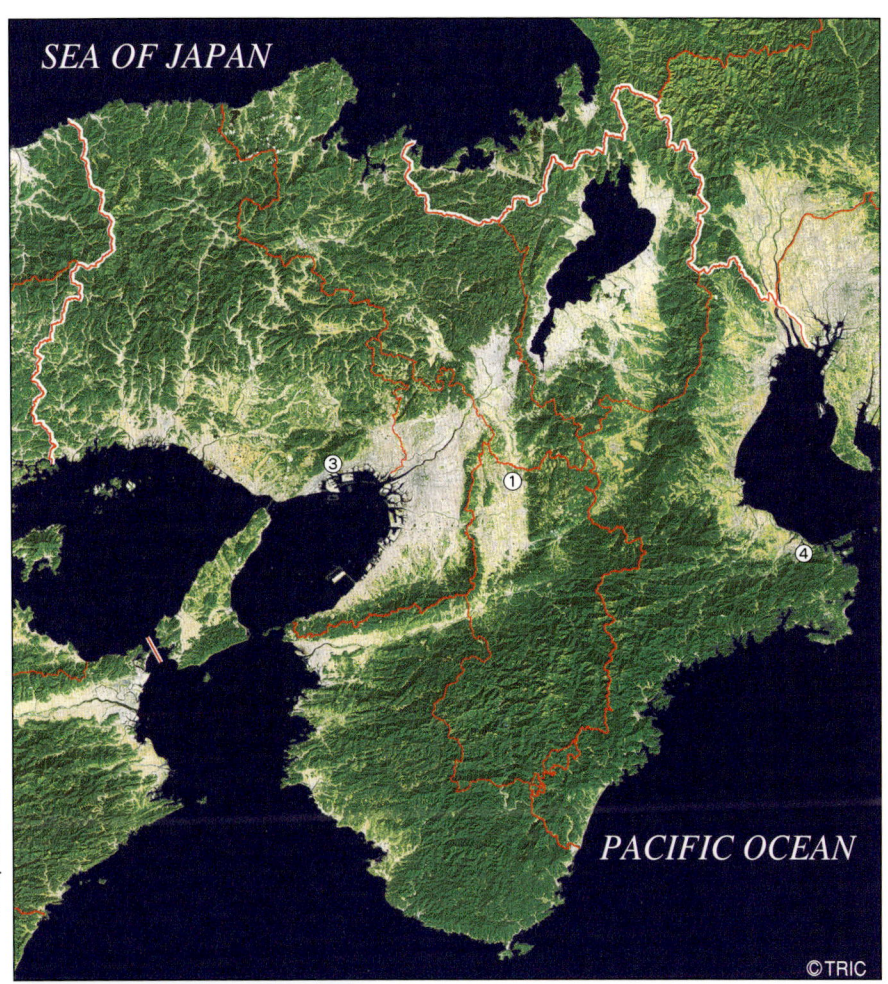

► ② **Satellite picture of the Kinki Region** The circled numbers correspond to the numbers of the figures in the text.

◄ ③ **Ijinkan in Kōbe (Kōbe City)** Kōbe first developed as a trading harbor following the opening of Japan in 1868, and during the latter half of the nineteenth century, many foreigners lived in the city. The nineteenth-century buildings that remain are an attractive feature of Kōbe.

► ④ **Ise-jingū Shrine and Isuzu River (Ise City, Mie Prefecture)** During the Edo period (1603-1867), many people from all over Japan came to worship at the Ise-jingū Shrine, one of the most revered Shintō shrines in the country. There are still many who visit the shrine today. Here we see the Isuzu River, which runs in front of the shrine and is well known for the transparency of its waters.

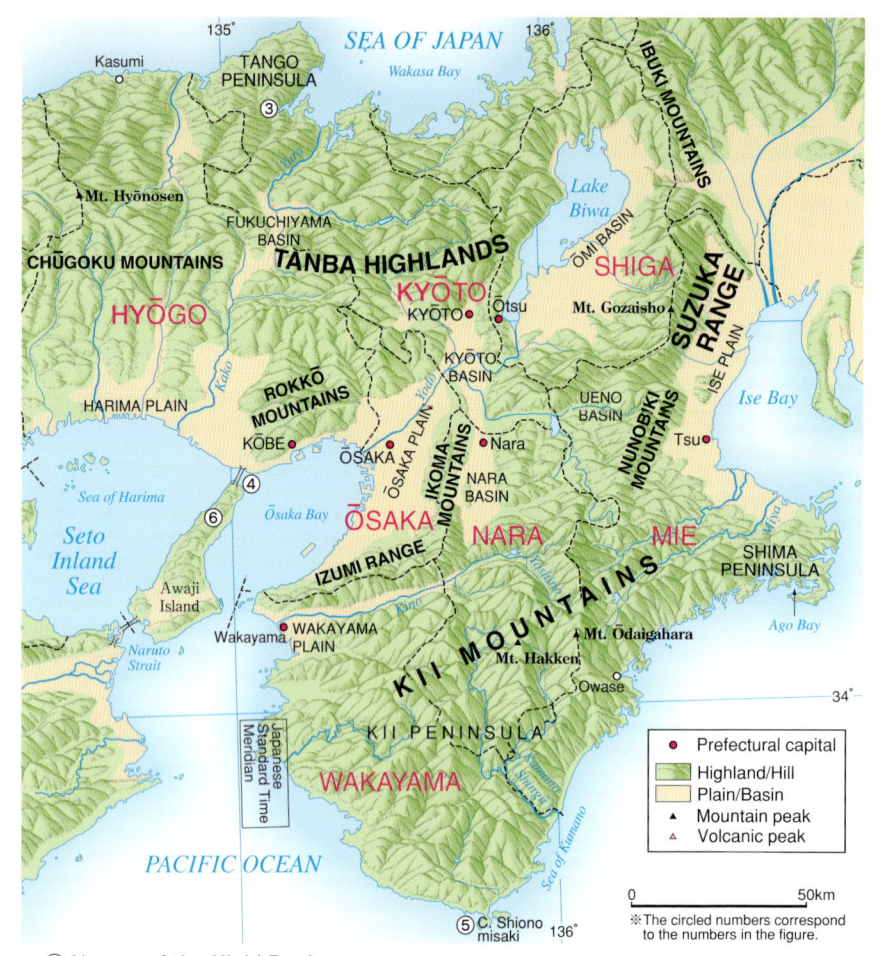

▲ ① **Nature of the Kinki Region**

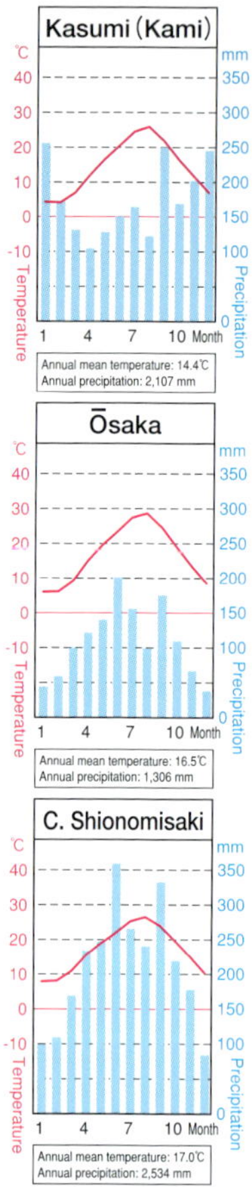

▲ ② **Temperature and precipitation in selected places**

▲ ③ **Amanohashidate (Kyōto Prefecture)** Pine trees grow on the sand dunes in Miyazu Bay, providing a beautiful landscape. Along with Matsushima (Miyagi Prefecture) and Itsukushima (Hiroshima Prefecture), Amanohashidate is said to be one of the three most beautiful views in Japan.

▲ ④ **Akashi kaikyo-ōhashi Bridge (Hyōgo Prefecture)** Opened in 1998, this is the world's longest suspension bridge. As it is close to Ōsaka and Kōbe, this bridge is the most heavily used of the three bridges across the Seto Inland Sea.

▲ ⑤ **Cape Shionomisaki (Wakayama Prefecture)** Located on the southern coast of the Kii Peninsula, the cape marks the southernmost tip of Honshū. The Kuroshio flows close to the shore and the cape bears the full brunt of the typhoons that arrive in Japan in late summer.

▲ ⑥ **Nojima fault (Hyōgo Prefecture)** Faults, the largest gap being 2.4m wide, appeared on the surface of the earth following the South of Hyōgo Prefecture Earthquake of 1995.

1 Looking at the map

The Kinki Region and three seas

Each of the constituent parts of the Kinki Region has its own natural environment, each part looking towards different seas: the northern part towards the Sea of Japan, the central part towards the sheltered Seto Inland Sea, and the southern part towards the Pacific Ocean.

In the northern part of the region, the Chūgoku Mountains and the Tanba Highlands stretch from west to east, while in the south of the region, the Kii Mountains run from east to west. In the eastern part of the region, the Ibuki Mountains run in a northwest to southeast direction and mark the region's northeast boundary. Other mountains and highlands are identified in Figure 1, as are the two main plains at the center of the region, namely the Ōsaka and Harima Plains. Lake Biwa, Japan's largest lake, lies at the center. Other important features are the Kyōto and Nara Basins.

The three climates of the Kinki Region

Snow falls during winter in areas facing the Sea of Japan. Along the sea coast, sand dunes like that of Amanohashidate have developed, reflecting the prevalence of the northwest seasonal winds.

By contrast, the parts of the region that face the Seto Inland Sea take advantage of the warm climate to produce rice and vegetables that are then shipped to important urban markets, such as those in Ōsaka and Kyōto Prefectures. The region's rainfall is relatively low, and for many centuries, local farmers have depended on irrigation systems and on many artificial reservoirs. From an early stage in history, the shipping routes of the Seto Inland Sea connected the Chūgoku Region with other regions of Japan, and with the Asian mainland, and along with the development of seaborne commerce, harbors and cities began to appear along the coast of Ōsaka Bay. Many of these settlements still exist today. In ancient times, the capital cities of Japan were located first in the Nara Basin and then in the Kyōto Basin, and these areas became the historic nuclei for the development of the Keihanshin Metropolitan Area, which today ranks as one of Japan's leading urban and industrial districts. Originating in Lake Biwa, the Yodo River flows from Kyōto to Ōsaka, where it enters the Seto Inland Sea. This river played a significant role in the early development of the Kinki Region's transport system.

To the south, the Kinki Region looks out over the Pacific Ocean. In this part of the region, strong seasonal winds blow, and plains are few and far between, especially in the Kii Peninsula, whose mountains slope steeply down to the sea. The Kii Peninsula is fully exposed to the rains of the *baiu* and typhoon seasons, and precipitation is much higher than the Japanese average. At Mt. Ōdaigahara and Owase, for instance, annual rainfall reaches about 4,000mm (see Figure 7), making the Kii Peninsula the area with the highest precipitation in Japan. Cedar and cypress afforestation has proceeded apace, reflecting successful exploitation of the opportunities offered by the physical environment.

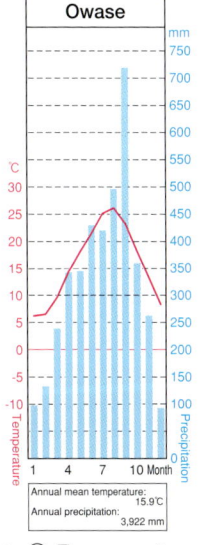

▲ ⑦ **Temperature and precipitation in Owase** (Mie Prefecture)

Annual mean temperature: 15.9℃
Annual precipitation: 3,922 mm

▲ ① Ōsaka Station (Ōsaka City)

▲ ② Kansai Science City (Seika Town, Kyōto Prefecture)

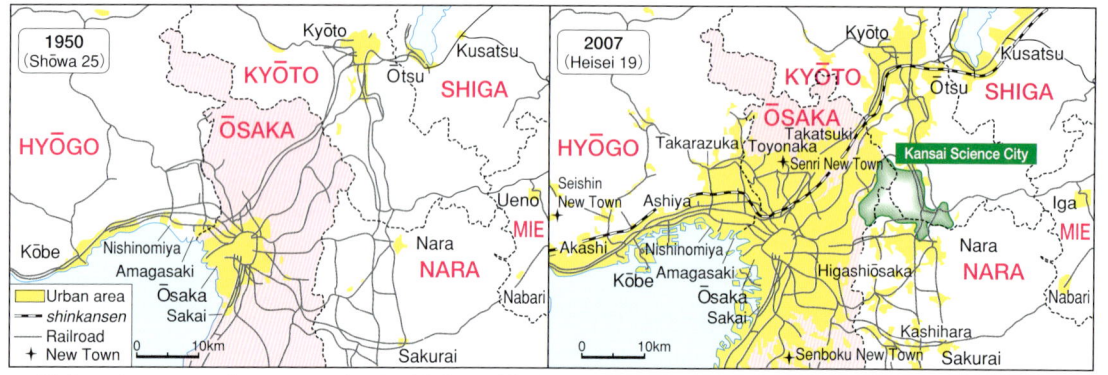

▲ ③ Development of transport in the Keihanshin Metropolitan Area <Railroad Outline, 2007, and other sources>

2 The Keihanshin Metropolitan Area and Ōsaka

One of Japan's most prominent metropolitan areas

The Keihanshin Metropolitan Area[1] is a major feature of the Kinki Region, and has the city of Ōsaka as its core. Centering on Ōsaka Prefecture, Kyōto Prefecture and the southern part of Hyōgo Prefecture, the sphere of the metropolitan area runs north-eastwards to the shores of Lake Biwa, and includes western Mie Prefecture in the east and the city of Wakayama in the south. A striking feature of the metropolitan area is the urban growth that has occurred along the railways that fan out from Ōsaka. After having reached the peak of its growth during the 1930s, Ōsaka, the center of the area, underwent a slow decline in population. However, the surrounding urban area has continued to develop, and includes several outer suburban[2] satellite centers that are linked to Ōsaka by railways. The continued growth of the urban area can be seen in the case of the large-scale Kansai

---

Notes (P.74)

[1] Centering on Ōsaka, and then on Kyōto and Kōbe, suburbs have spread far and wide. Daily commuting to the city centers for work, school, and shopping, as well as for political, economic and social activities, demonstrates the links that bind together the metropolitan area.

[2] Suburbs, the residential areas that surround big cities, have strong ties with the main cities by way of commuting for work, school, and shopping.

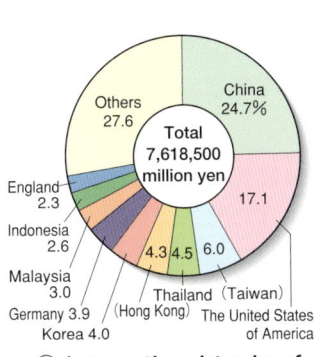

▲ ④ **International trade of Kōbe Port** (2005) <Foreign Trade Monthly Graph, 2005>

▲ ⑤ **Kōbe Port (**Hyōgo Prefecture**)** Kōbe ranks with Yokohama as one of the two great trading ports of Japan. Kōbe's cargo handling facilities were badly damaged in the South of Hyōgo Prefecture Earthquake of 1995, but have now been fully repaired.

Science City, which was recently constructed on the borders of Ōsaka, Kyōto and Nara Prefectures. In terms of the size of its population, the Keihanshin Metropolitan Area of the second largest urban area in Japan, after the Tōkyō Metropolitan Area.

Central City: the development of Ōsaka

Located on the shore of Ōsaka Bay, the ancient harbor of Naniwazu (the distant ancestor of Ōsaka) linked Japan with China and the Korean Peninsula, and functioned as a door through which cultures, people and goods entered Japan. From early times, Ōsaka also developed as a base for the growth of a system of nationwide shipping routes that ran from the Seto Inland Sea to other parts of Japan. Even today, Ōsaka remains important as a harbor city. In the southern section of the harbor, other than the container piers and Japan's largest ferry terminal, residential areas have been built and international trade facilities have been constructed.

During the Edo period, Ōsaka was the main center of Japan's domestic trade in rice, and specialty products from all over the country were bought and sold there. Because of this, Ōsaka was called "the kitchen of the country." With the beginnings of Japanese industrialization in the latter half of the nineteenth century, Ōsaka developed as an important city, and in size was second only to Tōkyō. Railway stations were built at the edge of the nineteenth-century built-up area of Ōsaka, and over time, these railway stations formed the nuclei of new urban sub-centers that also contained department stores and other commercial buildings . In 1929, Umeda Station, the terminal of the Hankyū Railway, became the first station in the world to be combined with a department store. Since then, there has been a proliferation throughout Japan of the same kind of development, in which department stores and other shopping centers are closely associated with stations. Another example of this kind of development in Ōsaka is the sub-center of Nanba.

Kōbe, an international city

Kōbe is one of the most important cities within the Keihanshin Metropolitan Area. Kōbe was opened to foreign trade in 1868. Trade prospered, and with trade came access to foreign cultures and foreign ways of living. Traces of the city's cosmopolitan past remain intact today, in districts such as Nankin-gai, the town of the former foreign settlement that

▲ ① **Collapse of the Hanshin Expressway during the South of Hyōgo Prefecture Earthquake** (Great Hanshin-Awaji Earthquake) (Kōbe, 1995)

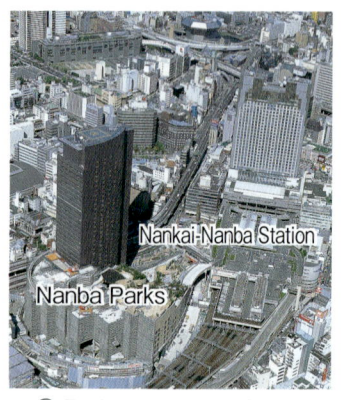

▲ ② **Redevelopment of central Ōsaka.** The Nanba Parks development, completed in 2003, was built on the site of the former Ōsaka baseball stadium. The center consists not only of offices and commercial facilities, but also contains apartments and rented rooftop gardens.

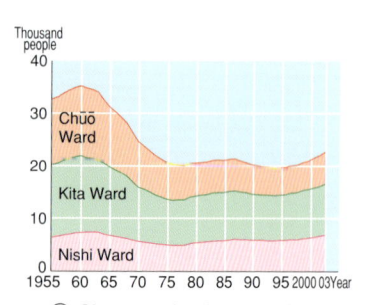

▲ ③ **Changes in the population of Ōsaka's three central wards.** <Source: Ōsaka City> The three wards are Chūō Ward, Kita Ward and Nishi Ward.

is nowadays a residential area inhabited by Chinese people, also in Ijinkan in Kitano-cho. Today, the presence of many consulates and the large number of foreigners who work in the central business district make Kōbe an international city.

In the nineteenth century, coastal land was reclaimed to provide port facilities, and Kōbe now contains one of Japan's leading international trade harbors. In 1995, Kōbe suffered severe physical damage as a result of the South of Hyōgo Prefecture Earthquake, and more than 6,400 lives were lost in Kōbe and in neighboring municipalities. Thanks to the efforts of many citizens and businesses, the damaged towns were quickly reconstructed. The street pattern in the old urban areas was improved, and wider roads were constructed. At present, further community development is under way, with a view to establishing measures to cope with natural disasters such as earthquakes.

Life in the suburbs

In the late nineteenth century, privately-owned railways began to fan out from Ōsaka and railway lines began to determine the directions in which urbanization proceeded. Following this pattern, in the 1960s, Japan's first large-scale outer suburban residential district, called Senri New Town, was constructed by the government on hills to the north of Ōsaka.

There are many other examples of the growth of residential areas along railway lines that in recent years have been modernized to carry fast suburban commuter trains. Towns and cities along the formerly state-owned JR line, which developed later than the private railroad lines, have exhibited especially rapid rates of population increase that have been the highest in Japan. Nowadays, people commute to the Keihanshin Metropolitan Area from as far afield as the eastern part of Shiga Prefecture, Nara Prefecture (in the case of the Kintestu line), the city of Nabari in Mie Prefecture, and Wakayama Prefecture.

While suburbanization continues to develop apace, the central urban area of Ōsaka is once again attracting residents, who are drawn there by the convenience of the efficient transport system and the other facilities offered by the main city. Living in Ōsaka itself means a shorter commuter journey, and the pleasant living environment within the big city also helps to explain the new inflow of people. In central Ōsaka, high-rise apartment blocks are being built one after another, evidence of the recent reversal of the city's population decline.

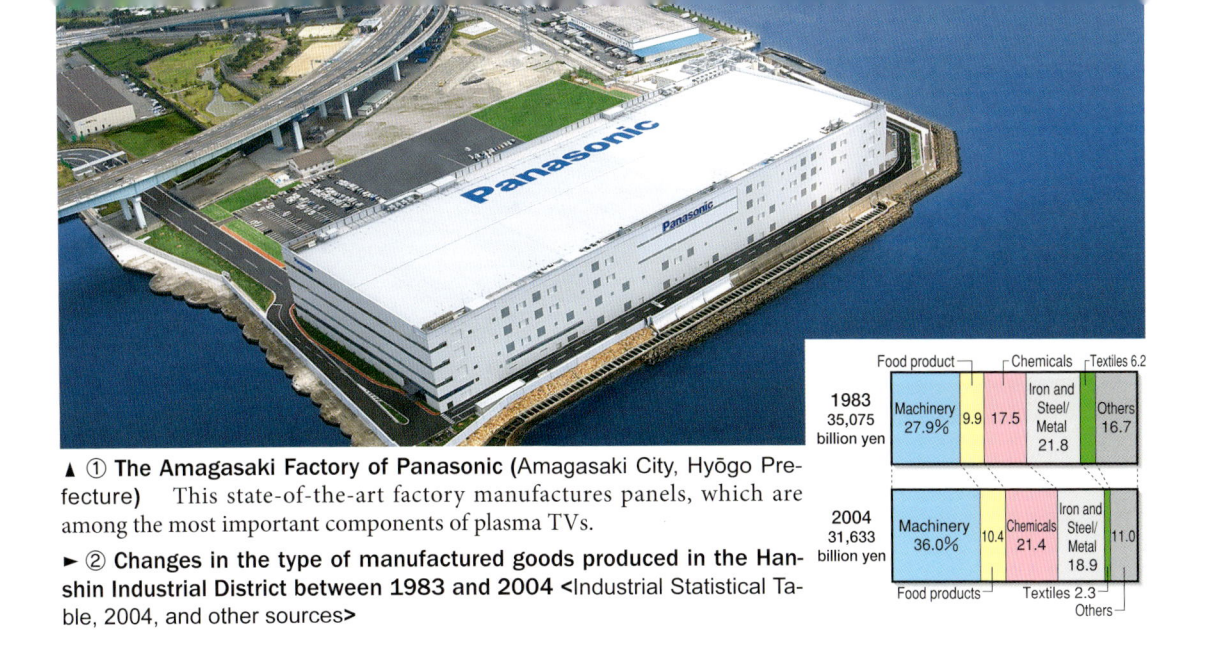

▲ ① **The Amagasaki Factory of Panasonic** (Amagasaki City, Hyōgo Prefecture)   This state-of-the-art factory manufactures panels, which are among the most important components of plasma TVs.

▶ ② **Changes in the type of manufactured goods produced in the Hanshin Industrial District between 1983 and 2004** <Industrial Statistical Table, 2004, and other sources>

1983 35,075 billion yen	Machinery 27.9%	Food product 9.9	Chemicals 17.5	Iron and Steel/Metal 21.8	Textiles 6.2	Others 16.7
2004 31,633 billion yen	Machinery 36.0%	Food products 10.4	Chemicals 21.4	Iron and Steel/Metal 18.9	Textiles 2.3	Others 11.0

3 Industries around the coast of Ōsaka Bay and Kansai International Airport

The structure of the Hanshin Industrial District

  The Hanshin Industrial District contains many factories that are concentrated around the coast of Ōsaka Bay. In the latter half of the nineteenth century, many factories were constructed on land reclaimed from Ōsaka Bay and also in the inland area that surrounded the seventeenth-century castle town of Ōsaka. In the eighteenth and early nineteenth centuries, Ōsaka lay at the center of a region in which traditional cotton spinning and weaving was an important rural occupation. From the 1880s onwards, there arose a modern textile (cotton) industry that processed imported cotton by using machine-driven spindles and looms. Meanwhile heavy industry also began to develop, beginning with the establishment of the National Mint, and later involving state-owned arsenals that made guns and military equipment for the army. In this way, Ōsaka developed as the center of a dynamic industrial district typical of the rapidly growing economy of early modern Japan.

  One of the characteristics of this industrial district is that compared with the Keihin and Chūkyō Districts, the steel and chemical industry remains relatively important. However, industry in the area has been in decline since the 1990s. This is due to tough competition from other Asian countries and to the slowness of the motor vehicles and high technology industries to respond quickly enough to the changing needs of the time. The closure of industrial plants, and the relocation of factories to suburbs and overseas sites has also contributed to Hanshin's contraction as an industrial district. Today, Hanshin ranks as Japan's third largest industrial district, after Keihin and Chūkyō.

  Nevertheless, there has been growth in some sectors of Hanshin's industry. Some of Japan's best-known electronic companies, including Panasonic, Sharp Corporation and San'yo Electronics, have established their headquarters in the Hanshin area. Plasma television sets are being exported from the world's largest factory of its kind in Amagasaki.

  Small and medium-sized factories have long been characteristic of the Hanshin Industrial District. Taking advantage of the city's location with respect to Japan's highway network, many companies have built warehouses and small factories at inland locations

▲ ① Assembling parts of a satellite (Higashiōsaka City, Ōsaka Prefecture)

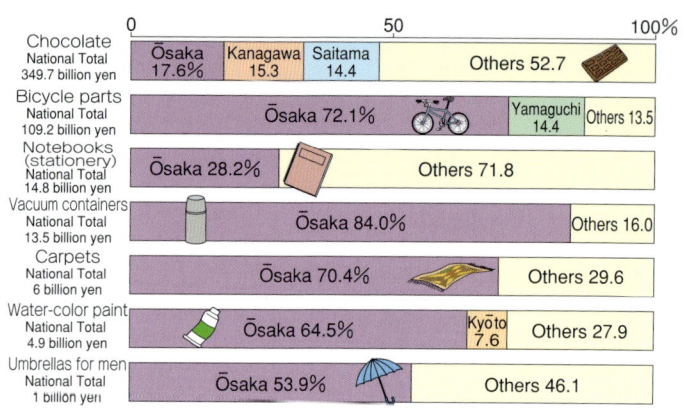

▲ ② Osaka's share in output of selected products, as a percentage of national output, 2004 <Industry Statistics Graph, 2004>

Product	National Total	Ōsaka	Others
Chocolate	349.7 billion yen	Ōsaka 17.6%, Kanagawa 15.3, Saitama 14.4	Others 52.7
Bicycle parts	109.2 billion yen	Ōsaka 72.1%, Yamaguchi 14.4	Others 13.5
Notebooks (stationery)	14.8 billion yen	Ōsaka 28.2%	Others 71.8
Vacuum containers	13.5 billion yen	Ōsaka 84.0%	Others 16.0
Carpets	6 billion yen	Ōsaka 70.4%	Others 29.6
Water-color paint	4.9 billion yen	Ōsaka 64.5%, Kyōto 7.6	Others 27.9
Umbrellas for men	1 billion yen	Ōsaka 53.9%	Others 46.1

such as Higashiōsaka. Many Hanshin factories also conduct joint research and development in cooperation with the laboratories belonging to large corporations and to universities, but at the same time, retain their own distinctive techniques[1] for competing against big companies. For example, one small factory in Ōsaka manufactures parts used in the NASA space shuttles. Although limited in size, small businesses in Hanshin are making strenuous efforts to upgrade their technical skills.

Developments along the coast of Ōsaka Bay

Large-scale land reclamation along the coasts of Ōsaka Bay began during the Edo period. Much later, in the 1960s and 1970s, hills were excavated to provide material for the creation of new coastal land areas, examples being Kōbe's Port Island and Rokkō Island. Sandwiched as it is between the steep slopes of Rokkō Mountains and the sea, Kōbe has always been particularly short of land, and the city has frequently turned to land reclamation. In one spectacular project, huge quantities of earth were cut out of a hillside to provide material for coastal land creation, while the new space made available by the excavation was later used for the development of Seishin New Town. In Ōsaka, redevelopment of an area that was once an industrial zone is under way. Elsewhere in Ōsaka, Universal Studio Japan, a Hollywood-movie theme park, has been constructed on a site that used to be occupied by factories and warehouses.

Meanwhile, in recent years the redevelopment of central urban areas has been making progress carried out, starting with the districts immediately surrounding some of the railway stations. An example is Ōsaka Business Park, a new development to the northeast of Ōsaka Castle. Here new business premises have been laid out on land that used to be occupied by an army arsenal. Meanwhile, development is going ahead on the north side of JR Ōsaka Station, on land that used to be occupied by an old railway freight depot. There are also plans for the construction of new apartment buildings, offices for commercial businesses and an academic research district, all of which will play a key role in Ōsaka's revival.

Notes (P.78)
[1] Involving Higashiōsaka companies that are equipped with advanced technology, a *san-kan-gaku* project (based on collaboration among Industry-Government-Academia groups) is under way in Hanshin. Research teams from the University of Tōkyō and elsewhere are collaborating with local companies and laboratories to develop a satellite, namely To be carried by the domestically produced space rocket, H-IIA. The first launch is planned for 2008.

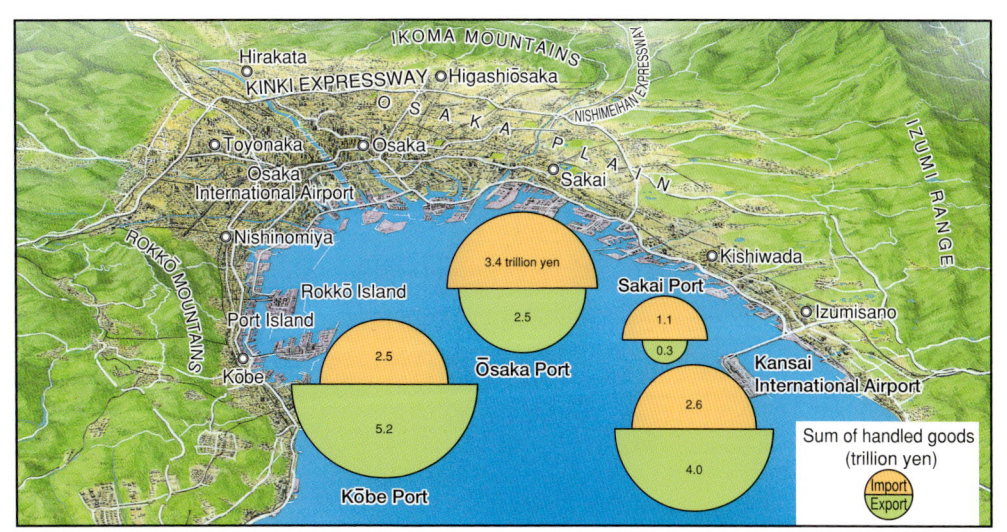

▲ ③ **Harbors and airport along the coasts of Ōsaka Bay**
<Chronological Table of Foreign Trade 2005, and others>

The airport: gateway to the sky

Besides conventional harbors, several airports exist along the coast of Ōsaka Bay. Within a radius of only 25km, there are three airports: Ōsaka International Airport, Kansai International Airport, and Kōbe Airport. The oldest of these, Ōsaka International Airport (in Itami), is now surrounded by housing, and there has been a rising number of complaints from residents concerning noise and security problems. In response to such problems, Kansai International Airport was laid out on reclaimed land in the sea off the coast of southern Ōsaka. The newest of the three airports is Kōbe Airport, built on reclaimed land off the coast of Port Island, and opened in 2006. Its proximity to Kansai International Airport and the great expenditure involved in its construction were controversial issues that led to protests against the airport's construction. However, as one of the projects aimed at reconstructing the city of Kōbe after the South of Hyōgo Prefecture Earthquake in 1995, the project went ahead as intended, under the guise of a disaster prevention programme.

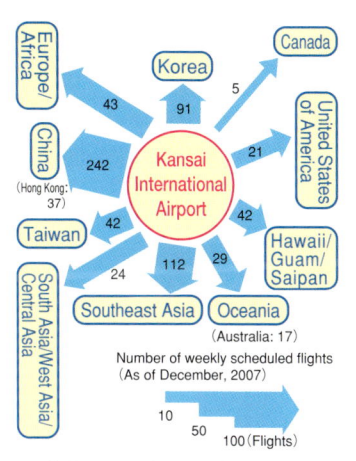

▲ ④ **International Flights using Kansai International Airport**
<JTB Timetable, December 2007>

Kansai International Airport operates around the clock and aircraft from around the world take off and land continuously, using broad and long runways the construction of which has been made possible by the airport's location on an artificial island surrounded by sea. However, other Asian countries are equipped with enormous international airports, examples being Incheon in South Korea, Shanghai in China, and Singapore, where air routes from all over the world converge. In fact all of the major airports of Asia are fighting to win a tough competition to be at the heart of the movement of people and goods throughout the Asian region. Owing to its expensive rent fees for arrival and departure, Kansai International Airport is making little progress in increasing its number of foreign air routes. Nevertheless, a second runway, which is 4,000 m long and one of the largest in Japan, was completed in 2007. Kansai International Airport is working to become the air base of Japan and Asia by dividing responsibilities with the other two neighboring airports.

79

▲ ① Bird's-eye view of central Kyōto (Kyōto Tower in the foreground)

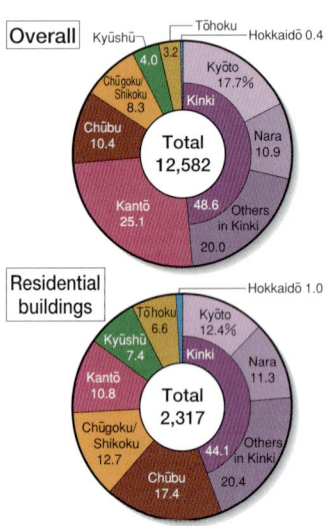

▲ ② **Number of cultural assets by region** (2007) <Source: Agency of Cultural Affairs>

Note) Important cultural asset including national treasures

▲ ③ **Nara Deer Park** (Nara City)

4 The ancient capitals and tourism

The ancient capitals: Nara and Kyōto

In the Kinki Region, Nara, Ōsaka[1] and Kyōto each became capital of Japan in early times, and they were the heart of Japan's politics and culture. In the Asuka district of central Nara Prefecture, many early Courts, called *miya*, were established, and Asuka became the early heartland of Japanese civilization. In this part of Japan, great imperial tombs were laid out, and the remains of many of these have survived to the present day, an example being the Takamastuzuka Tomb. Tombs such as this one are being carefully preserved, and some of them are being excavated and restored.

In 710, the new capital of Heijōkyō was built in Nara and was modeled on the Tang Dynasty capital of Chang'an. Heijōkyō lay at the center of an administrative system which united the entire country, with the Emperor and the Imperial court at the center, following the Chinese example. In due course, the capital moved to Heiankyō (present day Kyōto), and Nara developed as a temple town, accommodating important buildings such as the Tōdai-ji Temple, the Kōfuku-ji Temple and the Kasuga-taisha Shrine. The area that was occu-

---

Notes (P.80)

[1] Following the Taika political reforms of 645, Emperor Kōtoku built the Court of Naniwano-miya in the place that was to become Ōsaka, where land and water transport routes converged. The Court was maintained during the reigns of the Emperors Tenmu and Shōmu, and remained in existence up until the relocation of the capital to Heian-kyō in 794.

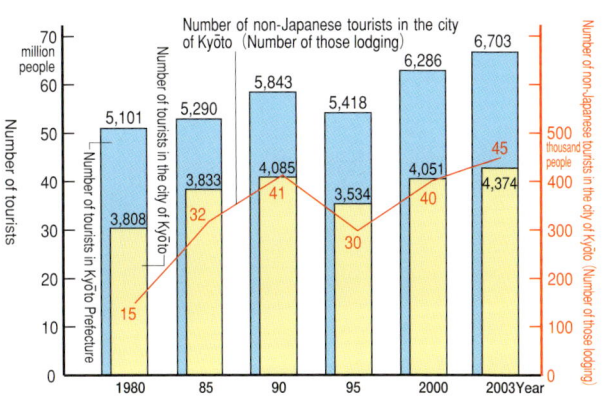

▲④ **Changes in the number of tourists in Kyōto** <Source: City of Kyōto and others>

◀ ⑤ **Yasaka-jinja Shrine (**above**) and a convenience store facing the shrine (**below**) (**Higashiyama Ward, Kyōto City**)** Because of its location just underneath the stairs of Gion, the color of the convenience store's sign uses deeper indigo than usual, and the roof was constructed taking into account the surrounding urban landscape.

pied by the old capital is now the center of the city of Nara.

In 794, the Emperor Kanmu relocated the Japanese capital to the northern part of the Kyōto Basin, choosing a site close to existing overland and river routes, and the new capital city was called Heiankyō. This city, designed along Chinese lines, was the ancestor of present-day Kyōto. The original grid-pattern layout of the streets of Heiankyō remains intact today. Heiankyō developed into Kyōto, and until 1869, Kyōto served as Japan's capital. As such, it was the home of the Japanese emperors for over a thousand years. In 1603, Edo became the political center of the country, but Kyōto continued to flourish as one of the most prominent cities in Japan. Many medieval monuments and buildings survive in Kyōto, including the Kyōto Imperial Palace, and many shrines and temples, as well as the *machiya* (homes of medieval merchants and craftsmen). The city also retains many national treasures and important cultural assets. Some of these assets, such as Kiyomizu-dera Temple and Rokuon-ji (Kinkaku-ji) Temple, are registered as World Cultural Heritage Sites. Moreover, traditional events, such as the summer *Gozan no Okuribi* (bonfire to pay homage to the spirits of the dead), and the harmonious landscape of Kyōto, are additional fascinating attractions. The Gion Festival, that dates from the Heian period continues to be held every year.

Historical tourism resources and new movements

As one of the Japan's principal tourist cities, Kyōto attracts more than 48 million tourists annually from both within and outside of Japan. However, the city not only has various cultural assets, but also makes great efforts to protect its urban landscape in order to preserve the finer aspects of its cultural tradition for future generations. In 1964, controversy was aroused over the construction of Kyōto Tower, which occupies a site in front of Kyōto Station. In particular, there was much concern over the height, design and appropriateness of this modern tower as part in the Kyōto landscape. Protests over the tower's construction led to the eventual implementation of a Law Concerning Special Measures for the Preservation of Historic and Natural Features in Ancient Cities[2] in 1966. This law now serves as a key regulation for preserving the historical landscapes of cities throughout Japan.

▲ ① An old *sake* brewery in Fushimi Ward, Kyōto City.

Nowadays, because of the need to preserve the landscape, electronic wires are buried underground and telephone and electrical poles have been removed in the historical districts of Kyōto, such as Gionhanami-kōji and Sanjō-dōri. Moreover, whenever new developments are planned, care is taken to respect and retain the city's unique landscape. For example, mild colors instead of garish ones are used for new convenience stores. Included in new city regulations[3] passed in 2007 was the standardization of the height of outdoor advertisements and buildings. These initiatives that have been taken in Kyōto to protect the historical landscape have had a considerable influence not just in Kyōto itself, but in many other cities, towns and villages of Japan.

There have also been growing calls for a move from mass tourism, which necessitates new large-scale developments, to individual tourism, which is less environmentally damaging.

Kyōto's industrial aspect

Kyōto is not only an important historical city, but also is one of the prominent industrial cities of Japan. In pre-modern times, various traditional industries developed, starting with *Nishijin* silk weaving, and including the production of cotton textiles, dyeing, ceramics such as *Kiyomizu-yaki*, and *sake* brewing in Fushimi. One section of this old-established industrial base has moved out to the suburbs.

In addition, some modern companies of more were founded in Kyōto and have taken root there. An example is Shimadzu corporation, founded in Kyōto in 1875 and today a world-famous maker of precision instruments. Nintendo, another Kyōto firm, began as a maker of cards and *hanafuda* (Japanese playing cards), before becoming one of the world's largest producers of computer games. These factories and bases are located in the western part of Kyōto, and along the highways in Southern Kyōto, where goods can be transported easily. Thus, side-by-side with Kyōto's ancient traditional industries are famous high-technology companies of today.

Notes (P.81〜82)
[2] The purpose of the Law is to preserve the historical character and cultural assets of the ancient capital, but the legislation also applies to the cities of Kamakura and Nara. The law regulates new development projects so as to protect the landscape of cities.
[3] A new regulation that was implemented from September 2007 for the preservation of the landscape of Kyōto. As a result, the permissible height of buildings in the city of Kyōto was reduced from a maximum of 45m to 31m.

▲ ① **A skiing ground in the Chūgoku Mountains** (Left: Kami Town, Hyōgo Prefecture) **and a view of a railway line in the southern Kii Peninsula** (Minabe Town, Wakayama Prefecture), **taken in the month of February.**

5 Contrasts between Northern and Southern Kinki

Northern Kinki, facing the Sea of Japan

The physical environment of northern Kinki differs considerably from that of the mild Setouchi side of the region. In north-central Hyōgo Prefecture, the gentle slopes of the mountains have long been given over to the breeding of livestock, a type of farming that remains profitable today, especially as regards the breeding of the local Tajima cattle. In northern Kinki, heavy snowfall makes it difficult to work on the land during winter, and in former times, farmers worked away from home in winter months, in the *sake* breweries in and around Nada, close to Kōbe. Northern Kinki contains the old province of Tanba, and it is significant that the term for a chief brewer in Nada is *Tanba tōji*.

The provision of new roads and railways has greatly improved communications between Ōsaka and other towns and cities in the region, and as a result, industry has grown in a number of inland locations. Industrial estates are being constructed in the outskirts of a number of inland cities, including the hitherto rather isolated city of Fukuchiyama, where sericulture once prospered.

Tourism based on North Kinki's natural attractions has also flourished. The development of the Kinosaki hot springs resort is an example of this trend. Moreover as one of the coastlands of the Sea of Japan, this region is rich in seafood such as squids and *Zuwai-gani* (the *Zuwai* crab also called the *Matsuba* crab). *Zuwai-gani* crabs unloaded at Taiza Port on the Tango Peninsula in Kyōto Prefecture are called *Taiza-gani* (*Taiza* crab), and is regarded in Tōkyō and Ōsaka as a high-quality delicacy.

Industries and tourism in the Kii Peninsula

Located in Southern Kinki, Wakayama is a long and narrow prefecture that is aligned from north to south. Even by boarding a direct express train, it takes three hours to travel from the city of Wakayama in the north of the prefecture, to the prefecture's southernmost city of Shingū. Along the coasts of the Kii Peninsula, the mountain slopes come right down to the shoreline, and railroads and roads follow difficult and winding routes along the coast. The climate is warm throughout the year, and the region experiences some of the heaviest rainfall in Japan.

The agriculture, forestry and fishing industry of the Kii Peninsula shows that good use

① Cultivation of pearls in Ago Bay (Mie Prefecture)
Pearls are cultivated in inlets along the intricate coastline.

is being made of the opportunities provided by the region's distinctive environment. The slopes of the mountains and the hilly areas are used for growing *Kishū-mikan* (*Kishū* tangerines) and *Nankō-ume* (*Nankō* plums). Forestry flourishes in the well-wooded Kii Mountains. Many of the forests, which consist mainly of cedars and cypress varieties, are privately owned. Among the tree species for which Kii is famous is the *Yoshino* cedar, a high-quality wood known for its straightness, beautiful color and strength, and for the dense pattern of its growth rings. The aroma of the wood is such that it is in much demand for making barrels. Efforts are continually being made to protect and cultivate the peninsula's mountain forests, in the face of competition from cheap imported timber and despite the aging of the communities that are involved in forestry. So far as marine resources are concerned, fish farming of red snappers flourishes in the sheltered waters of the intricate bay at Kushimoto Town, at the peninsula's southern tip. Fish farming specialists in Wakayama Prefecture succeeded in raising tuna, for the first time anywhere in the world, in 2002. In this part of Japan, as much effort is being put into the farming of marine products as it is into the conventional catching of fish in the open sea.

On the eastern side of the Kii Peninsula lies the smaller Shima Peninsula, which belongs to the territory of Mie Prefecture. The Shima Peninsula has a ria coastline, and is well known in Japan for its artificial pearl cultivation, and for its beds of edible seaweed. The peninsula contains many sites of historical interest, including the Ise-jingū Shrine, one of the most important Shintō shrines in Japan. Other famous sites of religious significance include Kumanosanzan[1] and Yoshino. Many religious sites are linked by a walkers' route known as the the Kumano-kodō, "the Sacred Sites and Pilgrimage Route in the Kii Mountains", registered as a World Cultural Heritage Site in 2004. Elsewhere in the Shima Peninsula, Shirahama onsen, a hot spring mentioned in the ancient *Nihon Shoki*[2], attracts many tourists. Futami-ura, on the coast of the Shima Peninsula, is famous in Japan for the unusual rock formation along its shore and is another popular tourist spot. In fact tourism is an important source of income throughout the entire peninsula, and especially in the Iseshima National Park, which stretches throughout most of the interior. Improvements in road and rail provision have made possible the emergence of the peninsula as a popular resort area for visitors from Ōsaka and Nagoya. In recent years, some of the railway companies have built theme parks in the area, an example of which is Parque España (Shima Spain Village), a resort built on a Spanish theme.

Notes (P.84)
[1] Name used to collectively call the three shrines of Kumano-hongu-taisha, Kumano-hayatama-taisha and Kumano-nachi-taisha Shrines.
[2] Compiled in Nara, this is Japan's oldest surviving official historical record.

Japan seen through its regions
Lake Biwa and environmental problems

▲ ① Lake Biwa and its surroundings (Shiga Prefecture)

- Use of synthetic detergent containing phosphorus within Shiga Prefecture is prohibited. Selling and presenting it as a gift are also banned.
- Vending machines cannot be placed in specified areas.
- Those who sell bottled drinks must place rubbish bins nearby.

▲ ③ One section of Shiga Prefecture's conventions to protect Lake Biwa <Source: Shiga Prefecture>

▲ ② Marshes in Japan registered under the Ramsar Convention <Source: Ministry of the Environment>

Lake Biwa is Japan's largest lake, and is the main source of the rivers that flow through central Kinki, including the Yodo River. In that it supplies two-thirds of the drinking water consumed in the Kinki Region, the lake plays a vital role in the lives of the region's people. Stretching along its coast are reed beds and marshes that provide habitats for a wide variety of wild plants and animals. Since the late 1920s, however, land reclamation projects have been carried out along the lake's shore to create new agricultural land. Furthermore, many commuters who work in the cities of the Kinki Region have chosen to live close to the lake, causing an increase in the local population, and much lakeside urban development. Perhaps inevitably, these changes have led to the contamination of the lake's water.

To counteract the deterioration of the lake's water quality, Shiga Prefecture took the lead in introducing a convention in 1979 that prohibited the local use of synthetic detergents containing phosphorus. Subsequently, another convention was implemented, in 1992, that protects the reed-beds which play an important role in purifying the lake's water. Administrative and legal attempts of this kind are continuously being made to enhance the water quality of Lake Biwa.

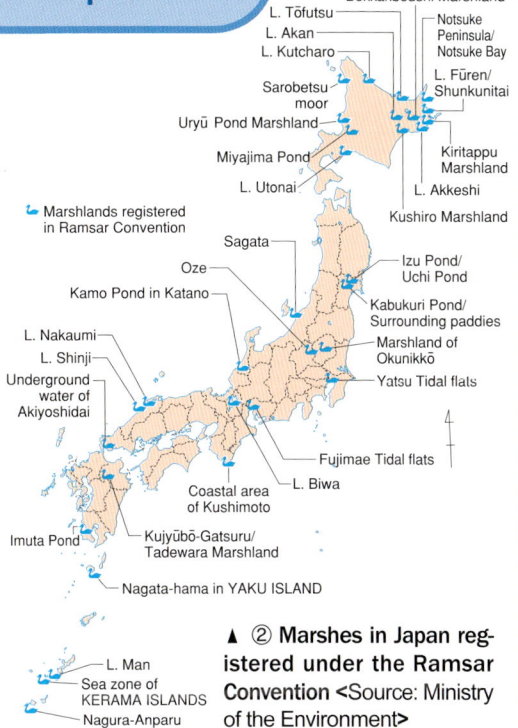

Initiatives of this kind, originally designed for Lake Biwa, are now spreading throughout the country. Based on the conventions of Lake Biwa, a national Law Concerning Special Measures for Conservation of Lake Water Quality has been established, aimed at preventing the deterioration of water quality of lakes and marshes across Japan. This law regulates the emission of waste water, not only by factories, but also by individuals and by farmers.

Lake Biwa is also registered under the Ramsar Convention, which bans the capturing of birds and land reclamation developments in lakeside areas so as to protect and conserve wetlands. Furthermore, the first World Lake Conference was held in the city of Ōtsu in Shiga Prefecture in 1984. The topics that were discussed related to the environmental problems of lakes and marshes throughout the world, and the measures that can be taken to control and eliminate these problems. The Lake Biwa Declaration was created at the conference, calling upon all countries of the world to preserve lakes and marshes. The World Lake Conference is now held on a regular basis, at different locations throughout the world.

Chapter 4
Chūbu Region

Chūbu Region

The Chūbu Region consists of the nine prefectures of Aichi, Shizuoka, Gifu, Nagano, Yamanashi, Fukui, Ishikawa, Toyama and Niigata. Chūbu occupies the central part of Honshū and lies between the Kinki and Kantō Regions.

As is shown in Figure 2 on page 39, the Chūbu Region straddles the three dō that lie to the east of Kinai: the Tōkaidō, the Tōzandō, and the Hokurikudō. Of the sixteen provinces of Chūbu, seven belong to Hokurikudō, six to the Tōkaidō, and three to the Tōzandō. The Chūbu Region is no longer divided according to historical usage. Divisions on the basis of the dō ceased to be included in geography curriculum of elementary schools in 1903, when the modern division of Japan into regions was adopted.

The adoption of a more modern system of regional division was done to give a clear identity to the Kantō and Kinki Regions, both of which had been divided by the former system into three dō. To begin with, Chūbu was referred to as the Honshū-Chūbu Region, but because this name was too long, "Honshū" was eventually dropped, and the region became known simply as Chūbu which means, literally, the middle part or section, and refers to the region's location in central Honshū.

As Figure 3 shows, the Chūbu Region is not only the widest part of Honshū, but is also home to Japan's largest and highest mountain zone in which several mountain ranges run across the central area of Honshū. Some would say that this rather complicated pattern of relief tends to fragment Chūbu, weakening its unity and cohesion as a region. Others, however, would argue that this fragmentation is itself a distinguishing feature, and one that sets Chūbu apart from the other major regions of Japan.

In recognition of Chūbu's internal physical arrangement, our study divides the area into the three sub-regions of Tōkai, Hokuriku, and Central Highlands, and highlights each of their characteristics, including relief and climate, industries and lifestyles, and sightseeing and present-day development.

Throughout the Chūbu region, we can see how the individuality of each sub-region has been shaped through the development of new industries, many of which have come about through the energy and inventiveness of local inhabitants. This latter point applies to all of the industrial developments in the region, whether they be the globally important automobile factories of the Nagoya area, or the much smaller but locally significant factories of the Central Highlands and Hokuriku. It also applies to the many different kinds of recent agricultural development within Chūbu. With its abundance of attractive natural landscapes, Chūbu has also emerged as an important new sightseeing area.

◀ ① **Mt. Fuji and Suruga Bay** (Shizuoka City, Shizuoka Prefecture)

▼ ② Regional division of the Chūbu Region

▲ ③ Satellite image of the Chūbu Region   The circled numbers corresponds to the numbers of the figures in the text.

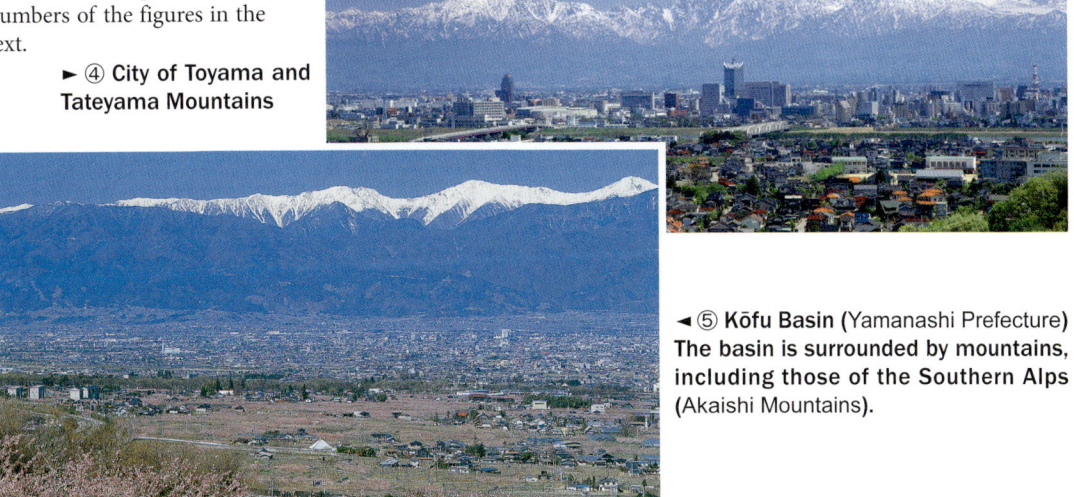

► ④ City of Toyama and Tateyama Mountains

◄ ⑤ **Kōfu Basin** (Yamanashi Prefecture) The basin is surrounded by mountains, including those of the Southern Alps (Akaishi Mountains).

87

◀ ① Nature of the Chūbu Region

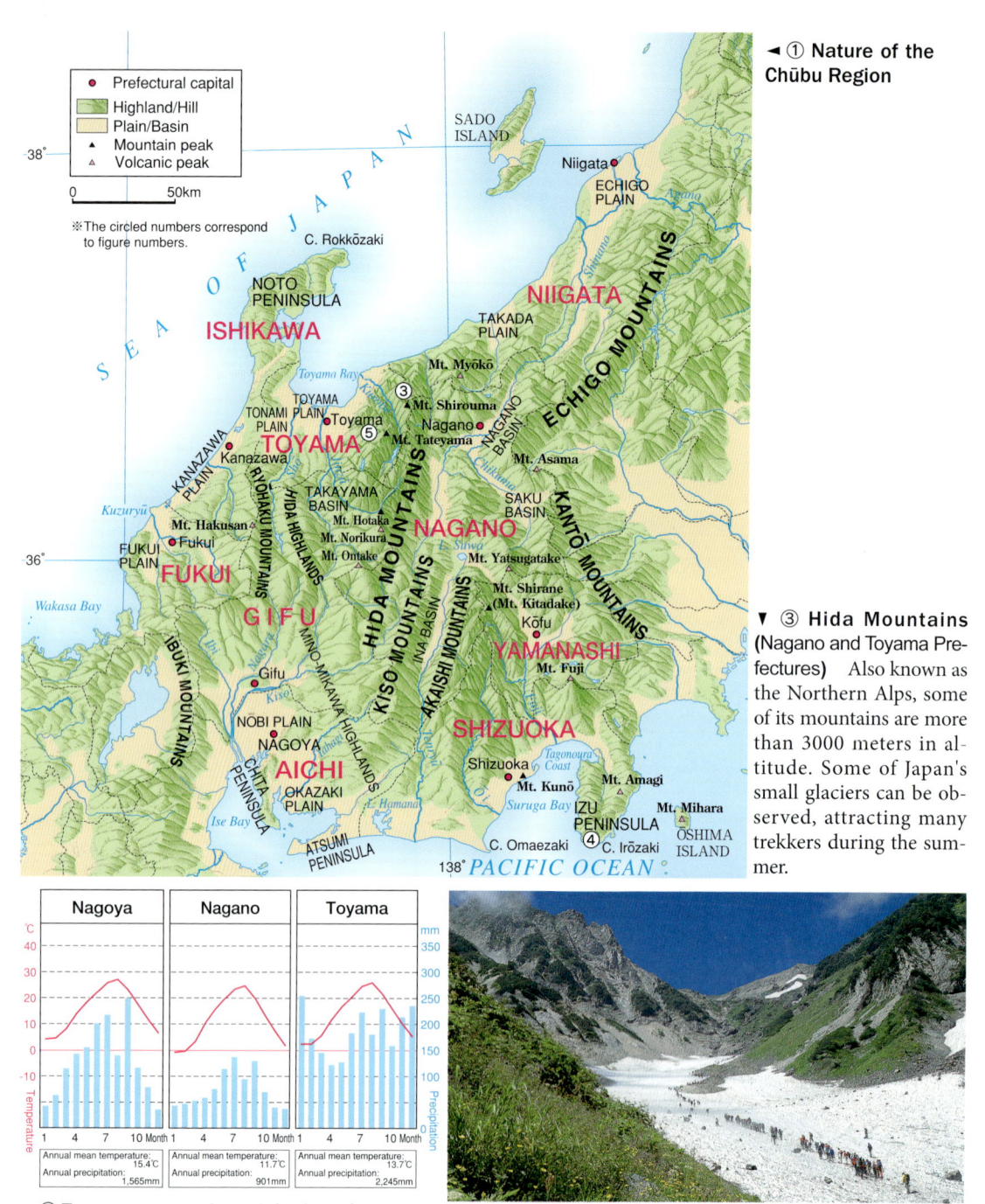

▼ ③ Hida Mountains (Nagano and Toyama Prefectures) Also known as the Northern Alps, some of its mountains are more than 3000 meters in altitude. Some of Japan's small glaciers can be observed, attracting many trekkers during the summer.

▲ ② Temperature and precipitation of selected cities

1 Looking at the map

The scenery which the "roofs" of Japan and river sources make

In the Chūbu Region, there is an extensive mountain area with an average elevation of 3000 meters above sea level. The mountains that make up this area are called the "roofs" of Japan. A major feature of the mountain zone is the presence of three great ranges: the Hida, the Kiso, and the Akaishi, that stretch across much of central Honshū, from south to north. These mountain ranges are collectively called the "Japan Alps," after the

88

Alps of Europe.

In the Japan Alps, rain and snow feed a number of streams that in turn become large rivers. The Shinano, the longest river in Japan, the Kurobe and the Jinzū all flow towards the Sea of Japan, while other rivers, such as Kiso, the Tenryū and the Fuji flow towards the Pacific Ocean.

In the Central Highlands, there are few plains, and population and industry are concentrated along the river valleys. Where rivers converge, there is enough flat land to allow the development of towns and cities, and these have become the region's main urban centers. In addition, alluvial fans have been formed along the edges of the valleys by small and medium tributary rivers, and these fans exhibit a distinctive land-use pattern, often with fruit orchards predominant.

Extensive lowlands occur on either side of the mountain region. On the Sea of Japan side, the Echigo and Toyama Plains provide wide expanses of productive lowland, and are important rice-producing areas of Japan. On the Pacific Ocean side, the main lowland area by far is the densely-populated Nōbi Plain, which contains the city of Nagoya. Other important physical features of Chūbu Region include volcanoes such as Mt. Fuji, Mt. Hakusan and Mt. Norikura. Numerous hot springs exist in association with these centers of volcanic activity.

▲④ **Cherry blossoms and rapeseed in the Southern Izu Peninsula** (Minamiizu Town, Shizuoka Prefecture)   Many tourists from outside the prefecture visit the Southern Izu Peninsula to catch a glimpse of the rapeseed that blooms from January to March, and of the cherry blossoms that bloom from February to March.

Three different climates

As a result of its location between the Sea of Japan and the Pacific, and because of its north-south alignment and predominantly mountainous nature, the Chūbu contains a variety of climatic types.

▲⑤ **Tateyama/Kurobe Alpen Route** (Tateyama Town, Toyama Prefecture)   Consisting of snow piled up during the wintertime, the snow wall reaches above 10m in height.

The Tōkai Area, which stretches along the Pacific Ocean, experiences warm summer weather with heavy rainfall because of the proximity of the warm Kuroshio. In particular, weather conditions in the Atsumi and Southern Izu Peninsulas are warm enough for rapeseed to blossom in January. Both of these areas are frost-free and enjoy mild winters.

In contrast, in January and in winter months generally, northwesterly seasonal winds bring heavy falls of snow to the areas that run parallel with the Sea of Japan. Winter landscapes on this side of Japan are very often white with snow-the *yukiguni* (snow country) of Japanese literature. During the winter, the Japan Alps experience the heaviest snowfalls in the world.

The temperature on the Japan Sea side of Chūbu Region does not drop as much because of the warm Tsushima Current that flows close offshore.

By contrast, being located more inland, the highly-elevated mountain country of central Highlands suffers severe coldness in winter and low rainfall throughout the year. During summertime, the relatively cool climate of the mountains attracts many people to summer resorts such as Karuizawa and the areas around Lake Fujigoko.

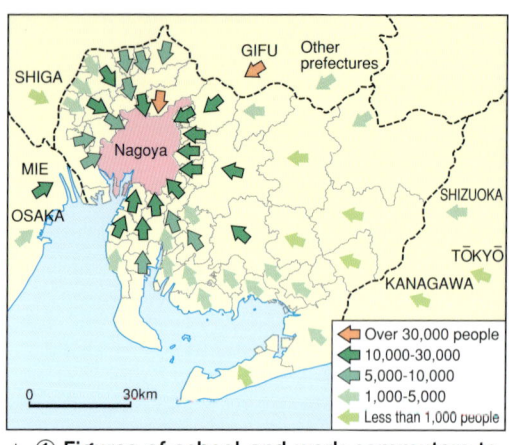

▲ ① **Figures of school and work commuters to Nagoya (2000)** <Population of commuters as well as the population during daytime 2000>

▲ ② **Chūbu International Airport (Tokoname City, Aichi Prefecture)** Opened in 2005, Chūbu International Airport (nicknamed *centrair*) can operate for 24 hours for it is laid out on land that has been reclaimed from the sea. It has become the air gateway of the Chūbu Region.

2 Industry and transport in the Tōkai Area

The growing metropolitan area of Nagoya

Centerd on the large city of Nagoya, the Nagoya Metropolitan Area[1] stretches into Gifu and Mie Prefectures, and it is nowadays the third most populated area of Japan, next to the Tōkyō and the Keihanshin Metropolitan Areas. After the Second World War, Nagoya, which had been virtually destroyed by bombing, was rebuilt according to a city plan that was based on a grid pattern of wide roads. The influence of this plan can be seen today in Nagoya's central business district(CBD), with its numerous offices and department stores.

Meanwhile, and accompanying rapid population growth in the area, transport systems were developed to connect Nagoya with the surrounding towns and cities. Within the metropolitan area, cities were equipped with JR and privately-owned railroad systems, resulting in an increasing flow of large numbers of commuters in and out of Nagoya. Subsequently, Nagoya and its area came to occupy a central position on the Tōkaidō *shinkansen*, completed in 1964, and the development of Chūbu International Airport marked further strengthening the area's ties with countries overseas, as well as with major cities elsewhere Japan.

Chūkyō, an industrial district that began with the growth of textile manufacturing

Centered on Nagoya, the Chūkyō Industrial District ranks second in Japan in terms of the value of its industrial shipments. The first industry to appear in Chūkyō was the textile industry which before the mid-nineteenth century depended on raw cotton cultivated in the villages of the plains surrounding Nagoya. The textile industry, including spinning and fabric production, was mechanized from the 1880s onwards, and successfully exploited domestic and overseas markets. Most of the textile industry was concentrated in the Nōbi Plain, where there is plentiful groundwater supplied from the Kiso River water system. During the 1960s, apparel production increased, not just in Aichi Prefecture but also in neighboring Gifu. Later, however, many of the textiles manufacturers relocated to other

Notes (P.90)
[1] Many commuters who travel to jobs and schools in Nagoya live within the region that lies within a 50km radius from Nagoya Station

▲③ **Chūkyō Industrial District** (Aichi Prefecture)　Iron and steel works and petrochemical complexes spread across the northeastern foreshore of Ise Bay.

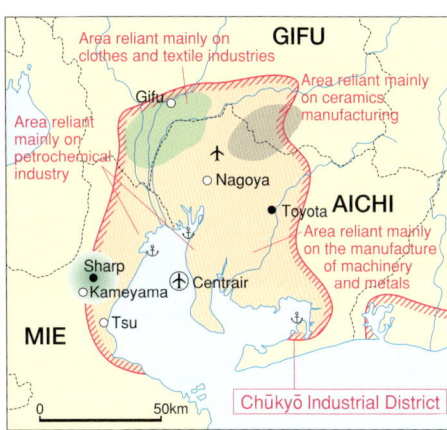

▲④ **The range of Chūkyō Industrial District**

Asian countries such as China, where labor costs were lower, leaving vacant spaces behind them. Many of these abandoned sites have been occupied by large shopping malls and other services.

Toyota City began its history as "the city of cars" when the Toyota Company, a local manufacturer of textile machinery, began to make motor vehicles in the 1930s. This developed mainly by military use, in the 1940s. However, the real development of the Chūkyō motor vehicles industry did not get under way until the 1960s. Toyota City has now become what is known as a company town, and accommodates the headquarters of the Toyota Motor Corporation, as well as car assembly plants, and the factories of motor parts makers.

Meanwhile, in the 1960s and early 1970s, the steel and petrochemicals industries also grew rapidly. Because of their dependence on imported raw materials and fuels, most of the region's heavy industrial plants became crowded together along the coast of Ise Bay. At the same time, rapid development of inland concentrations of industry went ahead in the Nōbi Plain, where amongst other things an aircraft parts factory is located, as well as at Seto and Tajimi, where the traditional pottery industry is switching into the production of advanced ceramics[2], and at Kameyama, where Sharp Corporation operates a factory for the manufacture of LCD television sets.

Nature and transport in the Tōkai Industrial District

The Tōkai Industrial District extends along the coastline of the Pacific Ocean into Shizuoka Prefecture. The earliest industries in Tōkai were based on local natural conditions and on the good transport links that developed between Tōkai and neighboring areas. Hamamatsu is famous as a center for the manufacture of musical instruments, an industry whose early growth was based on the availability of local timber resources and on the techniques applied in the nearby wood-processing industry, which in turn developed on the basis of timber transported along the Tenryū River. During the Second World War, musical instruments and textile factories were requisitioned and converted into factories for producing components for warplanes. This kind of industrial activity gave local manu-

---

Notes (P.91)
[2] A type of ceramics, also called "new ceramics", that gains new functions and features through alteration of the production process.

▲ ① The downstream area of the Kiso, Nagara and Ibi Rivers, where some *wajū* settlements still remain. (Aichi/Gifu/Mie Prefecture)

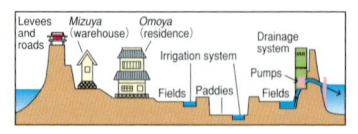

◀ ② **The structure of *wajū* settlements** Agricultural land is in the lower area, while *omoya* (residence) and *mizuya* (warehouse) occupy the artificial higher land. Waste water is removed from the *wajū* using pumps and drainage systems.

facturers valuable experience of advanced engineering, and after the war, firms such as Yamaha and Suzuki grew rapidly by putting to good use the techniques that they had used during the war to make motorcycles and cars.

Pulp and paper mills are concentrated at the foot of Mt. Fuji, where snow melt from the mountain helps to provide an abundant water supply. Attracted by the good connections with the Tōkyō Metropolitan Area offered by the Tōmei Expressway, electronics and biotechnology companies have constructed factories and research laboratories in places such as Gotenba and Susono.

People, plains and plateaus: life in the Tōkai lowlands

In the Tōkai Area, lowlands are concentrated close to where rivers enter the sea, and are surrounded by plateaus and hills. From early times, people living on plateaus and in the hills devised many techniques for drawing water supplies from nearby rivers for daily use and for agriculture. They also took steps to protect themselves from periodic floods.

In the lowlying downstream area of the Kiso, Nagara and Ibi Rivers, annual floods were a serious menace, but from the beginning of the Edo period (1603-1867), people began to construct *wajū*, hamlets enclosed by levees high enough to prevent flooding. First appearing in the lowlands of present day southern Gifu Prefecture, hamlets of this kind became characteristic of lowland zones throughout the western half of the Nōbi Plain.

However, since the Meiji period (1868-1912), the introduction of modern embankments reduced the incidence of severe flooding, and the *wajū* lost their importance gradualy. Subsequently, most of the *wajū* and their pre-modern embankments disappeared as a result of residential development and road construction.

In contrast to the lowlands, the plateaus suffer from a scarcity of water resources, and the spread of cultivation and settlements over plateau land occurred only slowly. On the

▲ ③ **Cultivation of house melons** (Aichi Prefecture)   The melons are grown in greenhouses under carefully controlled temperatures.

▲ ④ **Cultivation of chrysanthemums using electronic light** (Aichi Prefecture)   Uniquely, chrysanthemums can bloom just when daylight hours are getting short. Using this feature, growers use electronic light to create daytime conditions artificially within greenhouses so as to delay the blossoming season. The blooms are prepared for shipment around New Year's Day.

West Mikawa plateau, farming began in the latter half of the nineteenth century, when the Meiji Irrigation Canal was built to draw water from the Yahagi River to the plateau of Okazaki Plain. Later, after the Second World War, the Aichi Canal was constructed to transport water from the Kiso River to the Chita Peninsula, while the somewhat similar Toyokawa Irrigation Canal diverts water from the Tenryū River to the tip of the Atsumi Peninsula. These canals are still supplying water to agricultural and manufacturing industry as well as urbanareas in Aichi Prefecture.

The development of different kinds of market gardening

The main agricultural product of the Tōkai Area was previously rice. However, nowadays, the improvement of transport links with the major cities has made it possible to develop market gardening, which flourishes in the area's unusually mild climate. This type of agriculture produces high-value cash crops.

In the warm Atsumi Peninsula, crops such as vegetables, fruit and flowers are produced and distributed to the major cities. The peninsula is well-known for its cultivation of house melons and chrysanthemums using electronic light. Near the important urban market of Nagoya, in the Nōbi Plain and in the Chita Peninsula, even narrow strips of land are utilized in order to raise vegetable and fruit crops. Vegetables such as tomatoes and Japanese parsley are grown in greenhouses. From old times, this zone has been well known for its cultivation of garden shrubs and trees. The techniques that were used for shrub cultivation are nowadays employed in the growing of leafy plants. In Shizuoka, which lies astride the main transport routes linking Nagoya and Tokyo, tea fields and tangerine orchards thrive along with market gardens . The sunny and well-drained plateaus of Makinohara and Mikatahara are Japan's leading areas for tea production while the low hills along the coast of Suruga Bay are an important area for tangerine production. In recent years, fierce competition among tangerine producers within Japan and increasing imports of oranges from overseas have brought about a fall in the region's tangerine output. To counteract this decline, farmers in the area are striving to produce new varieties of this fruit, such as *dekopon*, and navel oranges, and are also trying to raise the quality of the fruit that they grow.

▲ ① **An apple orchard in the Nagano Basin** (Ogawa Village, Nagano Prefecture)

▲ ② **Vineyard and Winery** (Katsunuma, Kōshū City, Yamanashi Prefecture) Beyond the vineyards, there is a tourist facility with a wine and grape theme.

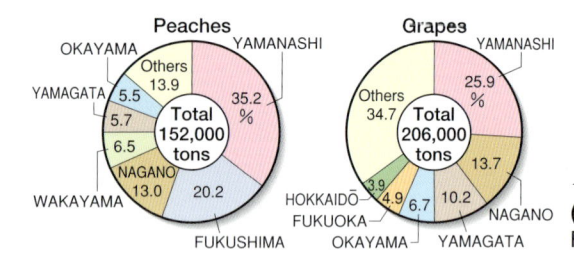

Peaches
- YAMANASHI 35.2%
- NAGANO 20.2
- WAKAYAMA 13.0
- OKAYAMA
- YAMAGATA 5.5
- 5.7
- 6.5
- Others 13.9
- Total 152,000 tons

Grapes
- YAMANASHI 25.9%
- NAGANO 13.7
- YAMAGATA 10.2
- OKAYAMA 6.7
- FUKUOKA 4.9
- HOKKAIDŌ 3.9
- Others 34.7
- Total 206,000 tons

FUKUSHIMA

◄ ③ **Grape and peach production by prefecture** (2003) <Source: Ministry of Agriculture, Forestry and Fisheries>

3 Nature, economy and life in the Central Highlands

Fruit orchards on alluvial fans

Alluvial fans can be seen inland, in locations such as the Kōfu and Nagano Basins, where rivers flow in from surrounding mountains. These fans have slopes that do not retain water, making them unsuitable for rice cultivation. Until the 1930s, they were used to cultivate mulberry to feed silkworms. However, following the decline of sericulture[1] after the Second World War, a shift in cultivation occurred, from mulberry to types of fruit that could grow on well-drained land. Farmers have succeeded in widening the range of fruit varieties that they grow, and have changed the shipping time so as to increase their income. These developments have enabled them to become some of the most important producers of apples and grapes in Japan.

Alluvial fans in the Kōfu Basin receive long hours of daylight and show big temperature differences between daytime and night-time. These features are well suited to fruit cultivation. So that peaches and grapes, in particular, have been grown here for centuries. Facing towards the sunny south, vineyards dominate the slopes of the Katsunuma alluvial fan in and around the city of Kōshū, in the eastern side of the basin. In fact the Katsunuma area is well-known throughout the country for its vineyards, and is one of Japan's leading centers for grape production. Such cultivation has given rise to a picturesque landscape and thus contributes to the thriving tourist industry in the Kōfu Basin. The opening of the Chūō Expressway greatly improved communications between the Kōfu Basin and the rest of Japan, enabling day trippers to visit the basin from the metropolitan areas. At harvest time, in late summer and autumn, farmers set aside parts of the vineyards for visitors to pick the grapes themselves[2]. Large wineries operated by the Mercian Corporation and Suntory are located close to the vineyards in Kōsyū City in Yamanashi Prefecture and

---

Notes (P.94)

[1] Sericulture is the production of raw silk from cocoons from the work of silkworms which feed on mulberry leaves.

[2] This refers to "pick-your-own" arrangements, whereby visitors are allowed to pick their own strawberries and grapes (and other fruit), which they then pay for. They can either eat the fruits that they have picked on the spot or take them home.

Ⓐ Silk-reeling mill in the mid 1920s

Ⓑ Factory of watch parts in the first half of the 1980s (Seiko Epson)

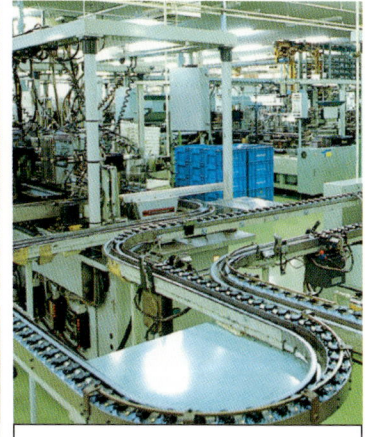

Ⓒ Music Box Factory in the first half of the 1990s (Sankyō Precision Machinery company <present-day Nidec Sankyo Corporation>)

▲ ④ **Changes in Industry (Nagano Prefecture)** Silk reeling was the first form of industry to develop around Lake Suwa, but from the 1950s onwards, the area saw the development of a precision machinery industry that produced clocks, watches and cameras. At present, there are factories producing computers and precisely machined metal parts.

Shiojiri City in Nagano Prefecture, and provide conducted tours for tourists.

From silk yarn to clocks to integrated circuits

From the middle of the nineteenth century to the 1930s, the Suwa Basin became an important center for the silk-reeling industry, and spinning mills became part of the landscape, especially around the cities of Okaya and Suwa. Raw silk yarn became a leading Japanese export, and the spinning industry boomed, using cocoons supplied by neighboring farmers and producing raw silk thread in mills that drew water from the Tenryū River. However, after the outbreak of the Second World War, many strategically important engineering factories were relocated into this basin from Tōkyō to protect them from air raids, and these factories displaced the area's silk mills as the main providers of local industrial employment.

In the post-war era, the factories for clock and camera production that were relocated here during the war merged with technologically advanced local businesses to become precision machinery factories. Furthermore, the opening of the Chūō Expressway in 1982 allowed for easier access and for the more efficient transport of raw materials and finished products, and with this development in transport, the region saw the emergence of factories producing ICs (integrated circuits). The manufacturers of ICs employed existing techniques for making precision machinery, and this in due course led an increase in the production of electronic products and components. For example, Seiko Epson Corporation in Suwa, which began as a maker of clocks and watches, now manufactures printers for computers.

▼ ⑤ **Semiconductor Factory near Suwaminami Interchange** (Fujimi Town, Nagano Prefecture)

In recent years, factories manufacturing electronic products, including electronic parts and integrated circuits, have been built not only in the Suwa Basin, but also in the areas that lie close to the highways between Kōfu and Matsumoto or Ina.

① **Kamikōchi during summer (**Matsumoto City, Nagano Prefecture**)** Surrounded by the beautiful mountains of the Northern Alps, Kamikōchi is a major tourist attraction in the Central Highlands of central Honshū. During summer, many tourists visit Kamikōchi for trekking and also to take refuge from the heat of the plains. In order to preserve the rich mountain environment, use of private cars has been regulated since 1975. Since 2004, entry of tourist coaches into the area has also been regulated at particular times of the year. When restrictions are in force, tourists must transfer on to low-emission buses, which can be seen in Figure 2, to reach their final destination.

② **A low-emission bus destined for Kamikōchi. (**Matsumoto City, Nagano Prefecture**). The buses that run in Kamikōchi are equipped with exhaust regulators for preserving the environment.**

Abundant nature - and various tourism

The Central Highlands of central Honshū consist of high mountains with an average elevation of 3000 meters above sea level, highlands and lakes rich in attractive scenery, and hot spring resorts. Several zones in the area are designated as national parks and quasi-national parks. Thus, this highland attracts many tourists all year round, and mostly from the metropolitan areas of Tōkyō and Nagoya. *Shinkansen* and modern highways were built in preparation for the opening of the Nagano Winter Olympics in 1998.

However, perhaps inevitably, the development of the tourist industry has caused damage to the environment. For example, the crowds of summer trekkers who visit places such as Kamikōchi and Mt. Norikura travel to the mountains by car and therefore bring with them problems of air pollution and also cause a negative impact on plants and animals. This is why the use of private cars in the Central Highlands has been restricted. Moreover, new types of tourism are coming to the fore. These include agritourism, in which visitors from outside can sample life in agricultural villages, and ecotourism, which focuses on the preservation of the natural environment.

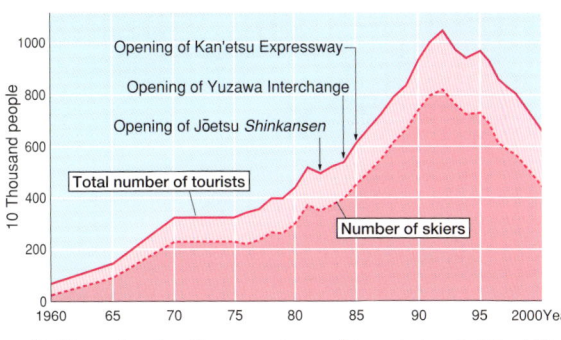

▲ ① **Changes in the number of tourists visiting Yuzawa Town, Niigata Prefecture** <Source: Yuzawa> From early times, Yuzawa has been a popular hot springs resort. With the opening of the Jōetsu *shinkansen* and the Kan'etsu Expressway, the skiing grounds and resort including the residential hotels in and around the town began to attract more tourists. However, tourist numbers have fallen somewhat in recent years.

▲ ② **Snow-melting pipe and snow disposal ditch** (Niigata Prefecture) Snow-melting pipes sprinkle ground water to melt snow. Snow disposal ditches are drains built below the roads to carry away the snow to rivers.

4 Life and economy in snowy Hokuriku

Living with snow

The Hokuriku Area experiences some of the heaviest snowfalls in the world. This is because northwesterly seasonal winds blowing out of Siberia during the winter become saturated with moisture while traveling over the warm waters of the Sea of Japan. When they reach Japan, the saturated air masses rise on contact with the mountains, and the moisture is released as snow. From December to February, most days in Hokuriku are either snowy or cloudy. In the mountains, where the snow can accumulate to a depth of three to four meters, and the people must remove snow from rooftops and from roads. Snow plows and snow-melting pipes have been introduced in the area to help with shifting the snow, but during heavy blizzards, snow can pile up on roads and railroads.

While snow causes big problems for the population, it also contributes to the area's life and industry. When temperatures rise, snow melts into the rivers to provide water for agriculture and factories. Water accumulated behind dams also generates hydroelectricity. In addition, the snowy areas have developed their own form of tourism, in the form of skiing grounds and other similar winter sports facilities. These provide employment opportunities for local people during the winter.

However, a wane in the popularity of skiing as well as a decrease in annual snowfall have brought about a fall in winter tourists in recent years, and many skiing grounds are closing down as a result. Several new initiatives[1] are being taken to overcome this problem. For example, skiing grounds are being transformed into forests in an attempt to regain the lost natural environment, and snow is being used in new ways for agriculture and tourism.

Besides issues concerning snow, the Hokuriku Area has experienced several major earthquakes in recent years. These include the Noto Peninsula Earthquake of March 2007, the Niigata Prefecture Chūetsu Earthquake of October 2004 and the Niigata Prefecture Chūetsu-oki Earthquake of July 2007. These earthquakes have prompted the machizukuri (restructuring of towns and villages) to start devising emergency measures to cope with natural disasters other than snow.

Notes (P.97)
[1] The carrots that have been harvested in the fall will be kept in snow to improve their sweetness, and will be shipped out in the spring. Tours to experience the snow country include recreational activities such as snowball fights and the viewing of snow caves.

▲ ① **Echigo Plain (Niigata Prefecture)**   Stretching downstream along the Shinano River, the Echigo Plain is one of Japan's main rice producing areas. As heavy snow makes any cultivation impossible during the winter, Echigo farmers grow only a single rice crop per year.

Rice cultivation in Snow Country

In the Hokuriku Area, where snow falls heavily in the winter, rice crops have been produced in lowland areas such as the Echigo Plain for hundreds of years, and abundant water supplies mainly melted snow have allowed Hokuriku to become one of the leading single-crop[1] areas of rice production in Japan today.

Since the Edo period, the maintenance of irrigation systems and the development of rice paddies on reclaimed land have been important features of Hokuriku's agriculture. Moreover, production of rice with an earlier than average harvest month, a variety called *hayabamai*[2], thrives in the Kanazawa and Fukui Plains. After the Second World War, the rice output increased following the mechanization of agriculture and the introduction of pesticides and fertilizers. However, from the 1970s onwards, the government began to provide farmers with subsidies to take rice land out of production, and many rice paddies were transformed into fields growing soybeans, barley and vegetables. The same policy led to an increase in the area of unused rice paddy land.

Not all parts of Hokuriku are given over to rice monoculture. In the Toyama Plain, for example, tulip bulbs have been introduced to cultivate before World War II as a second crop in the rice fields. Many of these bulbs are now shipped to destinations overseas as well as to buyers throughout Japan.

The price and the method of selling rice was formerly strictly controlled by the government, but since 2004, farmers and retail stores have been allowed to sell rice as they wish, without restriction. As a result, branded rice that advertises the high quality of its taste has been appealing to consumers. One such example is the *Koshihikari* rice variety, produced in Niigata and Toyama Prefectures.

Notes (P.98)
[1] Cultivation that is limited to one agricultural crop per year.
[2] Rice that is harvested in September, earlier than usual. It is cultivated in the Hokuriku Area, known for its heavy rains and sharp temperature drop in the fall. *Hayabamai*, which is harvested in July, is also being cultivated in southern Kyūshū, an area susceptible to typhoons.

ⓐ **Wajima lacquerware** (Ishikawa Prefecture)

ⓑ **Takaoka copperware** (Toyama Prefecture)

▲② **Major traditional handicrafts of the Hokuriku Area** <Source: Ministry of Economy, Trade and Industry>

ⓒ **Ojiya cotton crepe** (Niigata Prefecture)

ⓓ **Echizen Japanese paper** (Fukui Prefecture)

Why many traditional handicrafts remain in Hokuriku Area?

In Hokuriku, non-farming side jobs have been a feature of the local economy for hundreds of years. During the long, snowy winters, the area's farmers could not work in the fields so they occupied their spare time by engaging in side jobs. Over the course of time, the techniques used in these jobs provided the basis for the development of various types of traditional local industry, and these industries have survived to the present day.

Hokuriku's traditional industries have undergone continuous change through a process of technological evolution, and many of them successfully use new techniques and skills derived from industries that depend on mechanized mass production. Examples of the area's traditional industries include the Sanjō hardware industry, lacquerware making at Wajima, and the Takaoka copperware industry. These industries consist of clusters of very small enterprises which have traditional skills, and each cluster has strong economic and social ties with its surrounding area.

In recent years, old-established local industries of this kind are beginning to encounter a variety of problems including a lack of young people willing to take over the local traditional business, and strong competition from foreign products. However, some traditional local industries have advanced by way of new products and new business initiatives. Examples are Yamanaka lacquerware from Kaga, which has gained popularity on account of its low price, and Echizen lacquerware from Sabae that is now marketed for business use in hotels and restaurants.

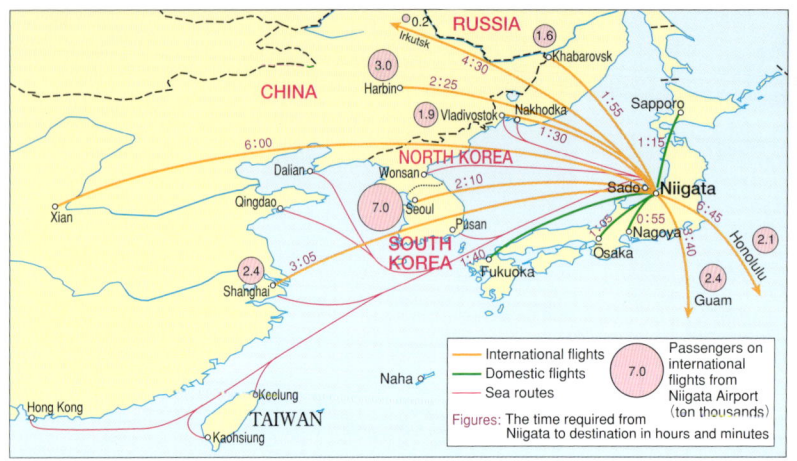

▲ ① **Connections between the city of Niigata and neighboring countries** (2000) <Source: Niigata, and others>

◀ ② **Preservation of a city landscape with canals (Kanazawa)** The parking lot (above) has been demolished to reveal an old canal (below).

Towards the formation of the Japan Sea coastlands as a single multi-national economic region

Hokuriku's cities are far away from Japan's metropolitan areas and are anxious to cement ties with cities both inside and outside Japan.

The central city of the area, Kanazawa, developed as a castle town during the Edo period, when it was known as the capital town of a very large fief in this area. Much of the traditional culture and historic landscape of the city remain intact today. During the Edo period, the feudal lord of *Kaga* fief placed a high value on culture and education and put great effort into the preservation and promotion of traditional handicrafts. Techniques used to produce traditional handicrafts such as *kagayūzen* (*kaga* dyeing products) and *kanazawa-haku* (*kanazawa* gold leaf) have been passed down over the centuries from one generation to the next. Furthermore, some buildings and views, such as the *machiya* (townhouses) and *bukeyashiki* (*samurai* residences built during the Edo period), and the city's picturesque canals, still retain traces from the distant past. With many historical resources for tourism that are characteristically Japanese, Kanazawa aims to become an international city of tourism that attracts people from both within and outside Japan.

▲ ③ **Kenrokuen (Kanazawa City)** Created as the garden of Kanazawa Castle during the Edo period, Kenrokuen is one of the most famous traditional gardens in Japan, and is visited every year by many foreigners.

Appointed as a government-designated city in 2007, Niigata, located on the coast of the Sea of Japan, is an old-established base of maritime transport. With the development of fast-transit roads and railways, Niigata is also well served by overland transportation and has connections with several other major cities in Japan. In addition, a regular international air service has been established, making it relatively easy to travel to cities in Russia, Korea and China. Niigata plays a vital role in a new economic region that encompasses the coastlands that surround the Sea of Japan- the so-called Economic Sphere for the Northwest Pacific Region-and a major function of this multi-national region is to promote economic exchanges with neighboring countries.

Japan seen through its regions
The light and shadow of nuclear power

▲ ① **Fukushima Dai-ichi** (No. 1) **Nuclear Power Plant** (Fukushima Prefecture, 2011)

◄ ② **Location of major power plants in Japan** (2003) <Details on Electricity Development 2003, and other sources>

- Thermal power plant (Maximum output over one million kW)
- Hydroelectric power plant (maximum output over 300,000 kW)
- Nuclear power plant
- Geothermal power plant (Over 10,000 kW)
- Wind power plant (Over 1,000 kW excluding private ones)

The sand dune area that extends through Kashiwazaki City and Kariwa Village in Niigata Prefecture, is home to the world's largest nuclear power plant, the Kashiwazaki-Kariwa Nuclear Power Plant of the Tokyo Electric Power Company. In the 1960s the challenge for the local governments of Kashiwazaki and Kariwa was how best to use the sand dune area so as to promote the development of the area's economy. The possibility of constructing nuclear power plants was considered as a way of increasing local employment and tax revenues, and local reactor construction became a reality in the 1970s. The local nuclear power station provides a stable supply of electricity to the metropolitan regions.

On the other hand, there have been several alarming incidents at nuclear power plants, such as at Ukraine's Chernobyl Nuclear Power Plant in 1986, and at the Mihama and the Monju Nuclear Power Plants in Fukui Prefecture. These incidents have raised questions concerning the safety of nuclear reactors. Moreover, on 11 March 2011, the tsunami that followed the Great East Japan Earthquake seriously damaged the Fukushima Dai-ichi (No. 1) Nuclear Power Plant. Power output failed, cooling systems broke down, and several units of the plant became uncontrollable. The release of hydrogen led to explosions and large quantities of radioactive material were ejected into the atmosphere, affecting not just Fukushima prefecture but an area that stretched from Miyagi prefecture in the north to the Kantō region in the south. Most affected was a zone with a radius of 20 km from the power station. The government ordered the evacuation of people living within this zone, and over 100,000 residents had to leave their homes, temporarily becoming refugees. Since this accident, concerns have grown apace over the safety of nuclear power plants throughout Japan.

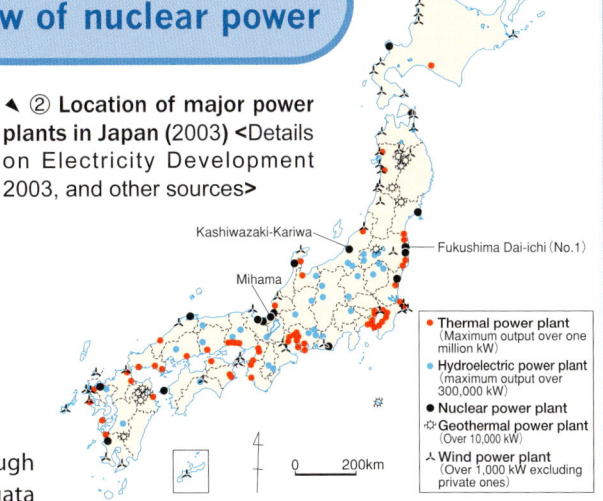

Nuclear power plants in Japan tend to be concentrated in certain areas, such as coastal areas in Fukushima, Niigata, and Fukui prefectures. In Aomori prefecture, there is not only a nuclear plant but also a reactor fuel cycle facility. Why are these nuclear power plants built so unevenly? Every nuclear power plant has the dangers of radioactive contamination when an accident happens. Therefore, they are unlikely to be built in populated regions. They are built in the regions where the population is decreasing and economy is declining. In such regions, local and municipal governments receive government subsidies to activate the local economy instead of accepting nuclear power plants. Another reason why they are built around coastal areas in Japan is water supply. Nuclear power plants require large amounts of water to generate power.

As is the case with nuclear power stations, hydroelectric power plants are rarely seen in metropolitan areas because they use water from dams in the upstream reaches of rivers. In contrast to the aforementioned types of power station, thermal power plants are generally located in and around metropolitan areas, as well in other places close to areas of mass consumption, and have often been constructed close to harbors equipped with facilities for handling imports of natural gas. Thus we can see that each type of power plant has its own geographical distribution as their distinctive requirements for location.

Chapter 5
Kantō Region

Kantō Region

The Kantō Region contains the capital of Japan, Tōkyō, and the six neighboring prefectures of Kanagawa, Chiba, Saitama, Gunma, Tochigi and Ibaraki.

As we can see from Figure 2 on page 39, the Kantō Region was in ancient times partly located in the Tōkaidō, and partly in the Tōzandō, however there has been an idea since Nara period (710 - 784) that the two sections were consolidated into the one area of Kantō. Kantō literally means "eastern side of (a certain) checkpoint". When Edo became the political center of Japan during the Edo period (1603 - 1867), the Hakone checkpoint became important for regulating the flow of travelers into and out of the strategically important region surrounding Edo, and as a result, "Kantō" came to refer to the eight provinces to the east of the checkpoint. This area is much the same as the present-day Kantō Region.

The area was formally designated as the Kantō Region in 1903 when the divisions shown on page 39 were abolished and replaced by modern regional divisions in elementary school geography textbooks. In fact, the dō divisions were replaced with regional divisions partly in order to emphasize the relatively new fact that Tōkyō was the capital of Japan, and not Kyōto. For this reason, the introduction of the new regions began with the demarcation of the Kantō Region, in which Tōkyō lies.

The Kantō Region is a physically diverse area and contains the Tone River basin, the Kantō Plain, which is Japan's largest area of lowland, and the mountains surrounding the plain. This diversity is one of the reasons why this part of Japan was described during the Edo period as the Kanhasshu, or the eight shū of Kantō.

Of the seven main regions of Japan, the Kantō Region is the smallest and occupies a mere 8% of Japan's land area. However, as many as 40 million people, close to a third of Japan's population, reside within the region. The Greater Tōkyō Area, we should remember, is the largest metropolitan area in the world. The primary reason why the status of the Kantō Region has risen to such prominence is because Tōkyō is the capital of Japan.

Vegetable farming and stock breeding flourish in the Kantō Region, and Kantō is Japan's leading region for vegetable production. This is partly because of the existence of plateau soils that are suitable for vegetable cultivation, and partly because of the presence of a huge consumer market in the form of the Tōkyō Metropolitan Area. In almost every respect, the Kantō Region is an area that revolves around Tōkyō.

◀① **Area around Shinagawa Station** (Tōkyō Prefecture) The area around Shinagawa Station was redeveloped with many of the new buildings occupying the site of a former freight marshalling yard. The Rainbow Bridge can be seen in the background.

▶ ② **Satellite image of the Kantō Region** The circled numbers correspond to the numbers of the figures in the text.

▶ ③ **Mt. Tanigawa (Gunma Prefecture)** Located in the upstream area of the Tone River, Mt. Tanigawa lies on the border of Niigata and Gunma Prefectures. The photograph captures the nature of the landscape in May. In the mountains, melting snow feeds the streams that become the Tone River, and the Tone provides water that is vital for people, farming and industry in the Kantō Plain.

◀ ④ **Kantō Plain (Aerial photograph taken above the city of Kasukabe City, looking northeastwards. Saitama Prefecture)** This is the largest plain in Japan, and extends over almost the whole of the Kantō Region.

▼ ② Temperature and precipitation of selected cities <Scientific Chronological Table, 2007> The region experiences its maximum rainfall not during the *baiu* season, but in September with the coming of the typhoons.

▲ ① Nature of the Kantō Region

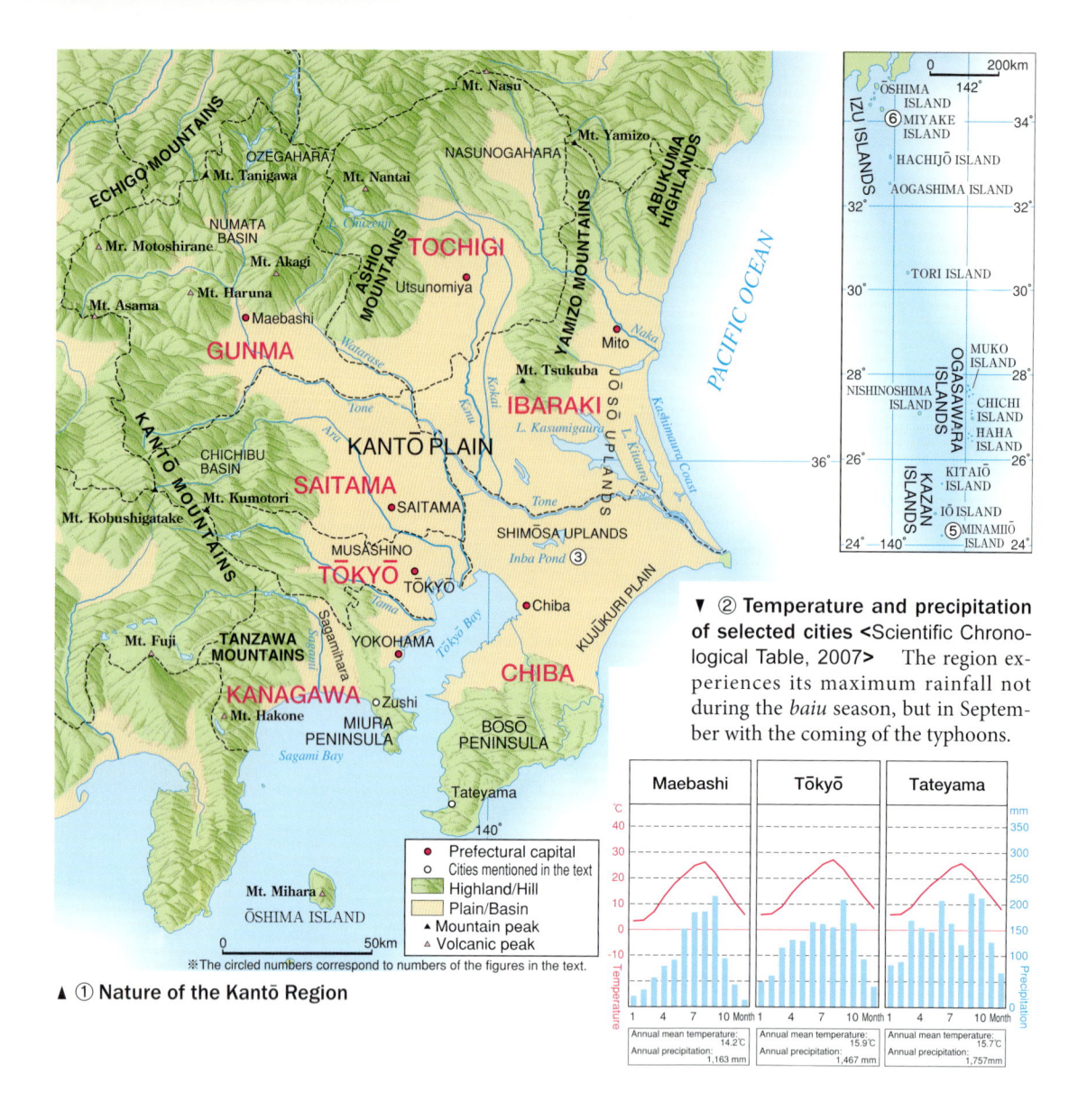

1 Looking at the map

The Kantō Plain, the largest lowland area in Japan

Many rivers run through the Kantō Region, including the Tone and its tributary the Kinu, the Tama, the Ara and the Sagami. Together, these rivers have formed the greatest and most important lowland area in Japan, the Kantō Plain. Irrigated rice fields stretches in low-lying tracts close to the rivers, but the plain is characterized above all by low plateaus that occupy a large portion of its surface area. The Shimōsa Uplands and the Jōsō Uplands are both mantled with the Kantō loam, a red earth derived from thick deposits of volcanic ash. These areas are used mainly for non-irrigated fields and for urban development, while many of the hills and plateaus around the margins of the plain have been transformed into golf courses.

In the Kantō Plain, built-up areas have developed along the railways and roads that fan out across the plain from Tōkyō. Meanwhile, the coasts of Tōkyō Bay have undergone drastic change as a result of land reclamation.

▲③ **Shimōsa Uplands and river lowlands** (Tomisato City, Chiba Prefecture)

▲④ **The uses of the water of the Tone River**

Mountains as river sources, and the southern islands

The Kantō Region is surrounded by mountains, such as Kantō Mountains in the west, and the Echigo Mountains and the Abukuma Highlands in the north. In the upstream sections of the rivers that flow through these hills and mountains, there are many multi-purpose dams that generate hydroelectricity, prevent floods from occurring, and provide water for industry, for agriculture and for millions of homes throughout the Kantō Region. The forests that surround these dams store rainwater and prevent erosion, but for these roles to be carried out efficiently, careful management of the forests is essential.

Tōkyō Prefecture also includes isolated islands, such as Izu and Ogasawara archipelagoes. These island chains were created by volcanoes, some of which are still active. In 2000, the volcano Mt. Oyama on Miyake Island erupted, forcing the residents to vacate the island for a period of almost four and a half years.

▲ ⑤ **Minamiiō Island in the Ogasawara Islands** (Tōkyō Prefecture) The Japanese government and Tōkyō Prefectual Government are working on a campaign to register the Ogasawara Islands as a World Heritage Site, in recognition of its rare and unique natural features.

Inland Kantō and coastal Kantō - two different climates

The inland area of the Kantō Region experiences little rainfall and enjoys plenty of sunny days during the winter. This is due to the northwesterly seasonal wind which, after leaving heavy snow in the mountains to the north of the Kantō Plain, turns into a dry wind, called the *karakkaze*.

Winter in the coastal areas[1] is much warmer than in the interior. Agriculture in the Bōsō and Miura Peninsulas, as well as tourist attractions such as Tateyama and Zushi, benefit from the relatively warm winter conditions.

In addition, great built-up areas such as the one that centers on Tōkyō exhibit higher temperatures than the surrounding areas. This phenomenon is called the urban heat island and is caused by the modification of the surface of the land caused by large-scale urban development as well as by the substantial quantity of artificial heat emitted by motor vehicles and air conditioners.

Notes (P.105)
[1] Precipitation is higher along the coast than inland.

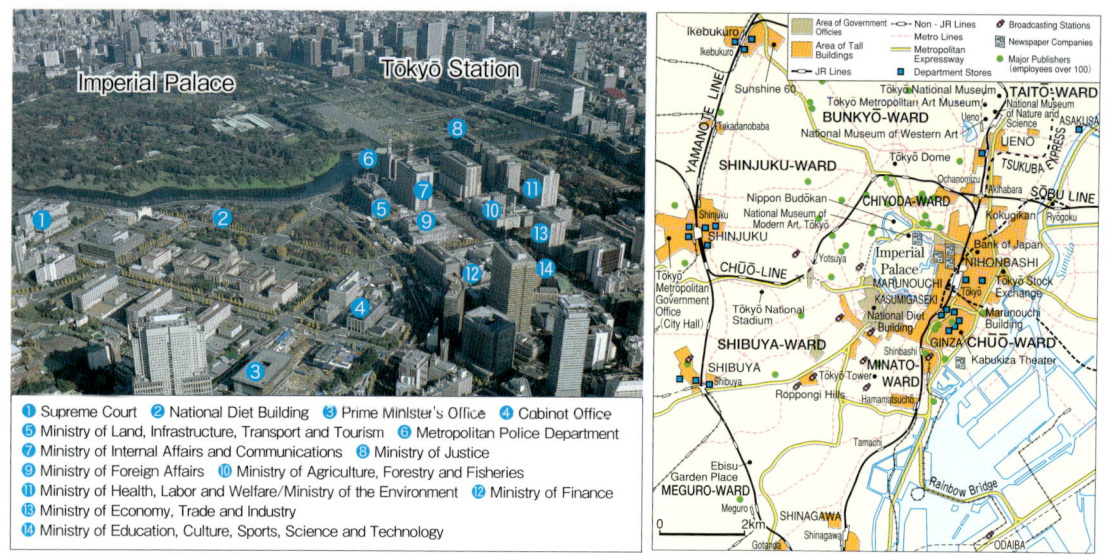

❶ Supreme Court ❷ National Diet Building ❸ Prime Minister's Office ❹ Cabinet Office
❺ Ministry of Land, Infrastructure, Transport and Tourism ❻ Metropolitan Police Department
❼ Ministry of Internal Affairs and Communications ❽ Ministry of Justice
❾ Ministry of Foreign Affairs ❿ Ministry of Agriculture, Forestry and Fisheries
⓫ Ministry of Health, Labor and Welfare/Ministry of the Environment ⓬ Ministry of Finance
⓭ Ministry of Economy, Trade and Industry
⓮ Ministry of Education, Culture, Sports, Science and Technology

▲ ① Kasumigaseki, home of the Japanese government, and its surroundings (Tōkyō Prefecture, photo taken in 2003)

▲ ② The landscape of downtown Tōkyō

2 Tōkyō in Japan, Tōkyō in the world

The capital of Japan, Tōkyō

In 1868, at the beginning of the Meiji period, Edo was renamed Tōkyō and became the capital city of modern Japan. Containing as it does the Diet Building, the Supreme Court, and the offices of various government ministries, such as Foreign Ministry and the Ministries of Education, Culture, Sports, Science and Technology, downtown[1] Tōkyō is the center of the Japanese political and bureaucratic worlds. In addition, the central business district contains the Tōkyō Stock Exchange, the head offices of banks, the headquarters of the major Japanese corporations, and the branch offices of foreign corporations, making it the heart of business not just of Tōkyō but of the whole of Japan as well.

Tōkyō is also the hub of the national transport network. Railway lines within the Tōkyō Metropolitan Area continue to be developed, while highways fan out to join Tōkyō and other regions across the country. There is also a network of air routes that connects Tōkyō International Airport at Haneda with other airports in Japan.

A Global City, Tōkyō

Tōkyō is not only the central city of Japan, but also a global city with an international importance that renders it capable of exerting a great influence on other countries in terms of politics, economy and culture. People, goods, money and information gather in Tōkyō, and are sent out by the city to the rest of the world. Alongside embassies and offices of foreign corporations, a large population of foreigners lives in downtown Tōkyō. The presence of the foreign community in Tōkyō is partly attributable to the fact that the Japanese capital is one of the world's three major financial centers. A wide range of economic activities including financial transactions, investment and trade take place in Tōkyō all day,

Notes (P.106)
[1] The central region of a big city with a significant concentration of political and economic facilities is called a downtown area. In Tōkyō, besides the central business districts, there are sub-centers that have grown up around the main commuter railway stations. Examples include Shinjuku and Shibuya.

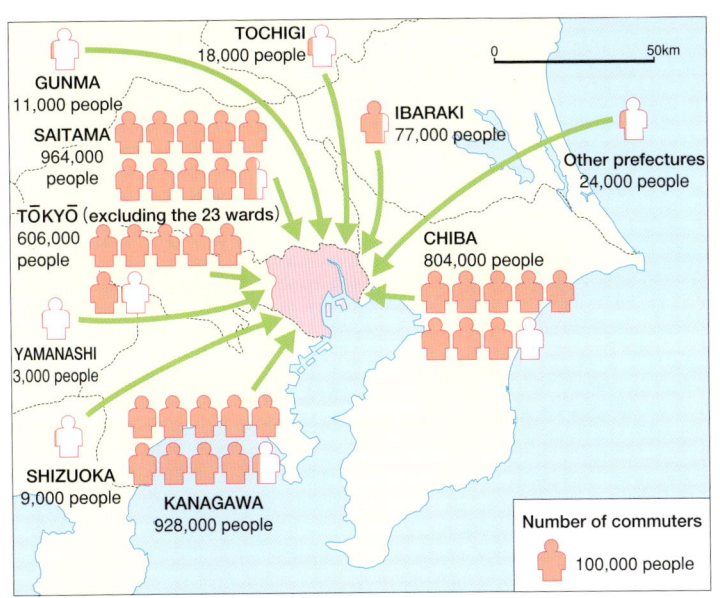

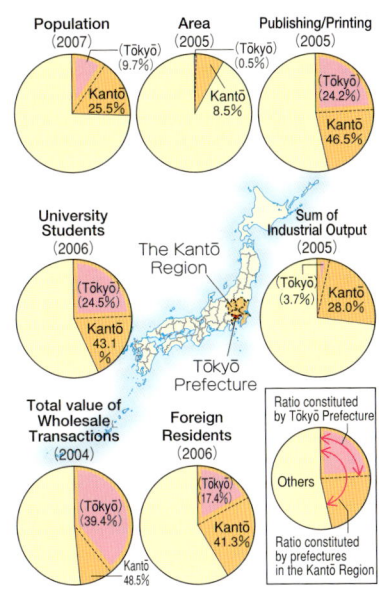

▲ ③ **Number of commuters** (for school and work) **to the 23 Tōkyō wards per day** (2000) (Census Report 2000)

▲ ④ **Concentration of economic activities and population in Tōkyō and the Kantō Region**

every day, and these financial and commercial services are closely linked to similar activities occurring in the other leading financial centers of the world. Because of this, Tōkyō has become a city that never sleeps.

Narita International Airport, located approximately sixty kilometers east of downtown Tōkyō, is Japan's main gateway to the sky. The air routes that connect Narita with the rest of the world transport goods as well as people, and among all the airports and harbors of Japan, Narita is the most important in terms of the annual value of cargo that it handles.

Tōkyō, a human magnet

Many department stores, name-brand shops, specialty stores and restaurants are located in Tōkyō. Famous foreign retailers and fashion houses have established shops under their direct management in the city. Tōkyō is home to many cultural facilities including art and science museums, and theatres and concert halls. Wholesale businesses, for example the Metropolitan Central Wholesale Market in Tsukiji that handles fish and vegetables, are a lively element of the Tōkyō scene. Wholesale companies as well as newspaper companies, publishing companies and broadcasting stations use Tōkyō as a base from which to disseminate information to Japan and to the world. Also located in the capital are universities that are engaged in various educational and research projects. These institutions attract many students from both Japan and overseas.

In this way, Tōkyō creates and offers a variety of abundant globally-connected services and jobs. People moving into Tōkyō to take advantage of these resources, in turn, generate new kinds of services and jobs. This never-ending cycle of activity invigorates the economy, society and culture of Tōkyō, and underpins its future development. In contrast to this buoyancy, regions other than Tōkyō are undergoing a decline in service provision, employment creation and the gathering of information, and the result has been the emergence of an increasingly wide gap between the capital and other regions.

The development of new centers

Many government and company offices are concentrated in downtown Tōkyō and those who work in this central zone commute daily from areas outside the main city. As is the case in other capital cities elsewhere in the world, the high concentration of offices in the centre has caused a variety of problems, including high land prices, and severe traffic jams during rush hours.

One way of solving problems such as these is to disperse the city-center concentration of offices. In Tōkyō, Shinjuku is being developed as a new center of the city, and other important zones outside the central district include the sub-centers of Shibuya and Ikebukuro. These sub-centers have grown up around railway termini which are located at points where the JR Yamanote Line, an inner city circle route, intersects with important commuter lines coming in from the suburbs, and the sub-centers are busy neighborhoods that contain various department stores, specialty stores, restaurants, bars and cinemas. The number of underground lines that serve the railway termini has increased in recent years. The improved accessibility of the sub-centers has made them increasingly attractive as sites for office development.

Meanwhile, Tōkyō prefecture has taken steps to move

▲ ① **The landscape on the western side of Shinjuku Station in the 1960s (top) and in 1999 (bottom)** In Shinjuku, a water filtration plant on the west side of the station was closed down and relocated elsewhere in 1965, leaving an empty site on which several super high-rise buildings were later constructed. The transformation of this area into an office district was accelerated in 1991 by the arrival here of the offices of Tōkyō Metropolitan Government, which had formerly been located close to Tōkyō Station.

some offices and other facilities out of Tōkyō altogether. "Makuhari New City Center" in Chiba Prefecture and "Saitama New Urban Center" in Saitama Prefecture are two new urban developments which accommodate facilities such as government and municipal offices, and multipurpose halls and shopping malls, and thus have taken on some of the roles that were formerly concentrated in downtown Tōkyō. In Ibaraki Prefecture, Tsukuba Science City was constructed to create a science and technology research center of Japan. The city has now developed into a new urban center with industrial complexes, shopping malls and residential zones, along with the laboratories of government ministries and university campuses that

▲② **Roppongi Hills**　Various new buildings have been constructed as part of this project, the most important (seen here) being a super high-rise structure with 54 floors above ground and 6 floors underground. Art museum and a broadcasting station are located within this building.

relocated from Tōkyō to the area's spacious plateau land. In 2005, a new, successful railway line was opened to carry the "Tsukuba Express", a fast train that connects Tsukuba and Akihabara on the edge of downtown Tōkyō.

The progress of redevelopment

Besides Marunouchi in downtown Tōkyō, and the neighboring areas of Roppongi, Akihabara and the coastal area, redevelopment[1] is also underway. In order to use the limited and expensive strip of land effectively, high-rise buildings and underground areas are being constructed in the places designated for redevelopment. The new high-rise buildings are equipped with highly developed communication systems that can handle large amounts of information within a short period of time, as well as security services and temperature control systems that can be monitored by computers.

From the late nineteenth century onwards, many warehouses and factories were built along the coast, close to the harbors of Tōkyō Bay. In recent years, the closure of factories and warehouses has made land available for development, and projects are being undertaken to construct offices, shopping malls and high-rise apartments in the coastal area, which is conveniently close to central Tōkyō.

Notes (P.109)

[1] In the context of Tōkyō, redevelopment means the demolition of old buildings and their replacement with buildings designed to meet a new urban purpose. Very often new offices are built as part of city redevelopment projects, but sometimes blocks containing urban apartments are sometimes provided, as well. When buildings that contain modern, spacious apartments (such buildings are called *manshon* in Japanese) are constructed as part of the redevelopment, many families move into the area over a short period of time and there is a drastic increase in the number of children. This can create temporary problems of overcrowding in the schools of the neighborhood, especially when the existing schools are small ones.

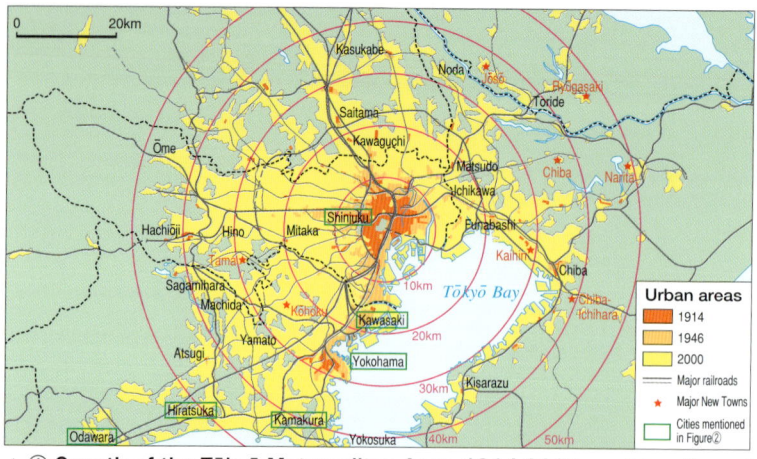

▲ ① **Growth of the Tōkyō Metropolitan Area, 1914-2000, and location of major new towns** <Census 2000 Population-concentrated wards of Japan, and other sources> Development of New Town and urban district mostly follow the maintenance of railroads.

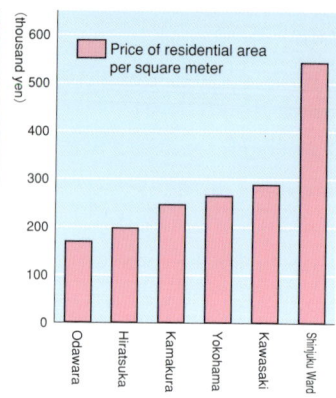

▲ ② **Residential land prices in Shinjuku Ward, Tōkyō, and five other Kantō cities** <Condition of cities, wards, towns and villages in statistical terms 2002> The price of residential land in downtown Tōkyō is several times higher than in the suburbs.

3 Life in the Tōkyō Metropolitan Area

The expansion of the built-up area towards the suburbs

Beyond the 23 wards of Tōkyō, built-up area expand into the neighboring prefectures of Kanagawa, Saitama and Chiba. Figure 1 shows the expansion of the built-up area along the major railway lines. Living near railway stations allows for fast access to the center of Tōkyō.

The emergence of commuter towns along railway lines began before the Second World War[1]. However, the development of large-scale modern residential areas by cutting open hills with bulldozers did not get under way until the 1960s. Due to high land prices and the rising cost of houses and rents in the downtown area of Tōkyō, people moved out of the center in search of inexpensive and spacious housing in the suburbs. Nowadays, however, lengthy commutes and overcrowding on the rush hour trains are currently drawing people back towards central Tōkyō.

▲ ③ **Shinjuku Station crowded with morning rush-hour commuters** (Tōkyō Prefecture)

Yokohama, a city with two aspects

Besides the 23 wards that make up Tōkyō, there are other large cities within the Tōkyō Metropolitan Area, and of these, Yokohama is the most important. The port of Yokohama was opened to trade in 1859 and until the early 1900s was the site of a foreign settlement, the foreigners being mainly European and American merchants. Later, along with Kōbe, Yokohama developed as a modern international trade port[2]. Large petrochemical plants and motor vehicles factories are concentrated on the reclaimed land along the waterfront. Moreover, redevelopment is under way in the form of the "Minato Mirai 21" project, which is located on the site of a former

Notes (P.110)
[1] The development of suburban towns first got under way after the Great Kantō Earthquake of 1923.
[2] Large scale piers exist in ports, where supertankers can berth and container ships can load and unload.

▲ ④ Central Yokohama from the air

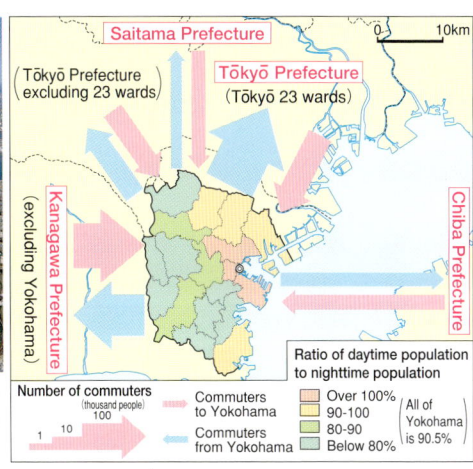

► ⑤ Commuters in and out of Yokohama (2000) <Source of Ministry of General Affairs, and others>

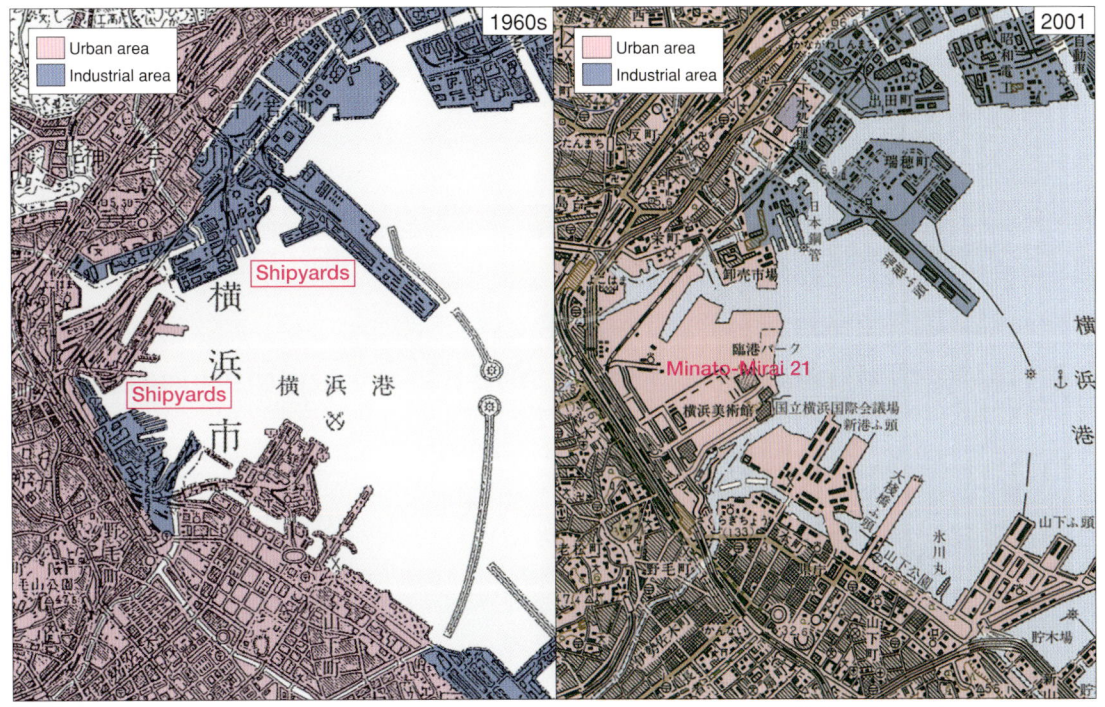

▲ ⑥ Land use changes around Yokohama Port, 1960 and 2001 (1:50,000 Geographical Survey Institute of Japan. Yokohama sheet.>

shipyard. The new development includes Yokohama Landmark Tower and international convention centers and museums, as well as the transformation of red brick warehouses into modern commercial facilities.

Yokohama is not just a port with an adjacent industrial area, but is an important city in its own right. In fact in terms of population size, Yokohama ranks second to Tōkyō with a population that in 2007 amounted to 3,560,000. Large urban areas such as Kōhoku New Town have been developed in the hills that border the suburbs of Yokohama.

As shown in Figure 5, Yokohama attracts a large inflow of commuters, but the population of commuters who travel out of Yokohama to the 23 wards of Tōkyō is even greater. People who commute to downtown Tōkyō live in Yokohama to take advantage of the several railways that connect the two cities.

▲ ⑦ Landmark Tower, the centerpiece of the "Minato Mirai 21" project (Yokohama City)

▲ ① **Printing works of the Yomiuri Shimbun, a major Japanese newspaper** (Chiyoda Ward, Tōkyō Prefecture) It is the largest printing works in the downtown area.

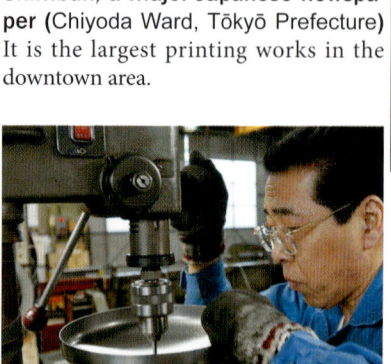

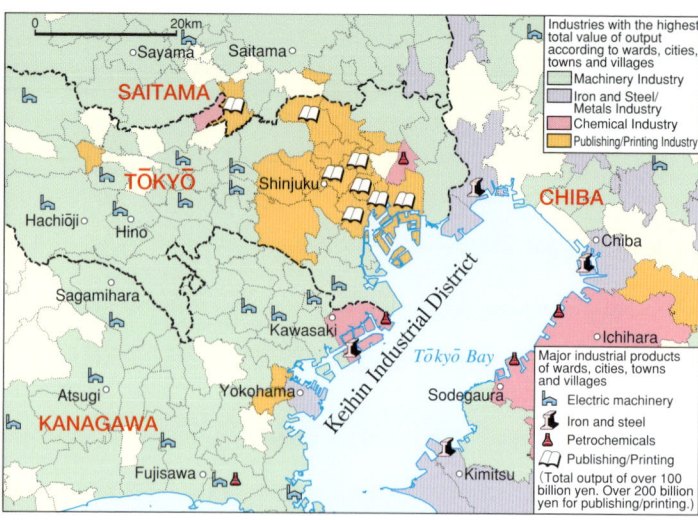

▲ ③ **Location of major industries in the Keihin Industrial District** (2001) <Industrial Statistical Table 2001>

◀ ② **Small factories with highly-skilled craftsmen** (Tōkyō Prefecture) A die is being produced using high-level manual techniques acquired through experience, and that cannot be performed by machines.

4 The Keihin Industrial District and its surrounding industries

Manufacturing in the Keihin Industrial District and adjacent areas

The Keihin Industrial District includes Tōkyō, Kanagawa, Saitama and Chiba Prefectures. Along the shores of Tōkyō Bay in the cities of Tōkyō, Yokohama and Kawasaki, land reclamation for industrial sites has been going on since the end of the Meiji period (1868-1912), and many large-scale waterfront factories were constructed as a result of this trend. After the Second World War, oil refineries petrochemical plants and steel works began to appear along the shores of Tōkyō Bay, especially in Chiba Prefecture. These are all industries that depend upon imported raw materials and fuels.

Within the 23 wards of Tōkyō, there is a concentration of publishing and printing companies. Tōkyō is at the center of Japan's political, economic and cultural life, and is therefore a highly favorable location for publishing and printing, both of which industries benefit from close proximity to sources of information. In addition, small factories equipped with advanced technical skills are located on the southwestern side of the capital, between Tōkyō and Kawasaki. Many of these factories are in the midst of a drive to improve their competitive strength by cooperating with one another and by collaborating with the research development branches of the big corporations.

There are also clusters of small engineering factories, many of them parts makers, to the west and northwest of Tōkyō, in cities such as Sagamihara, Atsugi, Sayama, and Kawagoe.

With its large concentrations of coastal and inland industries, Keihin is Japan's largest industrial district in terms of value of factory shipments. However, since the 1990s, the district's relative importance has declined following the increasing closure of urban factories and their transfer to other districts.

▲ ④ **Kiyohara Industrial Complex** (Utsunomiya City, Tochigi Prefecture)   Approximately 15,000 people work in the 40 factories that make up the complex, and the industries include food products and chemicals.

▶ ⑤ **Major industrial district in the Kantō Region**

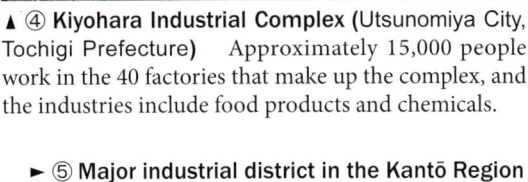

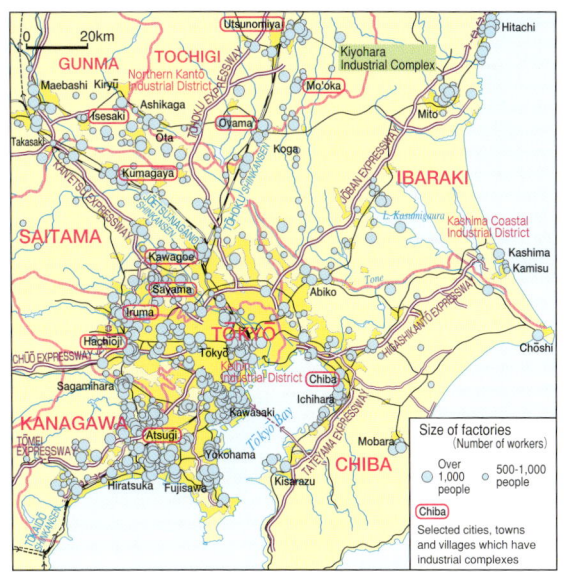

Factories going into northern Kantō

Industrial growth in northern Kantō began in 1870, with the construction of a government-owned silk-reeling mill in present-day Tomioka. This factory was a forerunner of other modern spinning mills in northern Kantō, and silk spinning and related textile manufacture became an important industry in Maebashi, Kiryū and Isesaki (Gunma Prefecture), and in Ashikaga (Tochigi Prefecture). Much later, during the Second World War, Fuji Heavy Industries[1] emerged as an important aircraft manufacturer, with its main factory in Ōta (Gunma Prefecture). After the war, this factory was converted into an assembly plant for motor vehicles production, and now makes Subaru cars.

Nowadays, motor vehicles and electrical goods production are northern Kantō's most important industries. Both are located in and around the aforementioned cities, and both have attracted into the region a large number of small and medium sized parts manufacturers. It is very difficult to find space for new factory construction in the existing cities, and companies wishing to build new factories often opt for locations in the countryside, close to major highways, where land costs are relatively low and where it is possible for firms to benefit from efficient freight transport using trucks. Many factories are located within industrial complexes. These complexes were built by prefectures and towns so as to create employment opportunities for the local population. In developments of this kind, local governments prepare industrial estates for use by incoming manufacturers.

One of the best-known industrial cities in northern Kantō is Hitachi, home of Hitachi Ltd, the electrical goods and engineering company. The company's factories are concentrated in and around Hitachi, a city located on the Pacific coast. Also on the Pacific coast is the great industrial harbor of Kashima, created in the 1970s, which is well equipped with spacious factory sites and with berths for large ocean-going vessels. Kashima is an important center for steel and petrochemicals production.

Thanks to these industrial developments, northern Kantō's total industrial shipments have remained stable while those of the Keihin Industrial District have fallen.

Notes (P.113)

[1] The relatively low-price Subaru 360 was developed in the 1950s. This vehicle ushered in an age in which people could afford to buy vehicles for private use.

▲ ① Cultivation of cabbages in a cool highlands area (Tsumagoi Village, Gunma Prefecture)

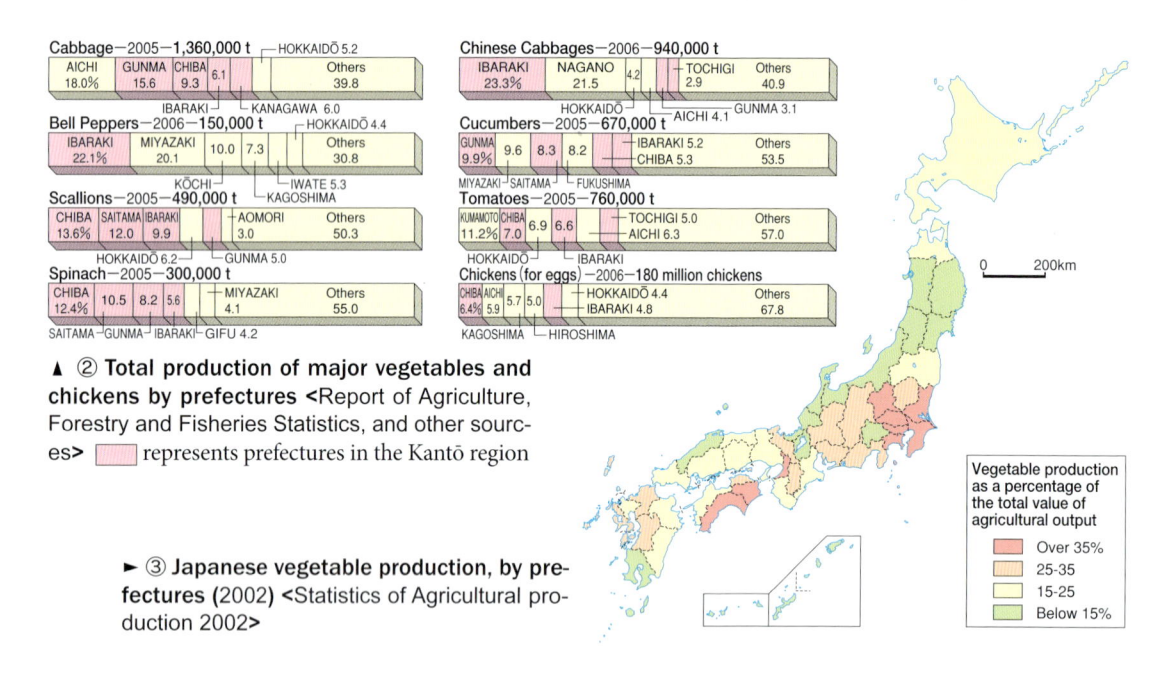

```
Cabbage—2005—1,360,000 t          ┌HOKKAIDŌ 5.2
┌─────┬─────┬─────┬───┐
│AICHI│GUNMA│CHIBA│6.1│       Others
│18.0%│15.6 │9.3  │   │       39.8
└─────┴─────┴─────┴───┘
        IBARAKI┘    └KANAGAWA 6.0
Bell Peppers—2006—150,000 t    ┌HOKKAIDŌ 4.4
┌───────┬───────┬────┬───┐
│IBARAKI│MIYAZAKI│10.0│7.3│    Others
│22.1%  │20.1   │    │   │    30.8
└───────┴───────┴────┴───┘
           KŌCHI┘    └IWATE 5.3
Scallions—2005—490,000 t      └KAGOSHIMA
┌─────┬───────┬──────┐ ┌AOMORI  Others
│CHIBA│SAITAMA│IBARAKI│ │3.0    50.3
│13.6%│12.0   │9.9   │ │
└─────┴───────┴──────┘
      HOKKAIDŌ 6.2┘  └GUNMA 5.0
Spinach—2005—300,000 t
┌─────┬────┬───┬───┐ ┌MIYAZAKI  Others
│CHIBA│10.5│8.2│5.6│ │4.1       55.0
│12.4%│    │   │   │ │
└─────┴────┴───┴───┘
SAITAMA┘ GUNMA┘ IBARAKI┘ └GIFU 4.2
```

```
Chinese Cabbages—2006—940,000 t
┌───────┬──────┬───┐ ┌TOCHIGI  Others
│IBARAKI│NAGANO│4.2│ │2.9      40.9
│23.3%  │21.5  │   │ │
└───────┴──────┴───┘
    HOKKAIDŌ┘    └AICHI 4.1 ┌GUNMA 3.1
Cucumbers—2005—670,000 t
┌─────┬───┬───┬───┐ ┌IBARAKI 5.2  Others
│GUNMA│9.6│8.3│8.2│ │CHIBA 5.3    53.5
│9.9% │   │   │   │ │
└─────┴───┴───┴───┘
MIYAZAKI┘ SAITAMA┘ └FUKUSHIMA
Tomatoes—2005—760,000 t
┌────────┬─────┬───┬───┐ ┌TOCHIGI 5.0  Others
│KUMAMOTO│CHIBA│6.9│6.6│ │AICHI 6.3    57.0
│11.2%   │7.0  │   │   │ │
└────────┴─────┴───┴───┘
  HOKKAIDŌ┘     └IBARAKI
Chickens (for eggs)—2006—180 million chickens
┌─────┬─────┬───┬───┐ ┌HOKKAIDŌ 4.4  Others
│CHIBA│AICHI│5.7│5.0│ │IBARAKI 4.8   67.8
│6.4% │5.9  │   │   │ │
└─────┴─────┴───┴───┘
KAGOSHIMA┘   └HIROSHIMA
```

▲ ② Total production of major vegetables and chickens by prefectures <Report of Agriculture, Forestry and Fisheries Statistics, and other sources> ▭ represents prefectures in the Kantō region

► ③ Japanese vegetable production, by prefectures (2002) <Statistics of Agricultural production 2002>

Vegetable production as a percentage of the total value of agricultural output
- Over 35%
- 25-35
- 15-25
- Below 15%

5 Agriculture serves the Tōkyō Metropolitan Area

Vegetable farming - a flourishing occupation

In the regions from which the city centers are easily accessible, suburban agriculture has developed to deliver fresh products to the urban markets. By taking advantage of their proximity to areas of mass consumption, Kantō farmers have turned to profitable vegetable production using plateau land and the slopes of hills. As Figure 2 shows, the Kantō Region is one of Japan's leading producers of vegetables. A recent development in vegetable farming in Kantō Region is the widespread adoption of direct delivery from farmers to consumers, a link that by-passes wholesale markets. This provides consumers with access to fresher and safer vegetables.

Besides vegetables, the Kantō Region is a leading area for milk and egg production. Good transport provision means that fresh milk and eggs can be delivered swiftly to consumers in this region.

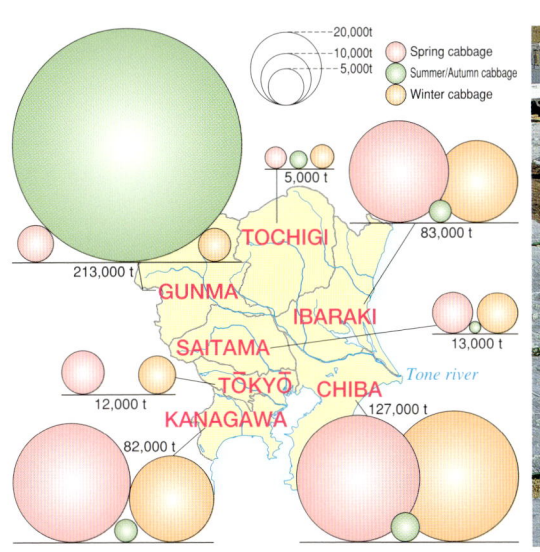

▲ ④ **Amount of seasonal cabbage cultivation in the Kantō Region** (2005) <Statistics of Vegetable production shipment 2005>

▲ ⑤ **Farmers rolling out covers to protect cabbages from the cold** (Chōshi City, Chiba Prefecture) Though in relatively warm areas, farmers use covers to protect vegetables from the sudden drops in temperature that can occur during the winter.

Variously contrived methods of agriculture

In order to use narrow strips of land effectively, producers of vegetables employ various methods to obtain high rates of profitability, such as cultivating two to three crops on the same field every year, and using greenhouses to control crop growth, so that produce can be ready for delivery at a time when a good profit can be had. An example of the ingenuity of Kantō farmers may be found in Hasaki district in the city of Kamisu, Ibaraki Prefecture. Hasaki has become a prominent location for bell pepper production by making good use of the area's well-drained sand dune soils and the warm local climate. Seedlings are planted three times a year and the techniques of accelerated and prolonged cultivation as well as greenhouses are employed, enabling farmers to ship bell peppers to market throughout the entire year.

As a consequence of continuous urban development, the areas where suburban agriculture can be practiced are located further and further away from the metropolitan area. Although located at a distance, vegetable production still prospers because of the good provision of road networks and the availability of long-distance transport using trucks. In Tsumagoi, Gunma Prefecture, cabbages are cultivated on a large scale in uplands areas which are between 800 meters and 1400 meters above sea level. Vulnerable as it is to high temperatures, the cultivation of cabbages is successful in these cool areas which experience heavy rainfall during the summer. Cabbages cultivated in Tsumagoi are marketed from summer to autumn. By cultivating fields located at different elevations, and therefore at varying temperatures, the time of shipment can be controlled.

On the other hand, cabbages shipped to Tōkyō from winter to spring are produced in warm areas such as the Bōsō and Miura Peninsulas. These areas also produce *daikon* (Japanese white radish), watermelon, and melon throughout the year.

▲ ⑥ **Shipment of cabbages** (Tsumagoi Village, Gunma Prefecture) Harvested cabbages are packed into boxes. Chilled in advance to maintain their freshness, they are then transported to the markets in refrigerated trucks.

▲ ① **Oze National Park (Gunma Prefecture)** Covering land that belongs to the four prefectures of Gunma, Tochigi, Niigata and Fukushima, Oze was registered as a national park in 2007. The park is equipped with wooden paths to keep tourists off the marshland.

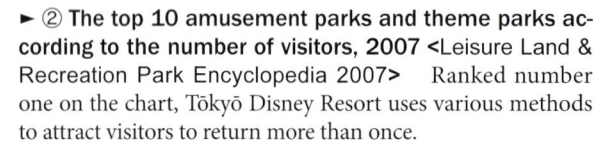

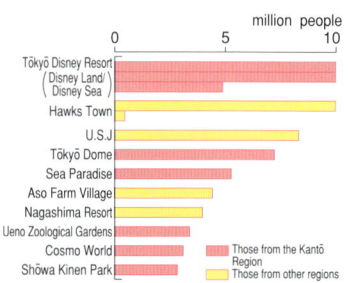

► ② **The top 10 amusement parks and theme parks according to the number of visitors, 2007** <Leisure Land & Recreation Park Encyclopedia 2007> Ranked number one on the chart, Tōkyō Disney Resort uses various methods to attract visitors to return more than once.

6 The leisure industry and nature conservation

Kantō's varied leisure industries

The Tōkyō Metropolitan Area is equipped with a wide range of leisure facilities, including places for eating out, shopping, sports, art and music entertainment, and amusement parks. Moreover with the development of the transport system, more people are able to make short weekend trips to Tōkyō. Constructed on reclaimed land in Tōkyō Bay near the downtown area, Tōkyō Disney Resort is designed for long family visits and offers amusement parks, hotels, restaurants and shopping malls. It attracts approximately 25 million visitors every year, including those from outside the Kantō Region, and sometimes from East Asia.

The development of tourism and nature conservation

The Kantō Region contains several national parks, such as Nikkō, Oze, Chichibu-Tama-Kai, Fuji-Hakone-Izu, and Ogasawara. Recently, people have tended to focus more on types of leisure that involve enjoying nature in the mountains and along the coasts, this type of recreation being a means of escaping from their routine daily lives in the cities.

At the same time, a tourist industry that makes good use of the area's natural environment, including hot springs, skiing grounds and beaches in the mountainous areas and islands, is seen as a way to energize the area's economy. However, nature preservation and environmental protection must be taken into account when exposing attractive places to the full brunt of tourism, so as not to damage the natural environment.

Japan seen through its regions
Initiatives for internationalism and multiculturalism

◀ ① **Pamphlet for Japanese-Brazilians at Ōta City Hall** It contains necessary information about daily life in Portuguese, the national language of Brazil.

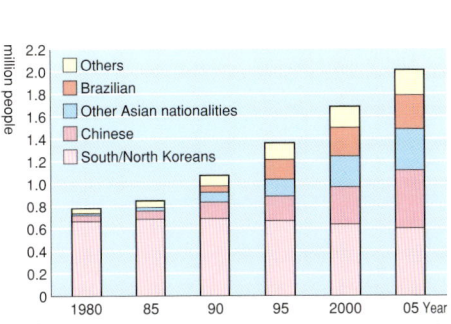

▲ ② **Changes in the number of registered foreigners by nationality** <Statistical Annual Report of Immigration Management 2003 version, and other sources>

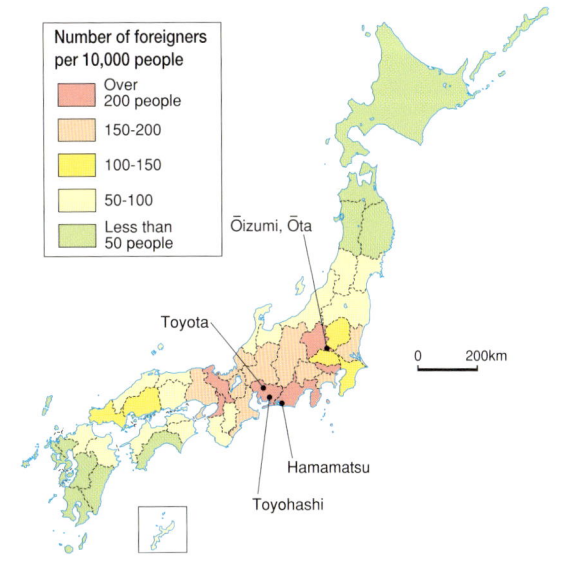

▲ ③ **Number of foreigners per 10000 by Prefecture** (2002) <Statistical Annual Report of Immigration Management 2003 version, and other sources>

Ōizumi Town, Gunma Prefecture, has a population of 42,000 (as of March 31, 2006), approximately 6,700 or 16 percent of whom are foreigners, the highest percentage of foreigners among all the municipalities of Japan. In the neighboring city of Ōta, many foreigners are the descendents of former Japanese emigrants to Brazil. Many of them work at factories, and it is not unusual to meet Brazilians who have been in Japan for over ten years.

The number of foreigners who live in Japan for work and study continues to rise. As can be seen on Figure 2, the nationalities of the foreign population in Japan altered drastically after 1990. Previously, foreigners needed special qualifications in the fields of media, research, the arts or technology in order to work in Japan. However, an amendment of the law in 1990 permitted not only those from Brazil and Peru with Japanese nationality to enter the country, but also allowed their children and grandchildren to work without qualifications. Until then, over 80% of the foreign population in Japan was made up of Koreans and those with Korean nationality, but following the amendment of the law in 1990, there has been a growing number of descendents of Japanese emigrants, mainly from Brazil. Japanese-Brazilians concentrate in districts with large motor vehicles factories in the Kantō and the Tōkai Regions. These districts provide services to help those who cannot familiarize themselves with Japanese culture to adjust to living in Japan, and one can find shops that sell Brazilian products, as well as schools that are approved by the Brazilian government to teach pupils for official diplomas that are recognized in Brazil.

In Ōta, Hamamatsu, Toyohashi, and Toyota, where many newly-arrived foreigners settle, the "Foreign Residents City Conference" was established in 2001 by regional bodies and international exchange associations. At the conference, topics such as how best to support the education of foreign youth are discussed. Initiatives are taken to understand each others' various cultures in order to build a society where people can coexist.

Chapter 6
Tōhoku Region

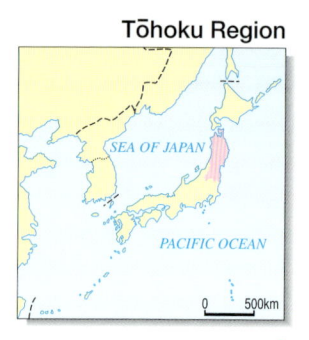

Tōhoku Region

The Tōhoku Region occupies the northeastern part of the island of Honshū, and consists of the six prefectures of Aomori, Iwate, Miyagi, Akita, Yamagata and Fukushima. Figure 2 on page 39 shows that the region originally consisted of seven provinces, but until 1868 (the beginning of the Meiji period), it in fact consisted only of two provinces, Mutsu and Dewa.

In ancient times, the Tōhoku Region was in administrative terms part of the Tōzandō but was in reality separate from the more southerly areas of Japan in both geographical and historical terms. This separateness was recognized by the middle of the seventeenth century, when the region was known as Ōu. The name Ōu was formed by taking a single character from the names of each of the two provinces, Mutsu and Dewa.

This definition and the name Ōu were used even after Japan adopted the prefectural system in 1903, and it was not until around 1955 that the name was changed to the Tōhoku Region (Tōhoku in Japanese means northeastern). The reason for the change is thought to stem from the fact that the geographical distinction was judged to be more appropriate than the historical one, and it was fitting to describe the region by a term that reflects its northeasterly position relative to the rest of Honshū. In fact, however, the name Tōhoku has been used informally since the latter half of the nineteenth century.

The Tōhoku Region, like the Hokkaidō Region, is geographically extensive. Tōhoku occupies 18 percent of Japan's land area but accounts for only 8 percent of the population. Although Tōhoku is roughly equal in size to Chūbu, its population is less than half of that of the Chūbu Region, and in fact Tōhoku's population is smaller than that of Tōkyō Prefecture. This reflects the fact that the economy of the Tōhoku Region has always centered on agriculture and fisheries.

In recent years, the region has become more nationally prominent thanks to the construction of factories by firms based in the Kantō Region. This development partly arises from the construction of better transport links with the Kantō Region, and follows from the establishment of shinkansen railway lines, rapid-transit highways, airports and other facilities that link Tōhoku with the Japanese capital.

Such changes mean that it is no longer sufficient to follow the traditional division of Tōhoku into an eastern half, looking out onto the Pacific, and a western half oriented towards the Sea of Japan. Today, an equally relevant division is a north-south one, reflecting differences in the ease of maintaining communications with the capital region. A further recent trend in Tōhoku has been the increasing dominance of Sendai, Tōhoku's largest city and the regional capital.

◀ ① *Imonikai* (the potatoes cooking) Festival (Yamagata City)   Taro, beef and leek are cooked in a large pot, 5.6 meters in diameter. This event is held not only Yamagata Prefecture, but also throughout the Tōhoku Region every year from autumn onwards.

► ② **Satellite image of the Tōhoku Region** The circled numbers correspond to the numbers of the figures in the text.

▼ ③ **View of Sendai City center from Aoba Castle** (Miyagi Prefecture)

119

► ① **Nature of the Tōhoku Region**

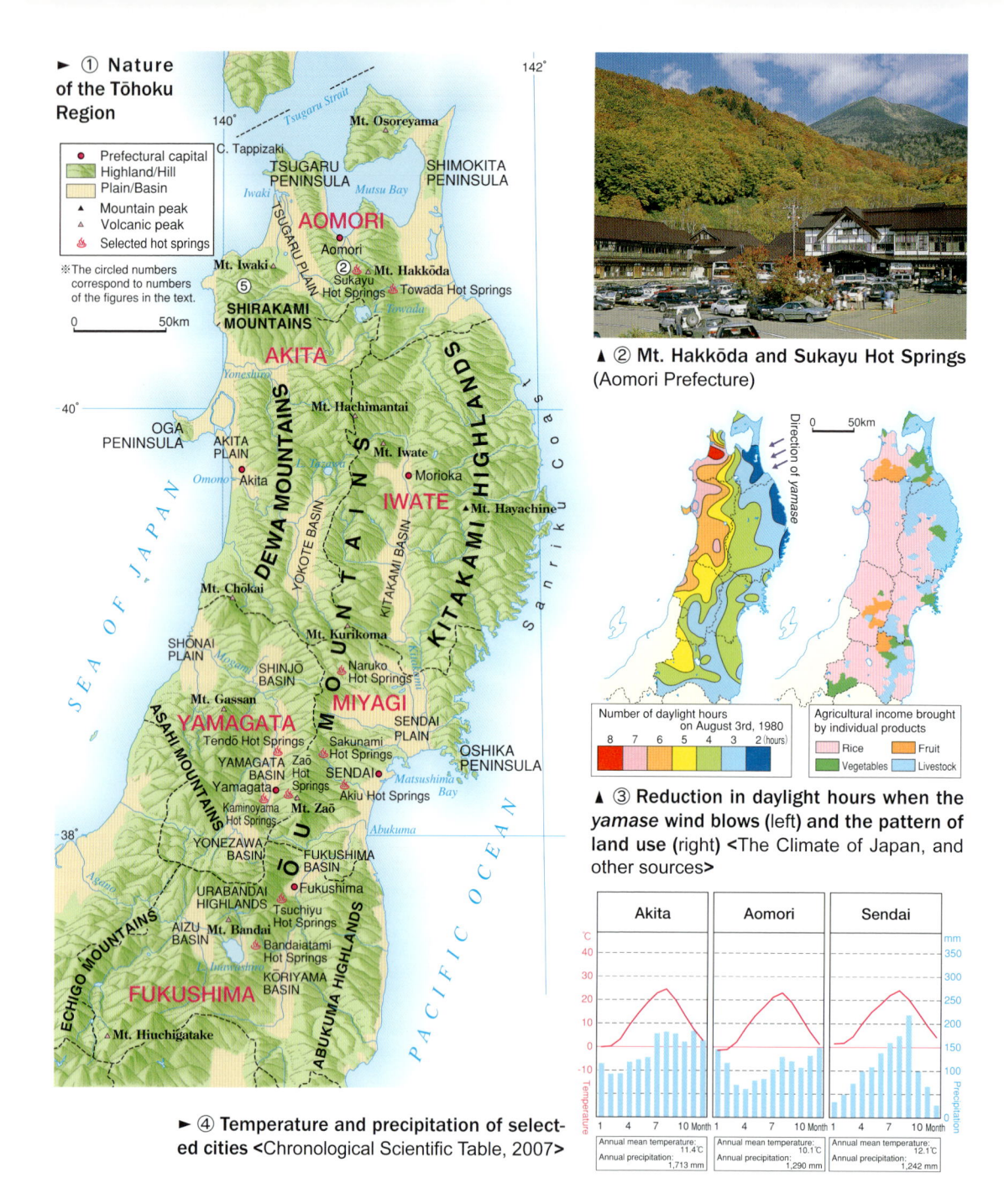

▲ ② Mt. Hakkōda and Sukayu Hot Springs (Aomori Prefecture)

▲ ③ Reduction in daylight hours when the *yamase* wind blows (left) and the pattern of land use (right) <The Climate of Japan, and other sources>

► ④ Temperature and precipitation of selected cities <Chronological Scientific Table, 2007>

1 Looking at the map

Mountainous areas, plains and basins extend from north to south

The Tōhoku Region extends from north to south with the Ōu Mountains running like a backbone along its center. At the foot of volcanoes such as Mt. Hakkōda, Mt. Iwate and Mt. Zaō, a plenty of hot springs have come out including the famous Naruko Hot Springs and Zaō Hot Springs. Especially during the autumn, many tourists visit the highlands of Hachimantai and Urabandai to enjoy the beautiful scenery, viewing autumnal leaves. To the east of the Ōu Mountains, and facing the Pacific Ocean, are the Kitakami and Abukuma Highlands, both consisting of low mountains with gentle slopes.

On the Pacific coast of Iwate and Miyagi Prefectures, there lies the Sanriku Coast which is famous as a ria coastline. In the calm waters of the inlets, fish farming flourishes. However, on the 11th March, 2011, a big earthquake, whose epicentre was off the coast of Miyagi prefecture, caused devastating tsunami. As a result, nearly twenty-thousand people were killed. By contrast, on the other side of the Ōu Mountains, rich deep forests like those of the Shirakami Mountains extend across wide tracts of land. Largely untouched by humans, the Shirakami Mountains contain a rare and extensive virgin beech forest. This mountainous region is registered as a World Natural Heritage Site.

Between the north-south mountain ranges are narrow lowland areas such as the Kitakami, Yokote, and Yamagata Basins. Along the edges of these basins, on alluvial fans and on gentle hill slopes, fruit cultivation thrives. In the lower valleys of the Kitakami and Mogami Rivers, the Sendai and Shōnai Plains carry broad expanses of fertile paddy land.

▲ ⑤ **Shirakami Mountains** (Aomori Prefecture) This area was registered as Japan's first World Natural Heritage Site, in 1993.

Climatic contrasts between east and west

In the Tōhoku Region, summers are cooler and winters more severe than in the rest of Honshū. Moreover there are variations, depending on latitude, within Tōhoku itself. Thus average temperatures in northern Tōhoku, in Aomori, Akita and Iwate Prefectures, are lower than in southern Tōhoku (Miyagi, Yamagata and Fukushima Prefectures).

▲ ⑥ *Yamase* wind blowing across fields (Aomori Prefecture)

As regards annual precipitation, however, the main contrast is between eastern and western Tōhoku. In winter, strong seasonal winter winds blow from the Asian mainland across the Sea of Japan and bring heavy snowfall to Akita and Yamagata Prefectures, the snow cover being deepest in the mountains. By the time this wind arrives on the eastern side of the Ōu Mountains, in Iwate and Miyagi Prefectures, it has become dry, and therefore causes far less snow.

During the summer, the Pacific coastlands of Tōhoku experience cloudy days with low temperatures as a result of the cold northeasterly wind that blows from the sea during June and July. This wind is called the *yamase*, and it is caused by sea air being cooled and made more humid during its passage over the cold Oyashio. The *yamase* has traditionally posed a threat for agriculture, for if the June temperature is too low, rice will not ripen in time for the autumn harvest. Throughout history, rice-cropping farmers in this part of Japan have been plagued by cold summers and by crop failures caused by a prevalence of the *yamase* wind.

▲ ① **A broad street in central Sendai flanked by rows of *keyaki* (zelkova trees) (Miyagi Prefecture)** Sendai is called "the city of woods," and with rows of *keyaki* in the central district, the city is rich in greenery. The name "city of woods" has its roots in the vast woods of the nearby *Samurai* residences in the Edo period (1603-1867). During the Second World War, Sendai lost those woods, but thanks to the contributions of a great number of citizens, the greenery of the city was gradually restored.

2 Transport development and urban growth

Transport and urbanization in Tōhoku

Because Tōhoku is characterized by parallel mountain chains that run north to south, it does not have natural unity as a region, and to rectify this situation, much attention has been given to the role of transportation in providing regional identity and cohesion. After the 1970s, highways and *shinkansen* were constructed to connect the Tōhoku Region with Tōkyō. As a result, cities located along these routes, such as Kōriyama, Sendai and Morioka, experienced a marked increase in population and an acceleration in industrial activity, while cities more distant from the new roads and railways lagged behind.

Sendai, Tōhoku's leading city

With a population of over a million, Sendai is the biggest city in Tōhoku. It is home to the high courts, to branch offices of various ministries and large companies, and to many universities including Tōhoku University. Called "miniature Tōkyō," Sendai has a central business district that contains high-rise buildings used for offices and stores, and high-rise residential apartments.

Sendai is positioned roughly at the center of the Tōhoku Region, where transport networks form a node. Recent years have seen an increase in the number of highway buses that run between Sendai and various parts of Tōhoku, and these bus services make it easier for people from other prefectures to commute and shop in the city.

▲ ① **Rice harvesting using a large machine in a very extensive paddy field.** (Daisen City, Akita Prefecture) The farming season begins in April, when the snow begins to melt, and the crops are harvested around the end of October and before the beginning of winter.

3 Farmers and fishermen respond to challenges

Rice production and its development

Tōhoku is one of Japan's leading rice-producing regions. Rice is grown not only on the Akita, Shōnai, and Sendai Plains, but also in inland regions such as the Yonezawa and Yokote Basins. Because heavy snowfall limits agricultural activities during the winter months, the area is a single-crop region of rice, and in this regard it closely resembles the Hokuriku Area. On the Pacific side of Tōhoku, where the *yamase* blows, cold-resistant types of tasty rice, such as *hitomebore* have been developed.

In Akita Prefecture, efficient production of rice was helped by land consolidation projects that were undertaken after the Second World War. These projects made it possible to use large agricultural machines in the paddy fields. Another development was the reclamation of Hachirōgata, formerly the second largest lake in Japan, to create a vast site for rice cultivation. As a consequence of these initiatives, Akita became Japan's leading prefecture for rice production. From the 1970s onwards, however, and in the context of a growing national rice surplus, government policy switched to the provision of farm subsidies to take rice land out of production. Farmers began to shift from quantity to quality with the aim of creating especially tasty rice varieties for consumers. "*Akitakomachi*" is one such variety, and has emerged as a well-known rice brand. In recent years, some farmers have begun to grow flowers and vegetables instead of rice.

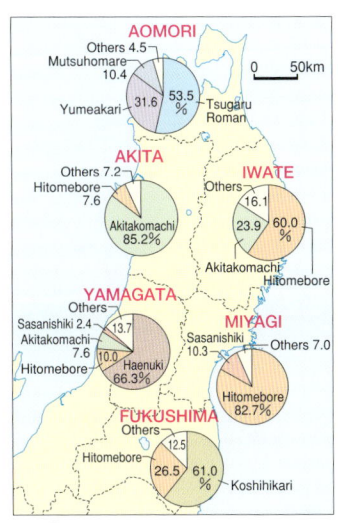

▲ ② **Main rice varieties of the Tōhoku Region, by prefecture.**

123

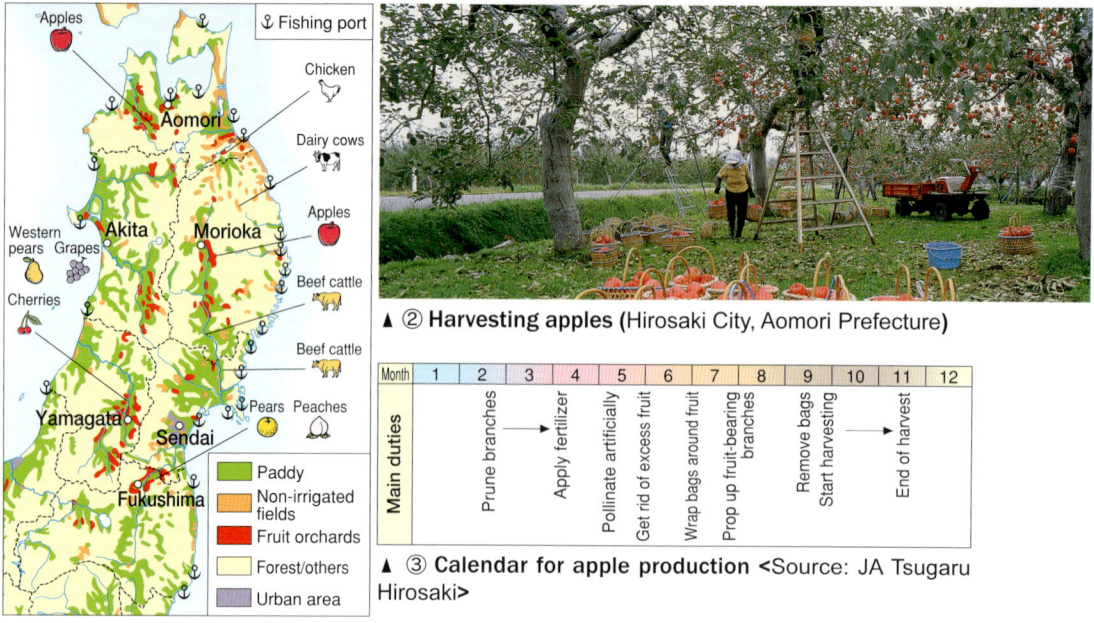

▲ ② Harvesting apples (Hirosaki City, Aomori Prefecture)

▲ ③ Calendar for apple production <Source: JA Tsugaru Hirosaki>

▲ ① Agricultural areas and major fishing ports in the Tōhoku Region

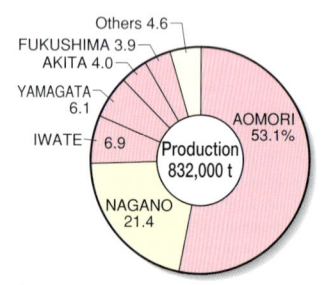

▲ ④ National production of apples (2006) <Source: Ministry of Agriculture, Forestry, and Fisheries>

Fruit cultivation and the development of recognizable brands

Well equipped as it is with suitable mountain slopes and alluvial fans, the Tōhoku Region cultivates a wide variety of fruit. In Aomori Prefecture, apples has been produced, while cherries and European pears are grown in Yamagata Prefecture, and peaches are cultivated in Fukushima Prefecture. Initiatives are being taken to establish brands that guarantee the quality of the product and that can be readily recognized throughout Japan. *Satōnishiki*, a high-quality type of cherry, is one of several fruit brands that are shipped all over the country.

The Tsugaru Plain surrounding the Hirosaki produces approximately one-half of all the apples grown in Japan. The crop is cultivated on the banks of the Iwaki River, and on the slopes of the mountains situated around the edges of the plain where water drains freely. The low temperatures of Aomori Prefecture have made apple cultivation an attractive alternative to rice, for apples are more resistant to the cold climate and their output is less prone to fluctuate. In response to consumer demand for juicier and sweeter apples, the brand *"tsugaru"* has been introduced.

Although apples are harvested in the months from September to November, work in the orchards begins in February with pruning. Much effort and time are spent on work such as grafting and wrapping apples in bags so as to ensure that the marketed product is of good quality. In recent years, attempts have been made to reduce costs and manpower in the cultivation process by using bees for pollination, and by growing short apple trees for easier harvesting. Among the initiatives that are being taken to improve profits is the installation of refrigerators to store apples harvested in the autumn. Refrigeration makes it possible to ship the apples to market during spring and summer when the supply decreases and the price rises. Other recent initiatives include the development of pure apple juice and sales of apples on the Internet.

▲ ⑤ A *Hatahata* fish catch (Akita Prefecture)

▲ ⑥ **Fishermen planting trees** (Mt. Yagoshi, Iwate Prefecture) <"Afforestation by fishermen" Kodansha Limited>   Saplings are being planted on a mountain slope above the upper reaches of the Ō River, which reaches the sea at the fishing port of Kesennuma.

Measures for fishery conservation

A vast marine environment rich in fishing grounds surrounds the Tōhoku Region. There are large fishing ports in the district, such as Shiogama and Kesennuma on the Sanriku Coast whose fishermen catch sardines and sauries in the zone where cool and warm sea currents converge . *Hatahata* (sailfin sandfish) is one of several fish varieties unique to the waters of the Sea of Japan offshore from Tōhoku. Fish culture and the farming of marine products are also thriving at various locations along the region's coastline. Examples include the cultivation of oysters along the Sanriku Coast and of scallops in Mutsu Bay.

However, the catch of sardines and *hatahata* has declined in recent years. To reverse this trend, it has become necessary to nourish and preserve aquatic resources, and to catch fish in such a way as to preserve fish stocks. For example, in Akita Prefecture, *hatahata* was hard to come by throughout the 1980s. In response, local fishermen of the prefecture banned the fishing of *hatahata* for three years from 1992, even though the ban caused a sharp drop in their income. The temporary sacrifice has been worthwhile, for there has been a rebound of the *hatahata* stock in recent years.

Kesennuma is known as an old-established center for oyster cultivation, but after the 1970s, the oysters grown there started to become too small in size. Until then, rain fell in the mountains, soaked into the earth through the trees, and formed rivers that flowed down to the sea. This river water, rich in mineral nutrients, served as the main source of food for the oysters. However, over-felling of trees and development projects that reduced the forest cover caused rainwater to flow over the land surface and enter the sea as mud water, without collecting any nutrients on the way. This is why the oysters stopped growing in size. In response, the fishermen who cultivate oysters are nowadays planting trees to revive the forests and thereby once again provide the sea with water rich in nutrients that the oysters can feed on.

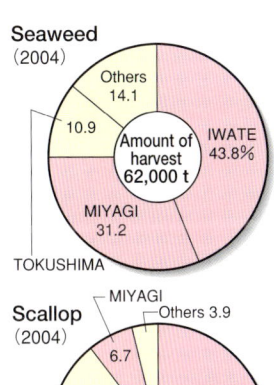

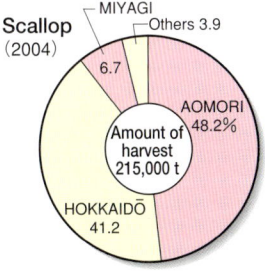

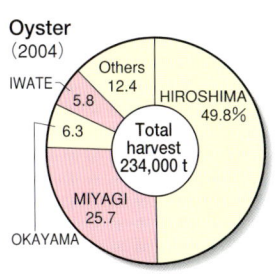

Seaweed (2004)
- IWATE 43.8%
- MIYAGI 31.2
- TOKUSHIMA 10.9
- Others 14.1
- Amount of harvest 62,000 t

Scallop (2004)
- AOMORI 48.2%
- HOKKAIDŌ 41.2
- MIYAGI 6.7
- Others 3.9
- Amount of harvest 215,000 t

Oyster (2004)
- HIROSHIMA 49.8%
- MIYAGI 25.7
- OKAYAMA 6.3
- IWATE 5.8
- Others 12.4
- Total harvest 234,000 t

▲ ⑦ **Cultivation of seaweed, scallops and oysters** <The 80th Statistical Table of the Ministry of Agriculture, Forestry, and Fisheries>

▲ ① **A craftsman making *shōgi-koma*** (Pieces for the game of *shōgi*. Tendō City, Yamagata Prefecture)

▲ ② **Miyagi traditional *kokeshi* dolls** (left) and ***Nanbu* ironware** (right).

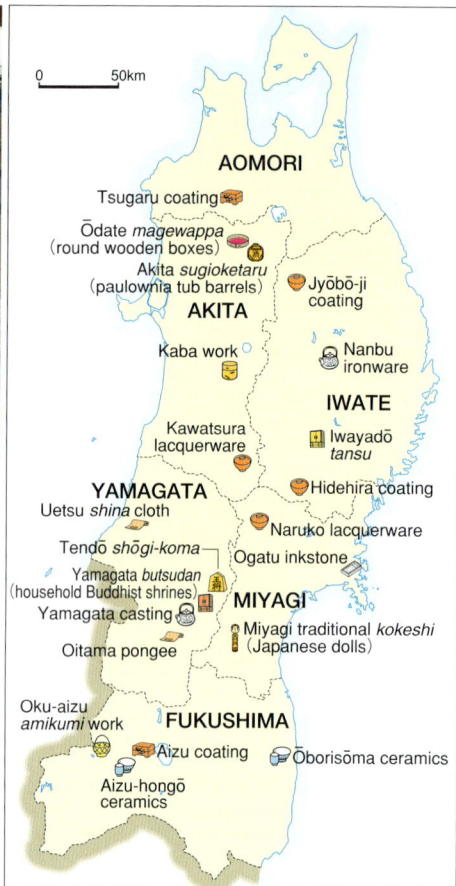

▲ ③ **The traditional crafts of the Tōhoku Region** <Source of Ministry of Economy, Trade and Industry>

4 Traditional industries and new industries

Characteristic traditional industries

As can be seen in Figure 3, the Tōhoku Region has various traditional industries, including lacquerware, textiles, pottery, woodwork and ironware. These industries make traditional handicrafts that are unique to this particular region of Japan, and the products include the *magewappa* (round, wooden boxes) of Ōdate in Akita Prefecture, the *nanbu* ironware of Morioka in Iwate Prefecture, the *shōgi-koma* (pieces for the game of *shōgi*) of Tendō in Yamagata Prefecture and the traditional *kokeshi* (Japanese wooden dolls) of Miyagi Prefecture. Using Tōhoku's resources of iron, lacquer and wood, the making of these handicrafts dates from the Edo period. Over time, most of these industries developed as side occupations for *bushi* (samurai warriors) and farmers.

Nowadays, however, these traditional industries face several threats to their future survival, the most important of which is the issue of aging craftsmen. It has become an important task to pass on ancient handicraft techniques to the next generation and not allow old-established skills to die out.

Transport and industrial growth in Tōhoku

Until recently, Tōhoku has been a region in which most of the working population has

▲ ⑤ A view of the Kitakami Industrial Complex (Iwate Prefecture)

▲ ④ Transport and industries of the Tōhoku Region

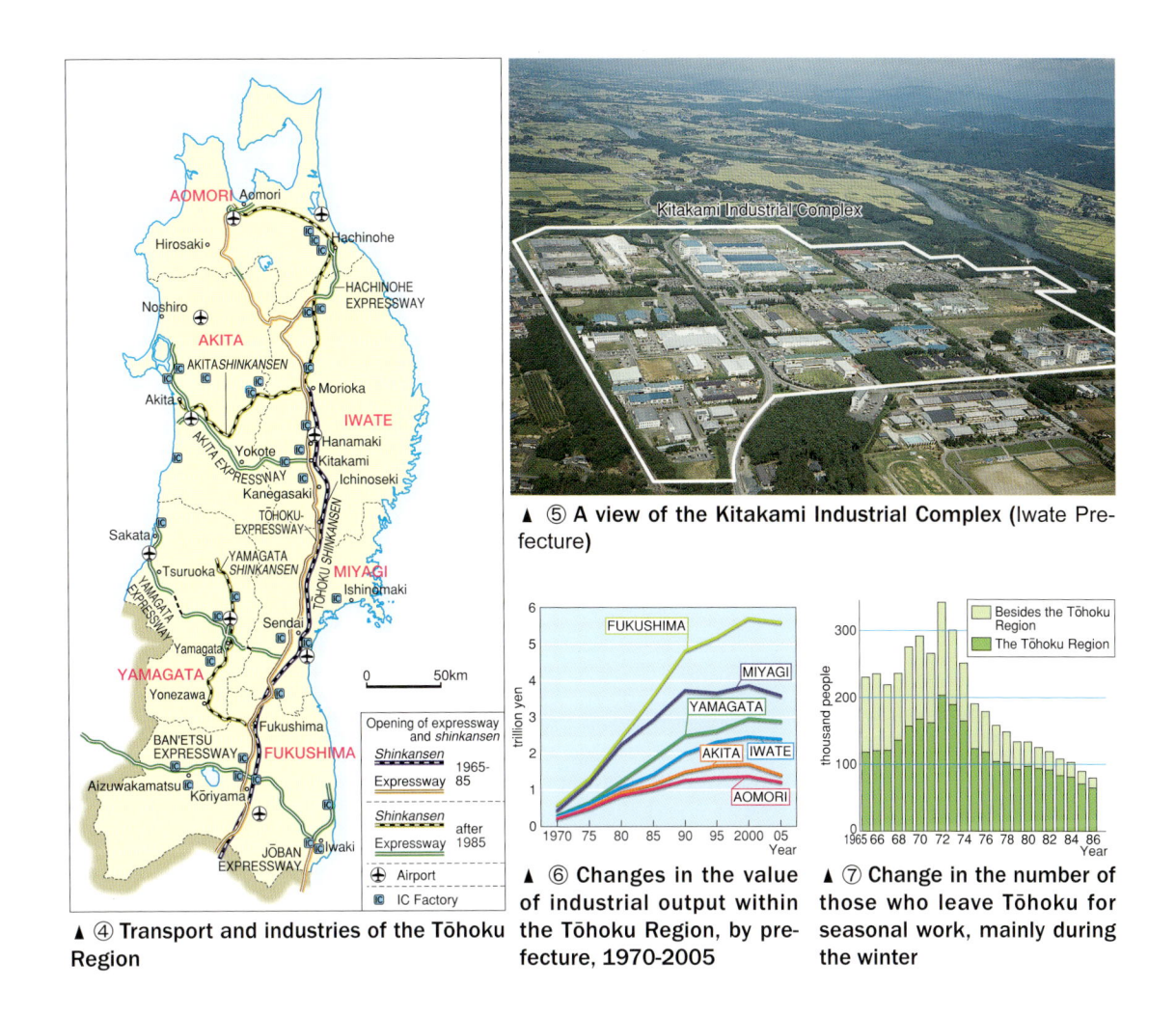

▲ ⑥ Changes in the value of industrial output within the Tōhoku Region, by prefecture, 1970-2005

▲ ⑦ Change in the number of those who leave Tōhoku for seasonal work, mainly during the winter

been engaged in agriculture, forestry and fisheries. However, with the introduction of the government policy to take land out of rice cultivation, and because of an inflow of cheap agricultural produce from overseas, farmers have found it increasingly difficult to depend solely on agriculture. During the 1960s and the 1970s, increasing numbers of farmers worked away from home during the winter when snow and low temperatures made it impossible to cultivate the fields. Many found seasonal jobs on construction sites, mainly in the Kantō Region.

In an attempt to develop their own industries and to create more local employment opportunities, many localities in the Tōhoku Region have set about the construction of industrial complexes. After the 1970s, fast transportation networks emerged, including the Tōhoku Expressway and the Tōhoku *shinkansen*, and these strengthened Tōhoku's ties with the Kantō Region, and greatly improved communication between southern and northern Tōhoku. As a result, many new companies and factories appeared, providing local jobs for the population. This development allowed a growing number of young people, who in days gone by migrated to the Kantō Region, to find employment locally. Furthermore, with side jobs available locally, the number of those working away from home during the winter has decreased annually.

▲ ① **An aerial view of the Kanegasaki factory of Kantō Auto Works, Ltd., one of Japan's leading car parts makers and a member of the Toyota Group. (Kanegasaki Town, Iwate Prefecture).** This factory is affiliated with Toyota Motors, which has its headquarters in Aichi Prefecture. Beyond the factory can be seen a recently established industrial estate which contains the factories of other motor parts makers.

New industries

Since the 1980s, many factories manufacturing integrated circuits (ICs) and electrical and electronic machinery began to appear along the Tōhoku Expressway and close to regional airports. The use of highways allows the swift transport of raw materials and products, and following the completion of a modern transport network in the region, many companies based in the Kantō Region established their second and third factories in Tōhoku. In this fashion, many new factories were built at various locations in the region, examples being IC and computer plants in Kitakami, Hanamaki, Yamagata, Yonezawa and Aizuwakamatsu, and loudspeaker and car stereo factories in Iwaki and Tendō.

Meanwhile, national and prefectural governments have taken initiatives designed to revitalize the more backward areas of the Tōhoku Region. An example is Rokkasho energy base in the hitherto remote Shimokita Peninsula of Aomori Prefecture, where facilities for petroleum stockpiles and nuclear fuel recycling are located.

A good example of recent trends in industrial growth in Tōhoku is the city of Kitakami, which contains a concentration of factories that make electrical and electronic machinery. This is the result of the city's energetic promotion of industrial estates and of an inducement policy that has attracted many new factories into the city. In the neighboring town of Kanegasaki, Toyota Motors in 1993 built a modern and large-scale factory that assembles Lexus cars. As a result of this initiative, many makers of vehicle parts have appeared in Iwate and Miyagi Prefectures, making it likely that the automobile industry will play a key role in Tōhoku's future development.

Japan seen through its regions
The role of professional sports in regional revival

► ① Players of the Vegalta Sendai club teaching soccer to local children (Vegalta Sendai Junior Soccer School in Ishinomaki, Miyagi Prefecture)

▼ ② Division of professional baseball (left) and J-league (right) teams

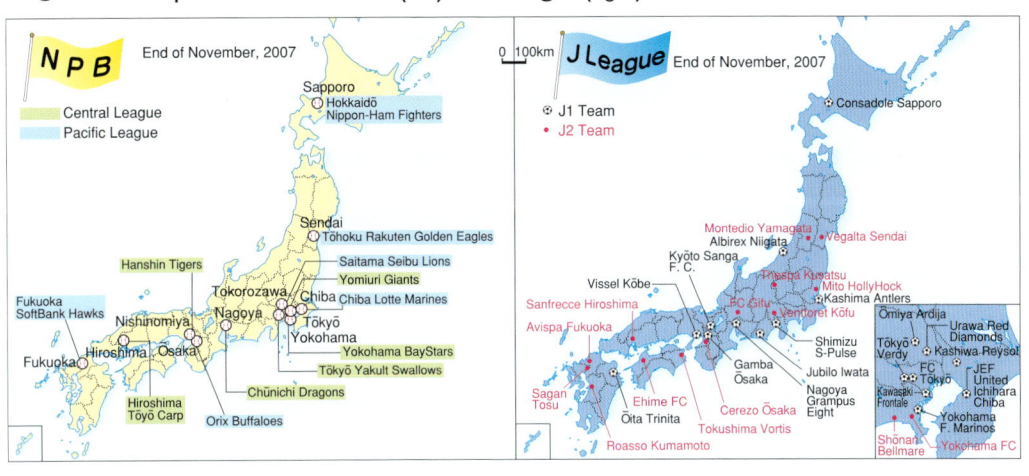

Several well-known professional sports teams are based in the Tōhoku Region. Examples include the Tōhoku Rakuten Golden Eagles baseball team, the soccer clubs Vegalta Sendai and Montedio Yamagata, and the 89ERS basketball team of Sendai. The existence of these teams has caused related activities to prosper and has strengthened the attachment of people to their localities and to the region.

"J Village", located in Naraha Town, Fukushima Prefecture, is a soccer facility with several pitches and overnight accommodation for soccer players and is used not only by Japan's national soccer team, but also by the public in general.

In this way and throughout Japan, sports facilities help to vitalize regions and promote interaction among people. Professional teams based in the provinces are becoming well known nationally, including those in professional baseball, in the J-League (Japan's leading soccer league), in volleyball's V-League and in basketball's bj-League.

Until the 1980s, the only professional sports league in Japan was the national baseball league, but since then, more and more Japanese have come to enjoy and to attach importance to leisure opportunities, and this trend has helped to create well-known sports teams in different regions across Japan. Far from being the "economic animals" of Western myth, the Japanese these days are far more focused on pleasure than they used to be, and are more concerned with the enrichment of their lives. Watching professional sports is nowadays a widespread recreation, and many people across Japan dream of one day having a professional sports team in their own town.

Chapter 7
Hokkaidō Region

Hokkaidō Region

Ancient Japan stopped at the Tsugaru Strait, which separate Honshū from Hokkaidō, and for many centuries, the island of Hokkaidō, which was called Ezochi, lay outside the Japanese realm.

It was not until the beginning of the Meiji period in 1869 that the island came to be referred to as Hokkaidō. The territory thereafter underwent extensive development by Japanese settlers. It was named Hokkaidō with the purpose of creating an eighth dō. The term was also thought to be appropriate because the existing circuit names that incorporated the element kai (sea) were the Tokaidō (eastern sea circuit), the Nankaidō (southern sea circuit), and the Saikaidō (western sea circuit), and given the fact that Ezochi was located in the northernmost part of Japan, it seemed reasonable to re-name it Hokkaidō (Hokkaidō literally means northern sea circuit). Like the other circuits, it was originally divided into provinces, of which there were eleven. It adopted the name Hokkaidō in 1910 and thus became the most recent of the seven major Japanese regions to be officially recognized.

Unlike the other Japanese regions, Hokkaidō was never divided into prefectures, apart from a very brief period in the middle of the nineteenth century (Hokkaidō's prefectures were abolished in 1886 when the Hokkaidō Prefectural Government was established). Because of the unusual historical development of Hokkaidō, it seemed appropriate to give the island the autonomy and importance of a prefecture. However, because Hokkaidō covers a large area that is 13 times the average size of the other 46 prefectures, 14 local government branch offices have been established throughout the island.

Hokkaidō, which formerly had been a distant island inhabited by the Ainu, was regarded by most Japanese people as a frontier region, and indeed after 1868, the island was developed as though it were a colony. Out of this unique historical background, and because the climate, relief and other physical features of the island were so different from those of the other regions of Japan, the special distinctiveness of Hokkaidō began to emerge.

One of the ways in which Hokkaidō is unusual within Japan is that despite having the largest area of all the major regions – Hokkaidō occupies about a fifth of the surface area of Japan – the island's population density is extremely low, and the population is less than 5% of that of Japan which is not even half of that of Tōkyō. Other unique characteristics of Hokkaidō make it unusually interesting. One of these features is the Northern Territories territorial dispute, a problem that has caused considerable tension between Japan and Russia, and that amongst other things has created serious problems for the Hokkaidō fishing industry.

◀ ① **The view from Mt. Hakodate (Hakodate City)** Looking out over the Tsugaru Strait, Hakodate for many years prospered as Hokkaidō's gateway. The spectacular night view from Mt. Hakodate is famous throughout the country.

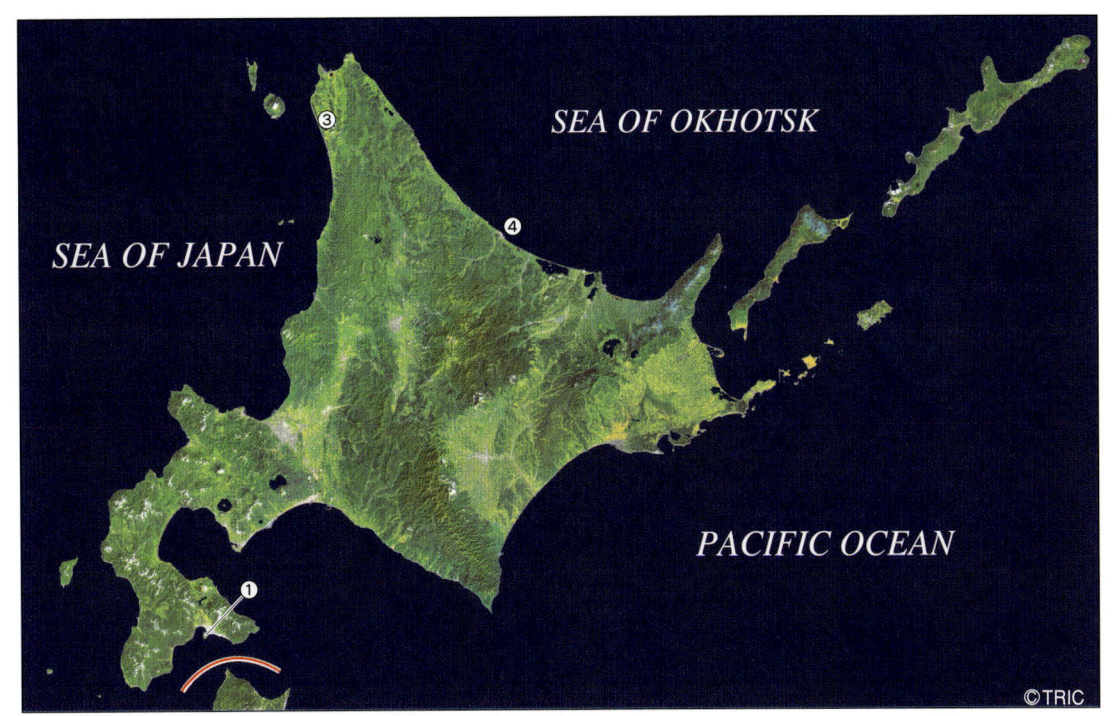

▲ ② **Satellite image of the Hokkaidō Region** The circled numbers correspond to the numbers of the figures in the text.

Column — **Japan's northern fringe: the Northern Territories**

Consisting of the islands of Kunashiri, Shikotan, Etorofu and the Habomai archipelago, the Northern Territories are an integral part of Japan, and were once inhabited by Japanese people. However, since the Soviet occupation of the islands in 1945, Russia has claimed these territories. Japan continues to demand the return of the Northern Territories.

◄ ③ **Rishiri Rebun Sarobetsu National Park (Toyotomi Town)** Mt. Rishiri (Rishiri-fuji) of Rishiri Island can be seen in the distance.

► ④ **The Icebreaker *Garinko* passing through a large ice floe (Monbetsu City)** From mid-January to April, the Sea of Okhotsk contains a large number of ice floes. Tourists on the ice breaker *Garinko*, can observe the sea creatures that live beneath the ice, while being entertained by the noise of grinding caused by the ship pushing its way through the ice floes.

◀ ① Nature of the Hokkaidō Region

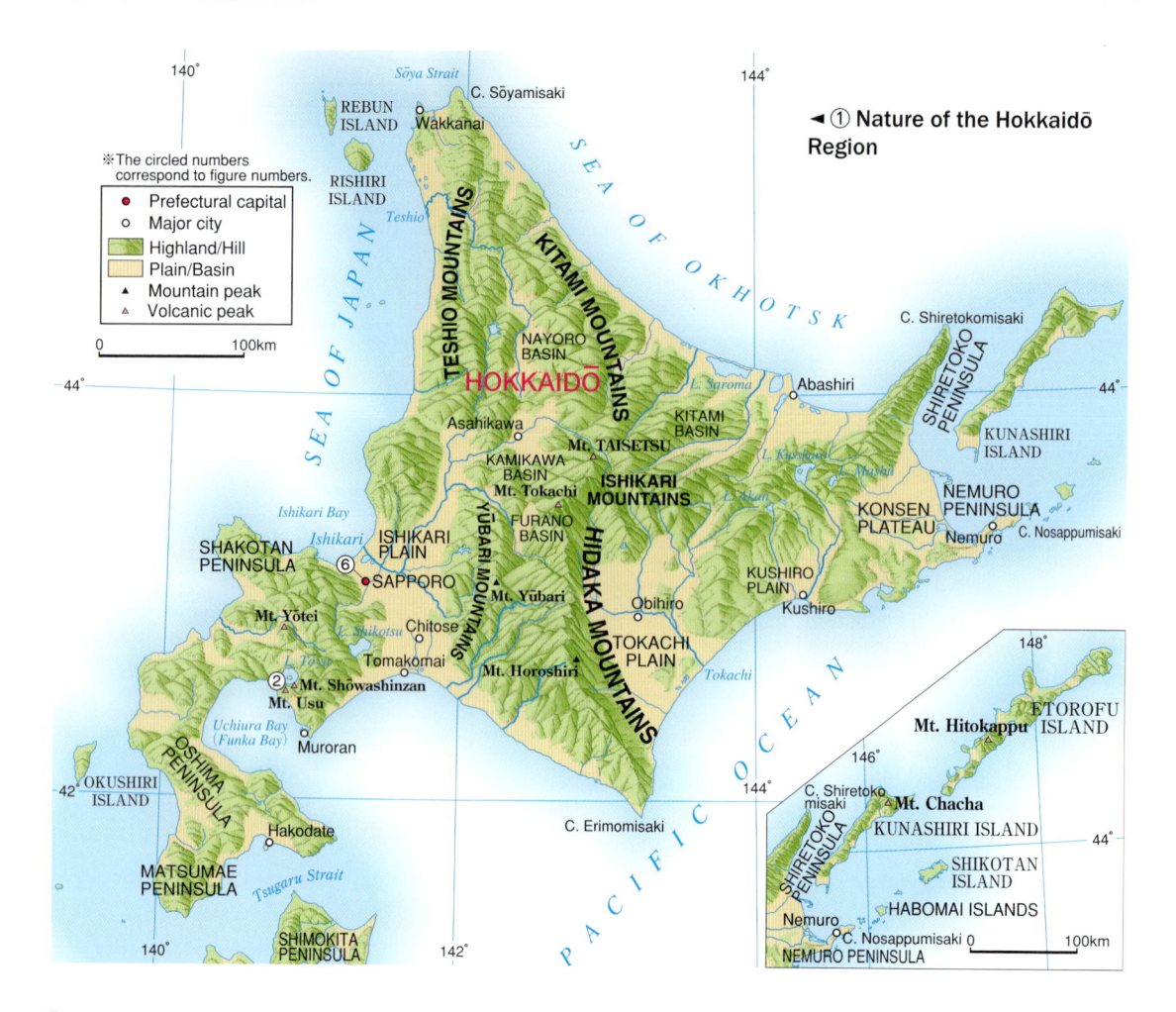

1 Looking at the map

Hokkaidō's wide open spaces

The northernmost of the four main islands that make up Japan, Hokkaidō faces both Honshū, across the Tsugaru Strait, and Karafuto (Sakhalin) across the Sōya Strait.

▼ ② Mt. Usu and Lake Tōya   Mt. Usu has erupted four times in the last hundred years. The crater on the right-hand side (where rising columns of steam can be seen) appeared as a result of the great eruption of March, 2000.

There is a saying in Japanese, "Dekkaidō, Hokkaidō!", which means "Hakkaidō is vast!", and indeed the island accounts for as much as a fifth of the Japan's surface area. The Hidaka Mountains, which runs north-south in the central part of the island, divides Hokkaidō into two contrasting regions. This mountains converges with the Ishikari Mountains, whose summits reach altitudes of above 2000 meters, and then continues northwards in the form of the Kitami Mountains. Although some of Hokkaidō's active volcanoes, including Mt. Taisetsu and Mt. Usu, have occasionally erupted with locally disastrous results, they have also engendered fine landscapes, including caldera lakes and hot springs, and these landscapes attract very many tourists. Hokkaidō's biggest river by far is the Ishikari, which rises in the Ishikari Mountains. The river, which is prone to flooding, has created lowland areas such as the

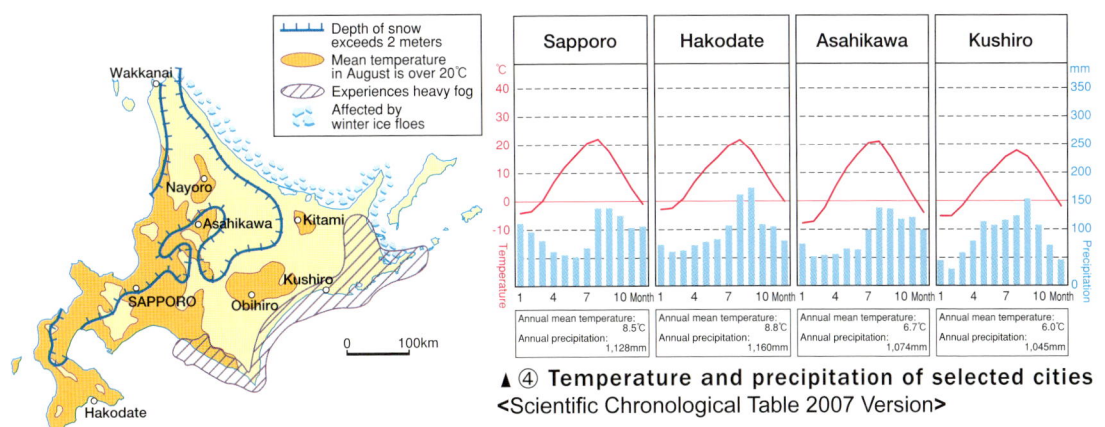

▲ ③ The Climate of Hokkaidō <Climate of Hokkaidō, and others>

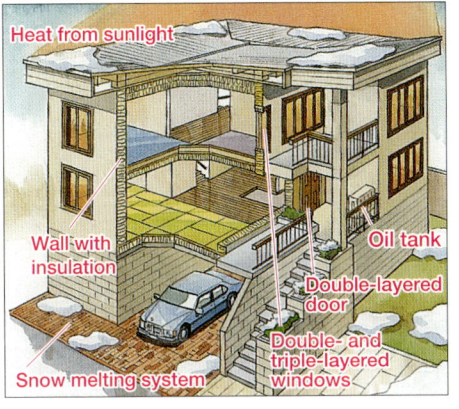

▲ ④ Temperature and precipitation of selected cities
<Scientific Chronological Table 2007 Version>

◀ ⑤ Measures for keeping houses warm in winter
Even in cold winters, central heating systems keep temperatures warm enough indoors short-sleeved shirts. Many measures are taken against snow accumulation.

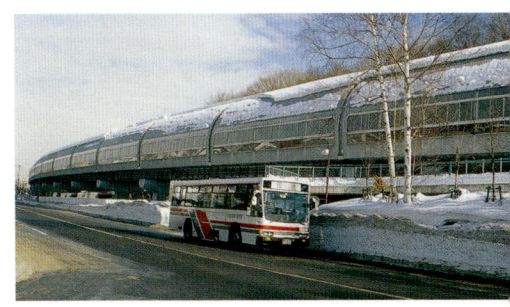

▲ ⑥ Shelter constructed over surface lines of the underground railway system (Sapporo City) This is to prevent snow from piling up on the tracks.

Kamikawa Basin and the Ishikari Plain. Other lowland areas that are important for farming include the Tokachi Plain and the Konsen Plateau in the east, and the Nayoro and Kitami Basins in the inland.

Land, covered with ice and snow

Belonging as it does to the subarctic zone, Hokkaidō has a climate that is generally cool. The long winter is characterized by severe cold, and the inland temperatures can drop below minus 20°C. In contrast to the heavy snowfall on the western side of the island, the area facing the Pacific Ocean experiences less snowfall and a larger number of cloudless days. From February to March, ice floes surge into the Sea of Okhotsk and reach the northern coasts of Hokkaidō. Summer in the interior of the island and in the Sea of Japan coastlands is mild, temperatures seldom exceeding 30°C. Along the eastern coasts, where the cold Oyashio (Chishima Current) flows close to the shore, dense fogs travel inland from spring to summer, and cool temperatures predominate. Hokkaidō does not have a marked rainy season and experiences few typhoons.

To pass the cold winters comfortably, the people of Hokkaidō insulate the walls of their houses, and windows and doors have two or three layers, to shut out the cold air. Furthermore, cities have built snow shelters over urban railway lines such as that shown in Figure 6, and have introduced snow melting systems.[1]

Notes (P.133)
[1] A system that melts snow by laying warm-water pipes and electric lines below the surface, thus raising the temperature of the ground. The pipes and electric cables melt the snow and prevent roads, sidewalks and parking lots from freezing over.

▲ ① **Atsushi-ori (Atsushi fabric)** Made from fibers of tree skins, *Atsushi* is a thick textile that is embroidered with *Ainu* patterns.

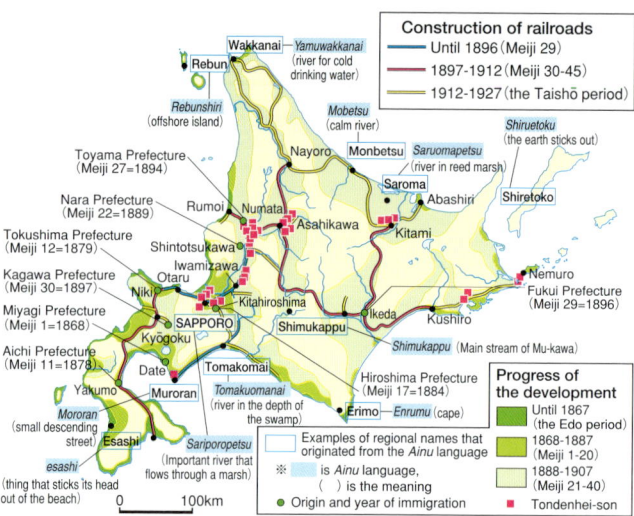

▲ ② **The development of Hokkaidō and the origins of place names** Some place names have been derived from the *Ainu* language, while others were coined by the early settlers, who named their villages after the places in Honshū from which they had come. Examples include Shintotsukawa (founded by settlers from Totsukawa, Nara Prefecture) and Kitahiroshima (founded by those from Hiroshima Prefecture).

2 The history of Hokkaidō's development and the growth of cities

The traditional culture of the *Ainu*

With their own unique culture, the *Ainu* people are the indigenous inhabitants of Hokkaidō, northern parts of the Tōhoku Region, and the southern half of Karafuto (Sakhalin). Believing that gods dwell in prominent natural features, the Ainu worshipped natural phenomena as *kamui* (a word meaning "gods"). There is no *Ainu* writing system, but numerous legends and stories were passed on by word of mouth from one generation to the next. Many place-names in Hokkaidō, including Sapporo and Muroran, have their roots to the *Ainu* language.

From the 1870s, the land inhabited by the *Ainu* people has been occupied as Japanese colonization proceeded and as development projects got under way. The *Ainu* population declined, and much of their traditional culture was gradually lost through the years. At present, many initiatives are being taken to revive and preserve the traditional *Ainu* way of life.

The era of Hokkaidō's development

The modern development of Hokkaidō[1] began in earnest with the establishment of the Colonization Office by the Japanese government in 1869. Many settlers from different backgrounds were gathered from across Japan, but *tonden-hei* (former samurai-turned-farmers) played a major role in opening up the island for cultivation and in securing the Japanese presence in these distant northern lands. Overcoming the chilly climate of the region, *tonden-hei* settlers cleared the vast plains and forests, assisted by the government, which created an orderly and geometrically planned system whereby plots of farmland

---

Notes (P.134)
[1] In the early years of the development of Hokkaidō, prisoners were made to work on road construction.

▲ ③ **The central area of Sapporo** Many events, including the famous "Sapporo Snow Festival" and the "*Yosakoi Sōran* Festival," are held in Ōdōri Park, a narrow recreational area that forms a an east-west axis in central Sapporo.

were allocated to settlers. The villages founded by the *tonden-hei* soldiers were called *Tondenhei-son*, and they were characterized by the systematic alignment of houses on both sides of wide roads. Some of Hokkaidō's present-day cities developed from *Tondenhei-son*, including Sapporo and Asahikawa.

Sapporo, metropolis of the north

Sapporo is a city created by the government in the nineteenth century as a base from which to organize the development of Hokkaidō. As can be seen in Figure 3, the city's streets are laid out in a grid pattern. The Hokkaidō Prefectural Government as well as several national government branch offices are located in Sapporo. Branch offices of companies from other prefectures have also moved in, and offices and services, continue to enjoy rapid development. As Hokkaidō's central city, Sapporo has attracted people from all over the island. In 2000, Sapporo and its surrounding suburbs contained approximately 2,510,000 people, or more than 40% of the population of Hokkaidō.

The development of transportation

As Hokkaidō's gateway to the sky, Shinchitose Airport is used by approximately 18 million passengers every year. The Shinchitose-Tōkyō (Haneda) route is Japan's most frequently traveled air route, carrying around 10 million people annually. In the 1960s, it took more than 17 hours to get from Sapporo to Tōkyō using railways and ferries, but aircraft have since reduced the traveling time to a mere hour and a half.

By contrast, ships are still used to transport freight. As Hokkaidō's gateway to the sea, Tomakomai has cargo ferry connections with several important ports in Japan. The introduction of large fast ferries has reduced shipping times, and has enabled Hokkaidō to export an increasing quantity of fresh goods to Tōkyō and Ōsaka. Moreover, the opening of the Seikan Tunnel (a railway tunnel that links Hokkaidō and Honshū) in 1988 marked an important improvement in rail transportation. In these ways, transport developments have exerted a strong impact on the economy of Hokkaidō and on the lives of the people who live in the island.

▲ ① **Paddy land in the Ishikari Plain**　In Hokkaidō, the typical rice-cropping farm produces approximately 31 tons of rice. This is equivalent to the annual rice needs of 500 Japanese consumers

3 Agriculture and stock raising in Hokkaidō's broad acres

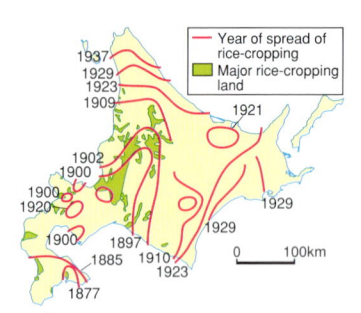

▲ ② **Northwards and eastwards spread of rice-cropping** <Kawaguchi Takeo, and others>

From "cold-resistant rice" to "tasty rice"

In the later half of the nineteenth century, when development of the island began, it was thought that the chilly climate of Hokkaidō was unsuitable for the cultivation of rice. However, the people who were involved in the early development projects made great efforts to overcome harsh environmental conditions and to produce the staple food that they had always eaten, namely rice.

The rice cultivation is common nowadays in Ishikari Plain, which spread widely in the basin of the Ishikari River. The environment of this plain was relatively warm by Hokkaidō standards, and where there was easy access to water. However, the plain was covered by marshy peat land[1] that was unfavorable for rice-cropping. So that, drainage systems had to be introduced and the soil had to be improved by mixing earths of different qualities[2] before the area could emerge as the prominent single-crop field of rice paddies that it is today. Rice cultivation began in the western lands of Hokkaidō, but thanks to the development of fast-maturing, cold-resistant rice strains, rice production became possible in almost all areas of Hokkaidō. In recent years, in response to consumer demands, rice that is especially tasty as well as cold-resistant has been developed, examples being the varieties "*Kirara* 397" and "*Hoshi-no-Yume*".

Notes (P.136)
[1] Dead plants piled up in marshlands and marshes did not decompose because of the cold, but over a long period of time became carbonized instead.
[2] To enhance the soil by mixing it with soil of different quality brought from elsewhere.

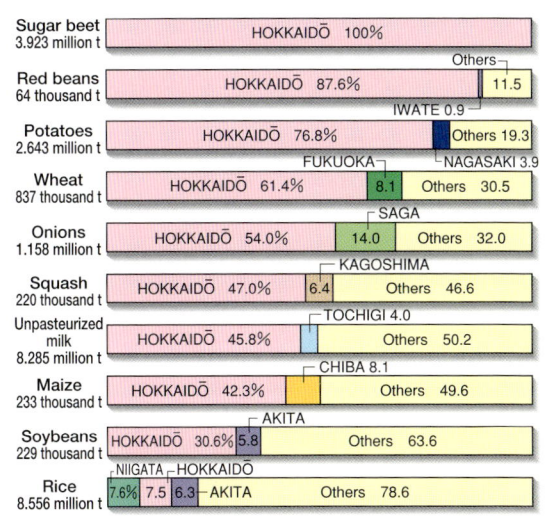

▲ ③ Hokkaidō's contribution to the national output of selected farm products, 2006 <Statistics for Milk and Dairy Products 2006, and other sources>

Product	Hokkaidō	Others
Sugar beet (3.923 million t)	HOKKAIDŌ 100%	
Red beans (64 thousand t)	HOKKAIDŌ 87.6%	11.5
Potatoes (2.643 million t)	HOKKAIDŌ 76.8%	IWATE 0.9 / Others 19.3
Wheat (837 thousand t)	HOKKAIDŌ 61.4%	FUKUOKA 8.1 / NAGASAKI 3.9 / Others 30.5
Onions (1.158 million t)	HOKKAIDŌ 54.0%	SAGA 14.0 / Others 32.0
Squash (220 thousand t)	HOKKAIDŌ 47.0%	KAGOSHIMA 6.4 / Others 46.6
Unpasteurized milk (8.285 million t)	HOKKAIDŌ 45.8%	TOCHIGI 4.0 / Others 50.2
Maize (233 thousand t)	HOKKAIDŌ 42.3%	CHIBA 8.1 / Others 49.6
Soybeans (229 thousand t)	HOKKAIDŌ 30.6%	AKITA 5.8 / Others 63.6
Rice (8.556 million t)	NIIGATA 7.6 / HOKKAIDŌ 7.5 / AKITA 6.3	Others 78.6

▲ ④ **Field farming (non-irrigated) in the Tokachi Plain** Large farm holdings stretch across the plain and the fields are wide enough to allow the use of big machines. Note the lines of trees, which are grown as windbreaks.

▼ ⑤ **Area of rice field per farming household** (2005) <2005 Agriculture and Forestry Census>

- Tokachi District: 31.9 ha
- Hokkaidō: 18.6 ha
- Japan (excluding Hokkaidō): 1.3 ha

▶ ⑥ **Dairy farms on the Konsen Plateau**

The wide green plains of Hokkaidō

The eastern area of Hokkaidō is prosperous in respect of both large-scale field farming (non-irrigated) and dairy farming. Hokkaidō is a leading producer of several agricultural products in Japan, as can be seen in Figure 3, and in many ways helps to support the typical Japanese diet. The farmers in this area have enlarged their operations and nowadays employ large agricultural machines. The green scenery of farmlands and meadows that stretches from horizon to horizon—a type of landscape typical of the island—has been shaped by the lasting efforts of generations of Hokkaidō farmers.

Field farming is undertaken in areas such as the Tokachi Plain and the Kitami Basin, both of which are well endowed with fertile soil, and where the average farm size is approximately 30 ha, which is 20 times greater than the national average. Vegetables such as potatoes, onions, sugar beet, maize, as well as red beans and soybeans are cultivated on the basis of crop rotation.[3] In recent years, cultivation of *daikon* (Japanese white radish), cabbages, and Chinese cabbages has been introduced, especially in the Furano Basin.

Dairy farming is mostly concentrated in eastern Hokkaidō. Grass meadows extend widely over the Konsen Plateau and along the coast of the Sea of Okhotsk. Pastureland has been developed despite the harshness of the environment in this part of Hokkaidō. Environmental obstacles have included the unusually severe winter, summers made cool by the incursion of dense cold fogs, and an unpromising soil that has developed from a thick layer of infertile volcanic ash.

Notes (P.137)
[3] To cultivate different crops in a fixed order over time on the same field.

▲ ① Unloading of cultivated scallops (Tokoro, Kitami City)

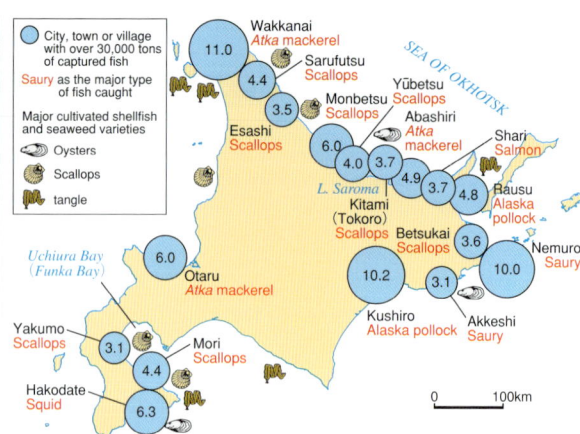

▲ ② Major sea products of Hokkaidō (2005) <Hokkaidō aquatic production 2005>

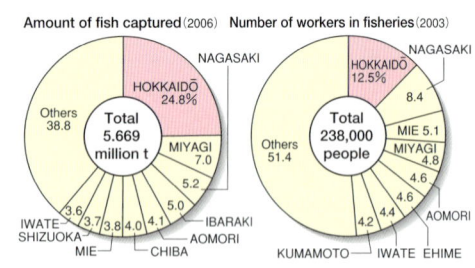

▲ ③ Quantity of fish caught in Japan and number of fishermen <Statistics of Fishery · Culture Production 2006, and others>

▶ ④ Changes in the amount of fish unloaded at Hokkaido ports by type <Hokkaidō aquatic production 2005, and others>

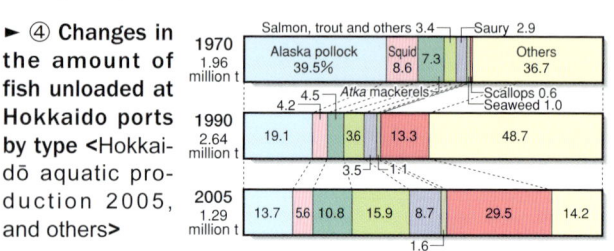

4 Changes in Hokkaidō's fishing industry

From catching fish to breeding them

Hokkaidō is surrounded by seas that are rich in marine resources, and is Japan's leading prefecture in terms of the size of fish catch.

Over the course of time, the nature of Hokkaidō's fish catch has changed substantially, reflecting changes in international circumstances. The ports of Kushiro and Nemuro, for example, formerly flourished as the bases of the Northern Sea fishery. Large fleets went fishing in the Bering Sea and the seas off the United States and Canada for salmon, trout and Alaska pollock. However, with the introduction of offshore Exclusive Economic Zones in the 1970s, various countries began to impose tight restrictions on Japanese fishing boats. Japanese fleets could not freely engage in fishing[1] in the Exclusive Economic Zones belonging to other countries and in the areas surrounding the Northern Territories, and as a result, the Northern Sea fishery received a great setback. What is more, operations on the open seas were regulated to allow salmon and trout to return to rivers before spawning.

While ocean fishing has been subject to an increasing number of restrictions, there has been a marked shift towards "aquafarming." Some enterprises are involved in artificially hatching salmon eggs and stocking rivers with them. Cultivation of scallops is flourishing along the coast of the Sea of Okhotsk and around Uchiura Bay, while cultivation fishery of urchins and herrings is also carried out.

Notes (P.138)

[1] Fish catches have been subdivided and are subject to limitations on the type of fish caught, and it has become necessary to pay large sums of money to obtain licenses to conduct fishing operations in these marine areas.

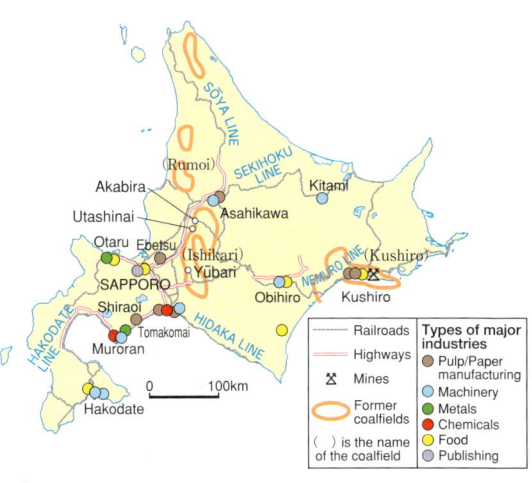

▲ ① **Mining and industry of Hokkaido** <Industry Statistical Table 2004, and others>

▲ ② **Cheese Factory of the Snow Brand Milk Product Company** (Taiki Town)　Gouda cheese, a type of natural cheese, is being stored to allow it to mature. Approximately 90% of Japan's natural cheese is produced in Hokkaidō.

5　The rise and fall of Hokkaidō's mining and industry

Coal-burning industries

Hokkaidō was formerly an important coal-mining region. The Ishikari Coalfield, in particular, was the largest of its kind in Japan, and cities such as Yūbari, Utashinai and Akabira, prospered as large mining towns. Coal mining was also carried out in and around Kushiro and Rumoi.

Coal from the Ishikari coalfield was used by various industries, including the Muroran Steel Works of the Nippon Steel Corporation. Several engineering and metal-processing industries that used steel as their raw materials developed in Muroran. In addition, the Ōji Paper Company constructed paper mills in Tomakomai and Ebetsu, while Daishōwa Paper Industry (now Nippon Paper Industry) followed suit in Shiraoi. Besides to abundant timber and water resources, Hokkaidō was rich in coal, the source of energy for paper production.

However, after the energy revolution of the late 1960s, mines closed down one after another, while the steel industry declined in relative importance. Since then, former coal and steel producing districts have had to develop new types of industries.

The beginning of a new industry

While its smokestack industries have declined, Hokkaidō has benefited from continued development of industries based on local agriculture, such as sugar refining and milling industries, and industries that make food products such as processed milk and cheese. Sapporo Beer and the Snow Brand Milk Product Company are examples of food and beverage companies that originated in Hokkaido.

In recent years, the city of Tomakomai has developed as a new industrial district. After the Second World War, a large-scale port was created at Tomakomai and in the 1970s, an industrial zone containing oil refining and assorted feed factories began to emerge on land surrounding the new harbor. In 1992, Toyota Motors built a new parts factory at Tomakomai, and this has attracted many related companies into the area.

▲ ① **Field of lavender in Furano (Kamifurano Town)** Originally, the lavender grown here was destined purely for the scent-making industry, but nowadays the lavender fields are maintained as a tourist farm.

▲ ② **Asahiyama Zoo (Asahikawa City)** "Displays of acts" by animals attract tourists from outside Hokkaidō.

▶ ④ **Number of tourists who visit Hokkaidō by month (2006)** <Inquiry Report of number of tourists in Hokkaidō 2006 Edition>

▲ ③ **Sapporo Snow Festival (Sapporo City)** One of many sets of snow sculptures in Ōdōri Park. In 2007, the number of visitors amounted to 2,190,000.

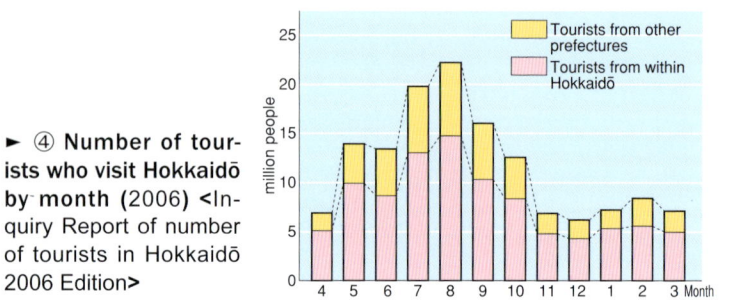

6 Tourism that supports the region

Hokkaidō's many attractions

Tourism is one of the most important industries in Hokkaido. Following improvements in air transportation, many tourists have visited the region from throughout Japan. In recent years, the number of tourists from neighboring countries has also begun to increase, and plans are underway to expand the number of international flights.

Summer is the major season for sight-seeing in Hokkaidō. Many people are attracted by the colorful landscapes of Furano and Biei with their beautiful flower fields. Others are drawn by the national parks of Shiretoko and Kushiro Marshland, and by hot springs such as the one at Noboribetsu. In contrast, winter was not as popular among the tourists. To eliminate this rather unbalanced situation, efforts are being made to promote skiing grounds, unusual features associated with coldness, and the snow of Hokkaidō as major winter tourist attractions. Snow-related events, including the "Sapporo Snow Festival" and the "Asahikawa Winter Festival," are held in various areas. In addition, icebreakers are attracting the attention of tourists in the Sea of Okhotsk, where there are many ice floes during the winter months.

Japan seen through its regions
"The Paradise of the Wild" -the ideal and reality of Shiretoko

▶ ① **World Heritage Sites in Japan**

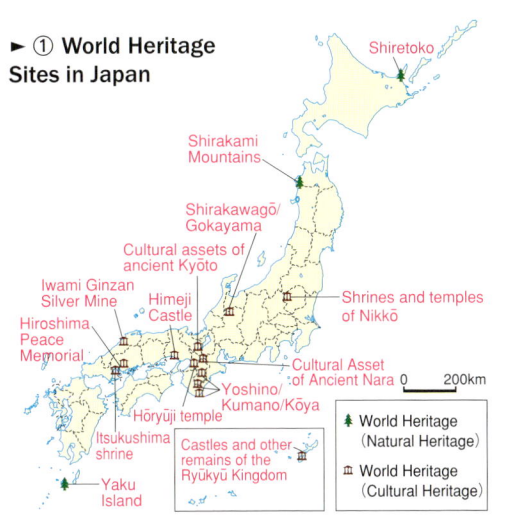

◀ ② **Shiretoko, registered as a World Natural Heritage Site** The photograph shows the "five lakes" of Shiretoko, surrounded by forest.

▶ ③ **Tourists strolling through the forest of Shiretoko** In order to maintain both tourism and the conservation of the natural habitat of the brown bears, a two-meter high overhead path has been constructed.

Untouched nature can still be found in the remote Shiretoko Peninsula. Because of its ecosystem, which contains many wild animals, the peninsula was registered as a World Natural Heritage Site by UNESCO in July 2005. There are currently only three areas in Japan that are registered as World Natural Heritage Sites: the Shiretoko Peninsula, Yaku Island in Kagoshima Prefecture, and the Shirakami Mountains in Aomori and Akita Prefectures.

Since its registration as a World Natural Heritage Site, Shiretoko has attracted a growing number of tourists. By trekking through the forest and observing plants and animals, people can come into contact with primeval nature. However, the increase in tourist numbers has caused a new problem. Wild animals have come to depend so much on tourists for food that they have stopped searching for food themselves. This is a serious issue that negatively affects the park's remarkable ecosystem. Sometimes, in the hope of obtaining food from tourists, ezo deer and ezo red foxes gather along the roads and consequently get involved in car accidents. Known as the "kings of the forest," brown bears, who once avoided contact with people, nowadays venture close to houses in an attempt to find food.

Japan's other World Natural Heritage Sites are experiencing similar problems. In order to prevent damage to the ecosystem caused by the increasing waves of tourists, restrictions have been imposed limiting entry into Shirakami Mountains. In Yaku Island, tourists must pay fees to enter the mountains. Being registered as a World Natural Heritage Site should not lead to the endangering of unique and valuable ecosystems. Shiretoko now faces the challenging problem of how best to balance conservation with the tourist exploitation of its natural environment.

Viewing Japan

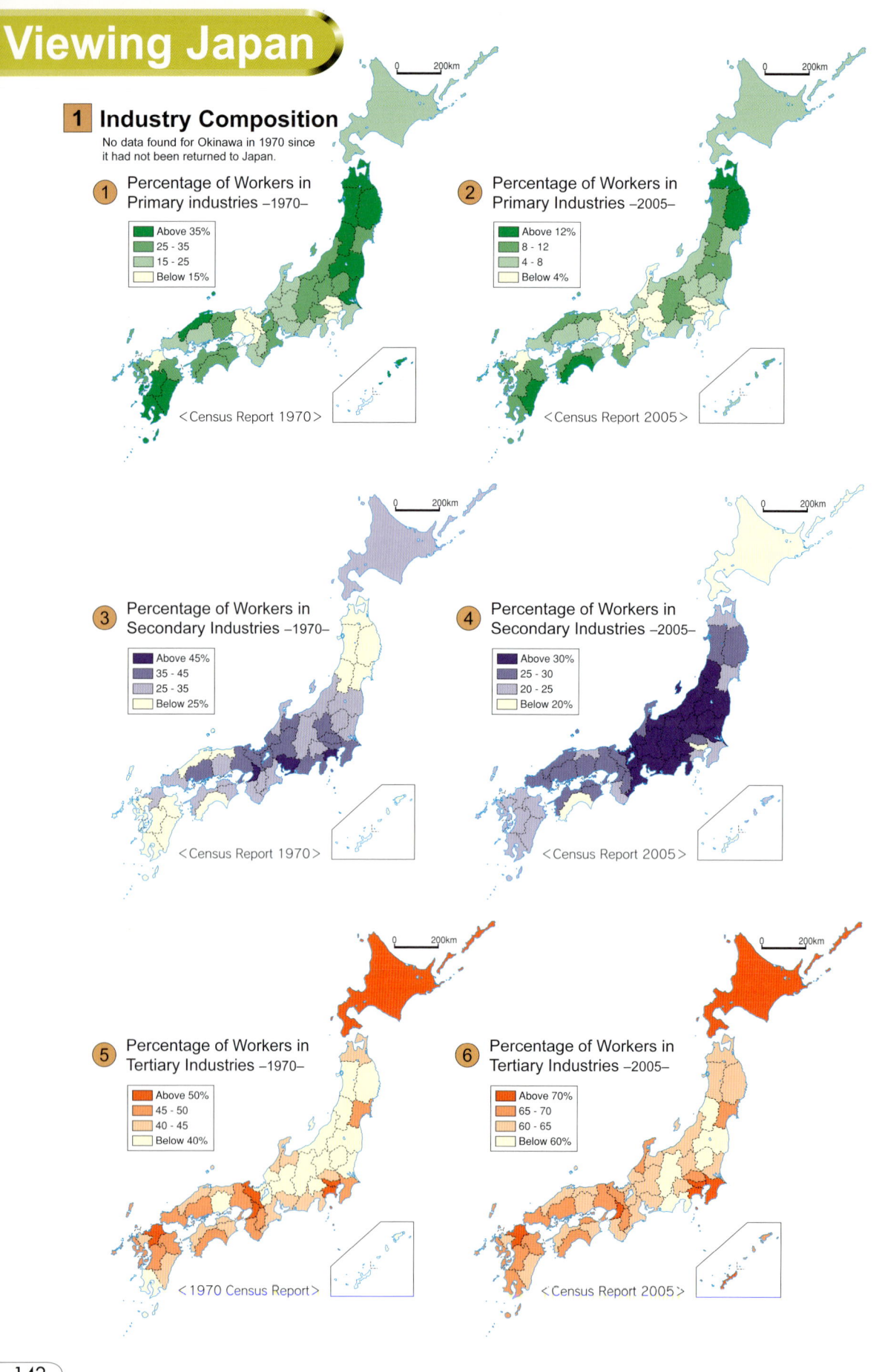

1 Industry Composition

No data found for Okinawa in 1970 since it had not been returned to Japan.

① Percentage of Workers in Primary industries –1970–

- Above 35%
- 25 - 35
- 15 - 25
- Below 15%

<Census Report 1970>

② Percentage of Workers in Primary Industries –2005–

- Above 12%
- 8 - 12
- 4 - 8
- Below 4%

<Census Report 2005>

③ Percentage of Workers in Secondary Industries –1970–

- Above 45%
- 35 - 45
- 25 - 35
- Below 25%

<Census Report 1970>

④ Percentage of Workers in Secondary Industries –2005–

- Above 30%
- 25 - 30
- 20 - 25
- Below 20%

<Census Report 2005>

⑤ Percentage of Workers in Tertiary Industries –1970–

- Above 50%
- 45 - 50
- 40 - 45
- Below 40%

<1970 Census Report>

⑥ Percentage of Workers in Tertiary Industries –2005–

- Above 70%
- 65 - 70
- 60 - 65
- Below 60%

<Census Report 2005>

2 Agriculture, Forestry and Fisheries

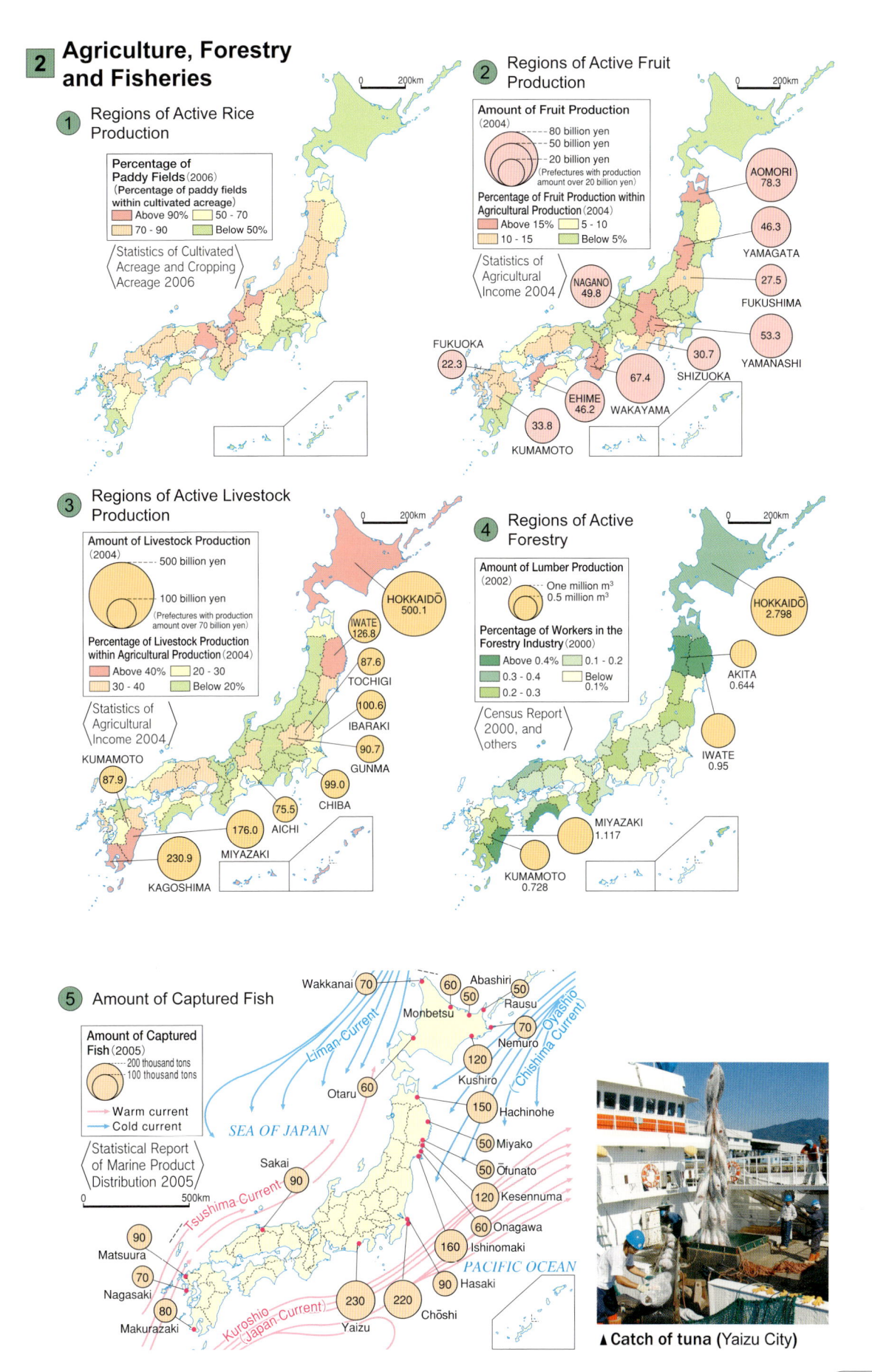

1 Regions of Active Rice Production

Percentage of Paddy Fields (2006)
(Percentage of paddy fields within cultivated acreage)
- Above 90%
- 70 – 90
- 50 – 70
- Below 50%

⟨Statistics of Cultivated Acreage and Cropping Acreage 2006⟩

2 Regions of Active Fruit Production

Amount of Fruit Production (2004)
- 80 billion yen
- 50 billion yen
- 20 billion yen
(Prefectures with production amount over 20 billion yen)

Percentage of Fruit Production within Agricultural Production (2004)
- Above 15%
- 10 – 15
- 5 – 10
- Below 5%

⟨Statistics of Agricultural Income 2004⟩

- AOMORI 78.3
- YAMAGATA 46.3
- FUKUSHIMA 27.5
- NAGANO 49.8
- YAMANASHI 53.3
- SHIZUOKA 30.7
- WAKAYAMA 67.4
- FUKUOKA 22.3
- EHIME 46.2
- KUMAMOTO 33.8

3 Regions of Active Livestock Production

Amount of Livestock Production (2004)
- 500 billion yen
- 100 billion yen
(Prefectures with production amount over 70 billion yen)

Percentage of Livestock Production within Agricultural Production (2004)
- Above 40%
- 30 – 40
- 20 – 30
- Below 20%

⟨Statistics of Agricultural Income 2004⟩

- HOKKAIDŌ 500.1
- IWATE 126.8
- TOCHIGI 87.6
- IBARAKI 100.6
- GUNMA 90.7
- CHIBA 99.0
- AICHI 75.5
- KUMAMOTO 87.9
- MIYAZAKI 176.0
- KAGOSHIMA 230.9

4 Regions of Active Forestry

Amount of Lumber Production (2002)
- One million m³
- 0.5 million m³

Percentage of Workers in the Forestry Industry (2000)
- Above 0.4%
- 0.3 – 0.4
- 0.2 – 0.3
- 0.1 – 0.2
- Below 0.1%

⟨Census Report 2000, and others⟩

- HOKKAIDŌ 2.798
- AKITA 0.644
- IWATE 0.95
- MIYAZAKI 1.117
- KUMAMOTO 0.728

5 Amount of Captured Fish

Amount of Captured Fish (2005)
- 200 thousand tons
- 100 thousand tons

→ Warm current
→ Cold current

⟨Statistical Report of Marine Product Distribution 2005⟩

- Wakkanai 70
- Abashiri 60
- Monbetsu 50
- Rausu 50
- Nemuro 70
- Kushiro 120
- Otaru 60
- Hachinohe 150
- Miyako 50
- Ōfunato 50
- Kesennuma 120
- Onagawa 60
- Ishinomaki 160
- Hasaki 90
- Chōshi 220
- Yaizu 230
- Sakai 90
- Matsuura 90
- Nagasaki 70
- Makurazaki 80

Currents: Liman Current, Chishima Current (Oyashio), Tsushima Current, Kuroshio (Japan Current)

SEA OF JAPAN
PACIFIC OCEAN

▲ Catch of tuna (Yaizu City)

3 Industry

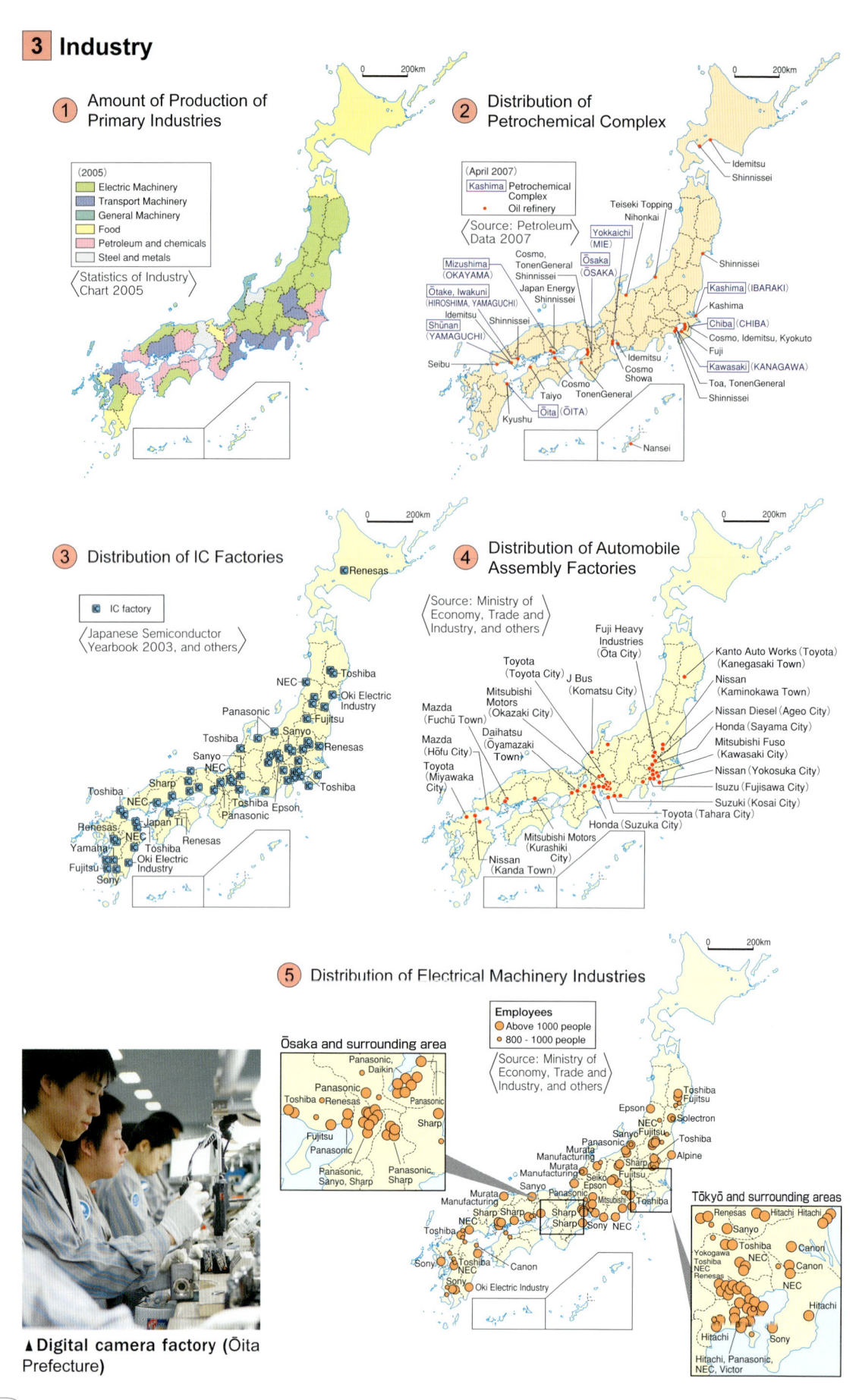

① Amount of Production of Primary Industries

(2005)
- Electric Machinery
- Transport Machinery
- General Machinery
- Food
- Petroleum and chemicals
- Steel and metals

⟨Statistics of Industry Chart 2005⟩

② Distribution of Petrochemical Complex

(April 2007)
- Kashima Petrochemical Complex
- • Oil refinery

⟨Source: Petroleum Data 2007⟩

- Idemitsu
- Shinnissei
- Teiseki Topping Nihonkai
- Shinnissei
- Mizushima (OKAYAMA)
- Cosmo, TonenGeneral Shinnissei
- Yokkaichi (MIE)
- Ōsaka (OSAKA)
- Japan Energy Shinnissei
- Kashima (IBARAKI)
- Kashima
- Ōtake, Iwakuni (HIROSHIMA, YAMAGUCHI)
- Idemitsu
- Shinnissei
- Chiba (CHIBA)
- Cosmo, Idemitsu, Kyokuto Fuji
- Shūnan (YAMAGUCHI)
- Fuji
- Kawasaki (KANAGAWA)
- Seibu
- Idemitsu Cosmo Showa
- Toa, TonenGeneral
- Cosmo
- Taiyo
- TonenGeneral
- Shinnissei
- Kyushu
- Ōita (ŌITA)
- Nansei

③ Distribution of IC Factories

■ IC factory

⟨Japanese Semiconductor Yearbook 2003, and others⟩

- Renesas
- NEC
- Toshiba
- Oki Electric Industry
- Panasonic
- Fujitsu
- Toshiba
- Sanyo
- Renesas
- NEC
- Toshiba
- Sharp
- NEC
- Toshiba
- Panasonic
- Epson
- Renesas
- Japan TI
- Renesas
- NEC
- Toshiba
- Yamaha
- Oki Electric Industry
- Fujitsu
- Sony

④ Distribution of Automobile Assembly Factories

⟨Source: Ministry of Economy, Trade and Industry, and others⟩

- Fuji Heavy Industries (Ōta City)
- Kanto Auto Works (Toyota) (Kanegasaki Town)
- Toyota (Toyota City)
- J Bus (Komatsu City)
- Nissan (Kaminokawa Town)
- Mazda (Fuchū Town)
- Mitsubishi Motors (Okazaki City)
- Nissan Diesel (Ageo City)
- Daihatsu (Ōyamazaki Town)
- Honda (Sayama City)
- Mazda (Hōfu City)
- Mitsubishi Fuso (Kawasaki City)
- Toyota (Miyawaka City)
- Nissan (Yokosuka City)
- Isuzu (Fujisawa City)
- Suzuki (Kosai City)
- Mitsubishi Motors (Kurashiki City)
- Toyota (Tahara City)
- Honda (Suzuka City)
- Nissan (Kanda Town)

⑤ Distribution of Electrical Machinery Industries

Employees
- ● Above 1000 people
- • 800 - 1000 people

⟨Source: Ministry of Economy, Trade and Industry, and others⟩

Ōsaka and surrounding area
- Panasonic, Daikin
- Panasonic
- Toshiba Renesas
- Panasonic
- Fujitsu
- Panasonic
- Sharp
- Panasonic, Sanyo, Sharp
- Panasonic, Sharp

Tōkyō and surrounding areas
- Renesas
- Hitachi Hitachi
- Sanyo
- Toshiba
- Canon
- Yokogawa Toshiba NEC Renesas
- NEC
- Canon
- NEC
- Hitachi
- Hitachi
- Sony
- Hitachi, Panasonic, NEC, Victor

- Toshiba
- Fujitsu
- Epson
- NEC
- Solectron
- Sanyo
- Panasonic Fujitsu
- Toshiba
- Murata Manufacturing
- Sharp
- Alpine
- Murata Manufacturing
- Sanyo
- Panasonic
- Epson
- Fujitsu
- Mitsubishi
- Toshiba
- Sharp
- Sharp
- Sony
- NEC
- Toshiba
- Sony
- NEC
- Canon
- Oki Electric Industry

▲ Digital camera factory (Ōita Prefecture)

4 Life-style

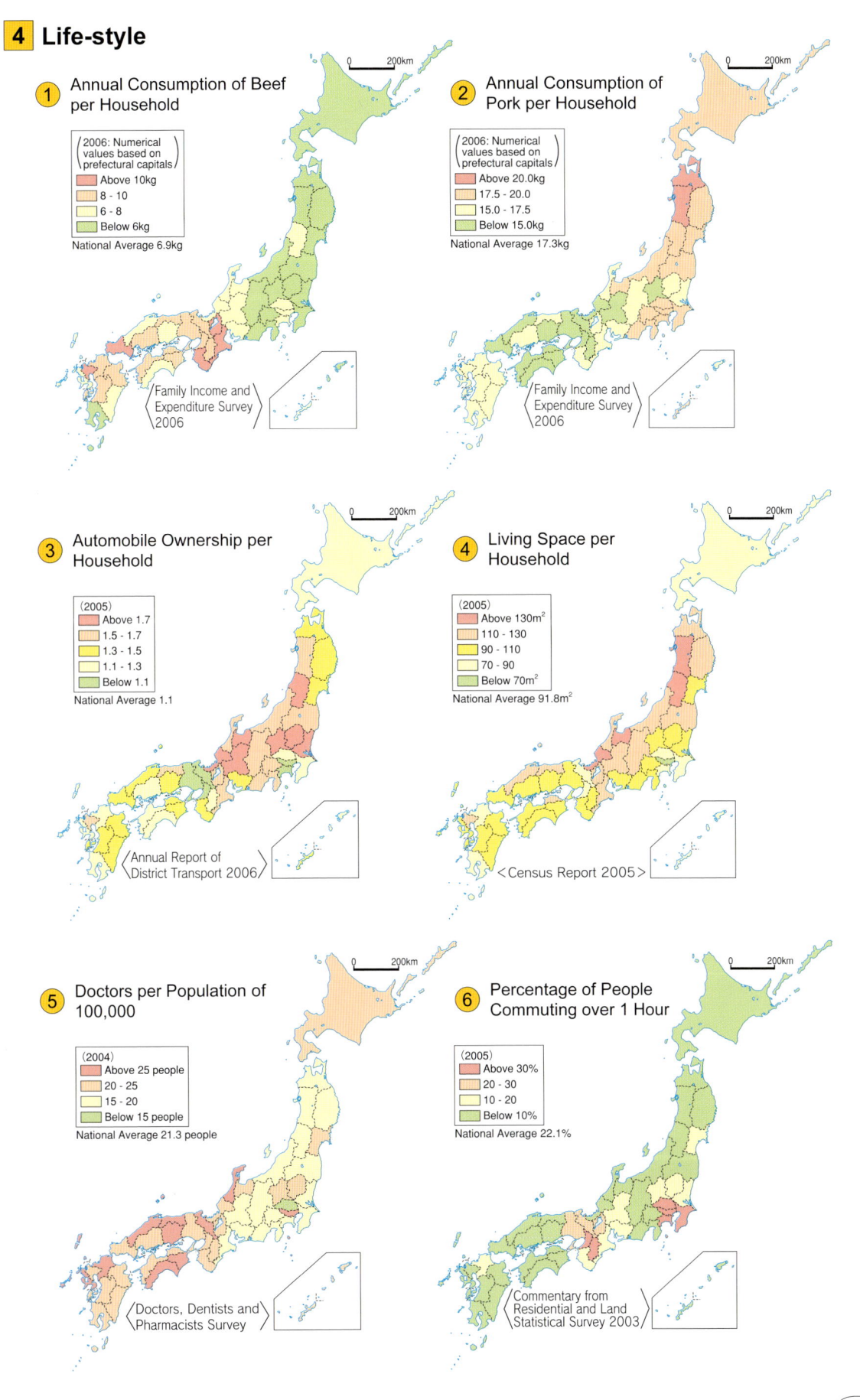

1 Annual Consumption of Beef per Household

2006: Numerical values based on prefectural capitals
- Above 10kg
- 8 - 10
- 6 - 8
- Below 6kg

National Average 6.9kg

Family Income and Expenditure Survey 2006

2 Annual Consumption of Pork per Household

2006: Numerical values based on prefectural capitals
- Above 20.0kg
- 17.5 - 20.0
- 15.0 - 17.5
- Below 15.0kg

National Average 17.3kg

Family Income and Expenditure Survey 2006

3 Automobile Ownership per Household

(2005)
- Above 1.7
- 1.5 - 1.7
- 1.3 - 1.5
- 1.1 - 1.3
- Below 1.1

National Average 1.1

Annual Report of District Transport 2006

4 Living Space per Household

(2005)
- Above 130m²
- 110 - 130
- 90 - 110
- 70 - 90
- Below 70m²

National Average 91.8m²

<Census Report 2005>

5 Doctors per Population of 100,000

(2004)
- Above 25 people
- 20 - 25
- 15 - 20
- Below 15 people

National Average 21.3 people

Doctors, Dentists and Pharmacists Survey

6 Percentage of People Commuting over 1 Hour

(2005)
- Above 30%
- 20 - 30
- 10 - 20
- Below 10%

National Average 22.1%

Commentary from Residential and Land Statistical Survey 2003

Statistics of Japan

1. Average Monthly Temperature and Precipitation in Selected Cities

<Chronological Scientific Table 2009>

1. Units: Temperature: °C Precipitation: mm
2. Red figures are maximum values: black and *blue italics* represent minimum values.

Climate Zone	City (height of observation point (m)) [prefecture]		January	February	March	April	May	June	July	August	September	October	November	December	Annual
Hokkaidō	Abashiri (37.6) [Hokkaidō]	Temperature	-5.9	-6.6	-2.5	4.1	9.2	12.8	17.2	19.4	16.0	10.3	3.3	-2.4	6.2
		Precipitation	58	*34*	49	55	65	59	78	98	109	76	67	54	802
	Asahikawa (120.0) [Hokkaidō]	Temperature	-7.8	-7.2	-2.4	5.2	11.7	16.5	20.5	21.1	15.6	8.8	2.0	-4.1	6.7
		Precipitation	74	*52*	54	56	65	64	99	138	136	118	121	99	1074
	Nemuro (25.2) [Hokkaidō]	Temperature	-4.0	-4.7	-1.7	3.2	7.3	10.5	14.4	17.3	15.5	11.1	5.0	-0.5	6.1
		Precipitation	43	*29*	52	78	106	93	101	118	163	114	86	47	1030
	Sapporo (17.2) [Hokkaidō]	Temperature	-4.1	-3.5	0.1	6.7	12.1	16.3	20.5	22.0	17.6	11.3	4.6	-1.0	8.5
		Precipitation	111	96	80	61	55	*51*	67	137	138	124	103	105	1128
Sea of Japan side	Aomori (2.8) [Aomori]	Temperature	-1.4	-1.1	2.0	7.9	13.1	17.0	21.1	23.0	18.9	12.6	6.4	1.3	10.1
		Precipitation	145	116	70	*61*	79	82	103	129	120	106	132	149	1290
	Akita (6.3) [Akita]	Temperature	-0.1	0.2	3.2	9.2	14.2	18.8	22.8	24.5	19.9	13.6	7.6	2.8	11.4
		Precipitation	114	*92*	93	118	123	128	178	182	178	161	184	164	1713
	Jōetsu (Takada) (12.9) [Niigata]	Temperature	2.2	2.1	4.9	11.3	16.3	20.5	24.5	26.0	21.6	15.6	10.0	5.1	13.3
		Precipitation	413	275	191	*95*	97	140	207	173	215	220	333	420	2779
	Kanazawa (5.7) [Ishikawa]	Temperature	3.7	3.6	6.5	12.2	16.9	20.9	25.1	26.6	22.2	16.7	11.3	6.5	14.3
		Precipitation	266	184	153	*144*	154	194	227	164	242	188	267	287	2470
	Tottori (7.1) [Tottori]	Temperature	3.9	4.0	7.1	12.9	17.4	21.5	25.6	26.6	22.1	16.3	11.3	6.6	14.6
		Precipitation	187	164	127	*110*	126	154	198	127	235	143	158	175	1898
Pacific Ocean side	Miyako (42.5) [Iwate]	Temperature	*0.2*	*0.3*	3.0	8.7	13.1	16.0	20.0	22.2	18.6	13.1	7.7	3.0	10.5
		Precipitation	53	80	86	96	98	117	139	181	229	106	86	*40*	1306
	Sendai (38.9) [Miyagi]	Temperature	1.5	1.7	4.5	10.1	14.9	18.3	22.1	24.1	20.4	14.8	9.1	4.3	12.1
		Precipitation	33	48	73	98	108	138	160	174	218	99	67	*26*	1242
	Fukushima (67.4) [Fukushima]	Temperature	1.4	1.8	4.9	11.3	16.5	19.9	23.5	25.2	20.7	14.8	9.0	4.2	12.8
		Precipitation	44	50	77	80	89	118	145	144	169	95	63	*33*	1105
	Tōkyō (6.1) [Tōkyō]	Temperature	5.8	6.1	8.9	14.4	18.7	21.8	25.4	27.1	23.5	18.2	13.0	8.4	15.9
		Precipitation	49	60	115	130	128	165	162	155	209	163	93	*40*	1467
	Shizuoka (14.1) [Shizuoka]	Temperature	6.6	7.0	10.0	14.8	18.6	21.9	25.5	26.8	23.8	18.7	13.8	8.8	16.3
		Precipitation	72	102	213	237	222	283	280	245	304	172	133	*60*	2322
	Owase (15.3) [Mie]	Temperature	6.2	6.5	9.6	14.4	18.1	21.5	25.1	26.1	23.2	18.1	13.2	8.3	15.9
		Precipitation	97	132	238	341	344	428	419	495	718	359	262	*92*	3922
	Kōchi (0.5) [Kōchi]	Temperature	6.1	6.9	10.5	15.5	19.3	22.7	26.4	27.2	24.1	18.8	13.4	8.2	16.6
		Precipitation	62	102	183	262	261	373	315	317	404	159	137	*52*	2627
	Fukuoka (2.5) [Fukuoka]	Temperature	6.4	6.9	9.9	14.8	19.1	22.6	26.9	27.6	23.9	18.7	13.4	8.7	16.6
		Precipitation	72	*71*	109	125	139	272	266	188	175	81	81	54	1632
	Miyazaki (9.2) [Miyazaki]	Temperature	7.6	8.3	11.7	16.1	19.4	23.0	26.8	27.0	24.1	19.2	14.3	9.4	17.2
		Precipitation	72	90	180	218	250	418	304	269	337	180	89	*52*	2457
Inland	Matsumoto (610.0) [Nagano]	Temperature	*-0.6*	*-0.2*	3.5	10.4	15.7	19.6	23.3	24.3	19.5	12.8	7.1	2.0	11.5
		Precipitation	31	43	74	87	93	136	133	96	162	89	53	*23*	1019
Setouchi	Ōsaka (23.0) [Ōsaka]	Temperature	5.8	5.9	9.0	14.8	19.4	23.2	27.2	28.4	24.4	18.7	13.2	8.3	16.5
		Precipitation	44	59	100	121	140	201	155	99	175	109	66	*38*	1306
	Hiroshima (3.6) [Hiroshima]	Temperature	5.3	5.7	9.0	14.6	18.9	22.8	26.9	27.9	23.9	18.0	12.3	7.5	16.1
		Precipitation	47	67	121	156	157	258	236	126	180	95	68	*35*	1541
	Takamatsu (8.7) [Kagawa]	Temperature	5.3	5.4	8.4	13.9	18.6	22.5	26.6	27.4	23.5	17.7	12.4	7.5	15.8
		Precipitation	39	48	73	86	100	159	135	92	187	108	62	*34*	1124
Nansei-Islands	Amami (Naze) (2.8) [Kagoshima]	Temperature	14.6	14.9	17.0	20.0	22.6	26.0	28.4	28.1	26.5	23.5	20.0	16.4	21.5
		Precipitation	187	167	228	236	277	401	228	277	341	239	176	*158*	2914
	Naha (28.1) [Okinawa]	Temperature	16.6	16.6	18.6	21.3	23.8	26.6	28.5	28.2	27.2	24.9	21.7	18.4	22.7
		Precipitation	115	125	160	181	234	212	176	247	200	163	124	*101*	2037

2. Cities and Population (2008)

Cities in red are prefectural capitals
City government-designated cities*

<Data from respective prefectures>

*Government-designated city: Cities designated by the government as having a population of over 500,000. Their public and financial administrative authorities are virtually on a prefectural level.

City	Pop. in 10,000s												
HOKKAIDŌ		Ashibetsu	1.8	Ōsaki	13.7	Shinjō	3.9	Ushiku	7.9	Yaita	3.5	Fujimi	10.5
		Akabira	1.4	Tome	8.7	Kaminoyama	3.5	Jōsō	6.6	Nasukarasuyama	3.0	Fujimino	10.4
Sapporo	188.3	Yūbari	1.2	Kurihara	7.8	Nan'yō	3.5	Kashima	6.5	**GUNMA**		Sakado	9.9
Asahikawa	35.7	Mikasa	1.1	Natori	6.9	Nagai	3.0	Hitachiōta	5.8	Takasaki	34.2	Higashimatsuyama	9.1
Hakodate	29.0	Utashinai	0.5	Kesennuma	6.5	Murayama	2.8	Moriya	5.8	Maebashi	31.8	Gyōda	8.7
Kushiro	19.1	**AOMORI**		Tagajō	6.3	Obanazawa	1.9	Bandō	5.7	Ōta	21.4	Hannō	8.4
Tomakomai	17.4	Aomori	30.6	Shiogama	5.8	**FUKUSHIMA**		Naka	5.5	Isesaki	20.4	Honjō	8.2
Obihiro	17.0	Hachinohe	24.2	Iwanuma	4.5	Iwaki	34.0	Omitama	5.3	Kiryū	12.5	Yashio	7.9
Otaru	13.9	Hirosaki	18.6	Higashimatsushima	4.3	Kōriyama	33.9	Yūki	5.2	Shibukawa	8.6	Wakō	7.9
Kitami	12.7	Towada	6.7	Shiroishi	3.9	Fukushima	29.6	Hokota	5.1	Tatebayashi	7.9	Okegawa	7.5
Ebetsu	12.4	Mutsu	6.2	Kakuda	3.3	Aizuwakamatsu	12.9	Kitaibaraki	4.8	Fujioka	6.9	Kuki	7.2
Muroran	9.8	Goshogawara	6.1	**AKITA**		Sukagawa	8.0	Inashiki	4.8	Annaka	6.2	Warabi	7.0
Chitose	9.3	Misawa	4.3	Akita	32.9	Minamisōma	7.2	Sakuragawa	4.7	Tomioka	5.3	Tsurugashima	7.0
Iwamizawa	9.2	Tsugaru	3.9	Yokote	10.1	Date	6.7	Hitachiōmiya	4.5	Numata	4.7	Kitamoto	6.9
Eniwa	6.9	Kuroishi	3.8	Daisen	9.1	Shirakawa	6.6	Shimotsuma	4.6	Midori	5.2	Chichibu	6.9
Ishikari	6.1	Hirakawa	3.5	Yurihonjō	8.8	Nihonmatsu	6.2	Kasumigaura	4.4	**SAITAMA**		Shiki	6.9
Kitahiroshima	6.1	**IWATE**		Ōdate	8.1	Kitakata	5.5	Tsukubamirai	4.2	Saitama	119.2	Kazo	6.8
Noboribetsu	5.3	Morioka	29.9	Noshiro	6.1	Tamura	4.2	Namegata	3.9	Kawaguchi	49.3	Hasuda	6.3
Hokuto	4.9	Ōshū	12.8	Yuzawa	5.4	Sōma	3.9	Takahagi	3.2	Tokorozawa	33.9	Yoshikawa	6.3
Takikawa	4.5	Ichinoseki	12.3	Kitaakita	3.9	Motomiya	3.2	Itako	3.1	Kawagoe	33.6	Hatogaya	6.0
Wakkanai	4.1	Hanamaki	10.4	Kazuno	3.6	**IBARAKI**		**TOCHIGI**		Koshigaya	31.9	Hanyū	5.7
Abashiri	4.0	Kitakami	9.5	Katagami	3.5	Mito	26.4	Utsunomiya	50.8	Sōka	23.8	Hidaka	5.5
Date	3.7	Miyako	5.8	Oga	3.4	Tsukuba	20.7	Oyama	16.2	Kasukabe	23.7	Satte	5.3
Nayoro	3.1	Ōfunato	4.2	Senboku	3.1	Hitachi	19.6	Ashikaga	15.8	Ageo	22.2	**CHIBA**	
Nemuro	3.1	Kamaishi	4.1	Nikaho	2.8	Hitachinaka	15.5	Sano	12.3	Kumagaya	20.5	Chiba	93.9
Bibai	2.8	Kuji	3.8	**YAMAGATA**		Koga	14.4	Nasushiobara	11.6	Sayama	15.7	Funabashi	58.7
Rumoi	2.6	Ninohe	3.1	Yamagata	25.5	Tsuchiura	14.4	Kanuma	10.4	Niiza	15.6	Matsudo	47.8
Monbetsu	2.6	Tōno	3.1	Tsuruoka	14.0	Chikusei	11.1	Nikkō	9.2	Iruma	14.8	Ichikawa	47.0
Furano	2.5	Hachimantai	2.9	Sakata	11.5	Toride	10.9	Tochigi	8.2	Fukaya	14.6	Kashiwa	38.9
Fukagawa	2.5	Rikuzentakata	2.4	Yonezawa	9.2	Kamisu	9.4	Ōtawara	7.0	Mioto	12.0	Ichihara	27.9
Shibetsu	2.3	**MIYAGI**		Tendō	6.3	Kasama	8.1	Mooka	6.7	Asaka	12.7	Yachiyo	18.5
Sunagawa	1.9	Sendai	102.9	Higashine	4.6	Ishioka	8.1	Shimotsuke	5.9	Kōnosu	11.9	Sakura	17.1
		Ishinomaki	16.4	Sagae	4.3	Ryūgasaki	7.9	Sakura	4.2	Toda	11.9	Narashino	15.9

City	Value	City	Value	City	Value	City	Value	City	Value	City	Value	City	Value
Urayasu	15.9	Tōkamachi	6.0	Toki	6.1	Kumano	2.0	Kasai	4.8	Kudamatsu	5.4	Taku	2.2
Nagareyama	15.7	Gosen	5.6	Ena	5.5	**SHIGA**		Awaji	4.8	Hikari	5.3	**NAGASAKI**	
Noda	15.3	Itoigawa	4.9	Minokamo	5.4	Ōtsu	32.9	Sasayama	4.4	Nagato	3.9	Nagasaki	44.9
Abiko	13.4	Agano	4.6	Mizuho	5.1	Kusatsu	12.4	Nishiwaki	4.3	Yanai	3.5	Sasebo	25.5
Narita	12.5	Uonuma	4.2	Gujō	4.6	Higashiōmi	11.7	Shisō	4.2	Mine	2.9	Isahaya	14.3
Kisarazu	12.4	Mitsuke	4.2	Mizunami	4.2	Hikone	11.1	Katō	3.9	**TOKUSHIMA**		Ōmura	8.9
Kamagaya	10.5	Ojiya	3.9	Kaizu	3.9	Kōka	9.4	Asago	3.4	Tokushima	26.6	Minamishimabara	5.2
Mobara	9.3	Myōkō	3.7	Gero	3.7	Nagahama	8.4	Aioi	3.2	Anan	7.7	Shimabara	4.9
Kimitsu	8.9	Tainai	3.2	Motosu	3.5	Moriyama	7.4	Yabu	2.7	Naruto	6.2	Unzen	4.9
Yotsukaidō	8.6	Kamo	3.1	Yamagata	2.9	Ōmihachiman	6.9			Yoshinogawa	4.5	Gotō	4.2
Katori	8.5	**TOYAMA**		Hida	2.8	Rittō	6.2	**NARA**		Komatsushima	4.2	Hirado	3.7
Yachimata	7.5	Toyama	42.1	Mino	2.3	Konan	5.5	Nara	36.7	Awa	4.0	Tsushima	3.6
Chōshi	7.2	Takaoka	17.9	**SHIZUOKA**		Takashima	5.3	Kashihara	12.5	Mima	3.4	Saikai	3.3
Asahi	6.9	Imizu	9.5	Hamamatsu	81.1	Yasu	4.9	Ikoma	11.5	Miyoshi	3.2	Iki	3.0
Tōgane	6.2	Nanto	5.7	Shizuoka	72.0	Yamatokōriyama	9.0			Matsuura	2.6
Inzai	6.0	Himi	5.3	Fuji	23.7	**KYŌTO**		Kashiba	7.3	**KAGAWA**			
Sodegaura	5.9	Tonami	4.9	Numazu	20.7	Kyōto	146.9	Tenri	7.1	Takamatsu	41.9	**KUMAMOTO**	
Sanmu	5.8	Uozu	4.6	Iwata	17.3	Uji	19.1	Yamatotakada	6.9	Marugame	11.1	Kumamoto	67.8
Shiroi	5.7	Kurobe	4.3	Fujieda	12.9	Kameoka	9.4	Sakurai	6.1	Mitoyo	6.9	Yatsushiro	13.4
Tomisato	5.2	Namerikawa	3.4	Fujinomiya	12.2	Maizuru	9.0	Gojō	3.6	Kan'onji	6.4	Amakusa	9.3
Tateyama	4.9	Oyabe	3.3	Yaizu	12.0	Fukuchiyama	8.1	Uda	3.6	Sakaide	5.7	Tamana	7.1
Futtsu	4.9	**ISHIKAWA**		Kakegawa	11.9	Jōyō	8.1	Katsuragi	3.5	Sanuki	5.5	Uki	6.3
Minamibōsō	4.4	Kanazawa	45.6	Mishima	11.2	Nagaokakyō	7.9	Gose	3.1	Zentsūji	3.5	Yamaga	5.7
Isumi	4.2	Hakusan	11.1	Shimada	10.2	Yawata	7.4	**WAKAYAMA**		Higashikagawa	3.5	Arao	5.6
Sōsa	4.1	Komatsu	10.9	Gotenba	8.8	Kizugawa	6.7	Wakayama	37.2	**EHIME**		Kōshi	5.3
Kamogawa	3.6	Kaga	7.4	Fukuroi	8.5	Tanabe	8.0	Matsuyama	51.5	Kikuchi	5.1
Katsuura	2.1	Nanao	6.0	Itō	7.2	Kyōtanabe	6.5	Hashimoto	6.8	Imabari	17.1	Uto	3.8
TŌKYŌ		Nomi	4.8	Susono	5.4	Kyōtango	6.1	Kinokawa	6.7	Niihama	12.3	Hitoyoshi	3.7
Tōkyō (23 Wards)	866.4	Kahoku	3.5	Makinohara	4.9	Mukō	5.5	Kainan	5.6	Saijō	11.3	Kamiamakusa	3.1
Hachiōji	56.7	Wajima	3.2	Izunokuni	4.9	Ayabe	3.7	Iwade	5.2	Shikokuchūō	9.2	Aso	2.9
Machida	41.4	Hakui	2.4	Kikukawa	4.8	Nantan	3.6	Shingū	3.3	Uwajima	8.7	Minamata	2.8
Fuchū	24.8	Suzu	1.7	Kosai	4.5	Miyazu	2.1	Arida	3.1	Ōzu	4.9	**ŌITA**	
Chōfu	21.9	**FUKUI**		Atami	4.1	**ŌSAKA**		Gobō	2.6	Seiyo	4.3	Ōita	46.7
Nishitōkyō	19.3	Fukui	26.9	Izu	3.6	Ōsaka	264.5	**TOTTORI**		Yawatahama	4.0	Beppu	12.7
Kodaira	18.6	Sakai	9.2	Omaezaki	3.5	Sakai	83.5	Tottori	20.0	Iyo	3.9	Nakatsu	8.4
Mitaka	18.1	Echizen	8.7	Shimoda	2.6	Higashiōsaka	50.9	Yonago	14.9	Tōon	3.6	Saiki	7.9
Hino	17.9	Tsuruga	6.8	**AICHI**		Hirakata	40.6	Kurayoshi	5.1	**KŌCHI**		Hita	7.3
Tachikawa	17.6	Sabae	6.7	Nagoya	223.9	Toyonaka	38.7	Sakaiminato	3.6	Kōchi	34.3	Usa	5.9
Tama	14.9	Ōno	3.7	Toyota	42.0	Suita	35.5	**SHIMANE**		Nankoku	5.0	Usuki	4.2
Higashimurayama	14.7	Obama	3.1	Toyohashi	37.7	Takatsuki	35.4	Matsue	19.6	Simanto	3.7	Bungoōno	4.0
Ōme	14.2	Awara	3.1	Ichinomiya	37.6	Yao	27.3	Izumo	14.6	Kōnan	3.4	Yufu	3.5
Musashino	13.9	Katsuyama	2.6	Okazaki	37.1	Ibaraki	27.2	Hamada	6.1	Tosa	2.9	Kunisaki	3.3
Kokubunji	11.9	**YAMANASHI**		Kasugai	30.1	Neyagawa	23.9	Masuda	5.1	Kami	2.9	Kitsuki	3.3
Higashikurume	11.5	Kōfu	19.9	Anjō	17.6	Kishiwada	20.1	Unnan	4.3	Susaki	2.6	Taketa	2.5
Koganei	11.5	Kai	7.4	Toyokawa	16.2	Izumi	17.9	Yasugi	4.3	Sukumo	2.4	Bungotakada	2.4
Akishima	11.2	Minami-alps	7.2	Komaki	14.9	Moriguchi	14.6	Ōda	3.9	Aki	2.1	Tsukumi	2.1
Higashiyamato	8.1	Fuefuki	7.1	Kariya	14.5	Kadoma	13.0	Gōtsu	2.7	Muroto	1.8	**MIYAZAKI**	
Inagi	8.1	Fujiyoshida	5.2	Inazawa	13.7	Minoo	12.8	**OKAYAMA**		Tosashimizu	1.7	Miyazaki	36.9
Akiruno	8.0	Hokuto	4.8	Seto	13.2	Matsubara	12.5	Okayama	70.1	**FUKUOKA**		Miyakonojō	16.9
Komae	7.8	Yamanashi	3.8	Handa	11.8	Tondabayashi	12.2	Kurashiki	47.2	Fukuoka	143.0	Nobeoka	13.2
Kiyose	7.4	Kōshū	3.5	Tōkai	10.7	Habikino	11.8	Tsuyama	10.9	Kitakyūshū	98.7	Hyūga	6.3
Kunitachi	7.3	Tsuru	3.4	Nishio	10.7	Kawachinagano	11.4	Sōja	6.7	Kurume	30.5	Nichinan	4.3
Musashimurayama	6.8	Nirasaki	3.4	Kōnan	10.0	Ikeda	10.4	Tamano	6.6	Iizuka	13.2	Kobayashi	4.1
Fussa	6.0	Chūō	3.2	Chita	8.5	Izumisano	9.9	Kasaoka	5.6	Ōmuta	12.7	Saito	3.3
Hamura	5.7	Ōtsuki	2.9	Ōbu	8.3	Kaizuka	9.0	Maniwa	5.0	Kasuga	10.8	Ebino	2.2
KANAGAWA		Uenohara	2.8	Gamagōri	8.2	Settsu	8.4	Ibara	4.4	Chikushino	9.9	Kushima	2.1
Yokohama	363.1	**NAGANO**		Nisshin	8.1	Izumiōtsu	7.8	Akaiwa	4.4	Munakata	9.5	**KAGOSHIMA**	
Kawasaki	137.4	Nagano	37.8	Kitanagoya	8.0	Katano	7.8	Bizen	3.9	Ōnojō	9.4	Kagoshima	60.5
Sagamihara	70.6	Matsumoto	22.7	Owariasahi	7.9	Kashiwara	7.6	Setouchi	3.9	Yanagawa	7.3	Kirishima	12.8
Yokosuka	42.1	Ueda	16.2	Inuyama	7.5	Fujiidera	6.6	Takahashi	3.8	Yukuhashi	7.0	Kanoya	10.6
Fujisawa	40.3	Iida	10.7	Hekinan	7.3	Sennan	6.5	Asakuchi	3.7	Dazaifu	6.9	Satsumasendai	10.1
Hiratsuka	26.0	Saku	10.0	Toyoake	6.9	Takaishi	6.0	Niimi	3.5	Maebaru	6.8	Izumi	5.7
Chigasaki	23.1	Azumino	9.7	Chiryū	6.8	Ōsakasayama	5.9	Mimasaka	3.2	Ogōri	5.8	Hioki	5.1
Atsugi	22.5	Ina	7.2	Tahara	6.7	Shijōnawate	5.7	**HIROSHIMA**		Asakura	5.8	Amami	4.8
Yamato	22.3	Shiojiri	6.8	Tsushima	6.6	Hannan	5.7	Hiroshima	116.4	Nōgata	5.7	Ibusuki	4.5
Odawara	19.9	Chikuma	6.3	Aisai	6.5	**HYŌGO**		Fukuyama	46.1	Koga	5.7	Soo	4.1
Kamakura	17.4	Chino	5.7	Kiyosu	5.7	Kōbe	153.1	Kure	24.6	Fukutsu	5.5	Minamikyūshū	4.1
Hadano	16.9	Okaya	5.4	Tokoname	5.3	Himeji	53.6	Higashihiroshima	18.8	Tagawa	5.0	Minamisatsuma	4.0
Zama	12.8	Suzaka	5.3	Shinshiro	5.1	Nishinomiya	47.7	Onomichi	14.8	Chikugo	4.8	Shibushi	3.4
Ebina	12.6	Suwa	5.3	Iwakura	4.8	Amagasaki	46.1	Hatsukaichi	11.5	Nakama	4.6	Ichikikushikino	3.2
Isehara	10.1	Nakano	4.6	Takahama	4.3	Akashi	29.2	Mihara	10.3	Kama	4.4	Isa	3.1
Ayase	8.2	Komoro	4.5	Yatomi	4.3	Kakogawa	26.8	Miyoshi	5.8	Yame	4.2	Makurazaki	2.4
Zushi	5.9	Komagane	3.5	**MIE**		Takarazuka	22.2	Fuchū	4.4	Miyama	4.2	Akune	2.4
Miura	4.9	Ōmachi	3.1	Yokkaichi	30.7	Itami	19.4	Shōbara	4.2	Ōkawa	3.8	Tarumizu	1.8
Minamiashigara	4.4	Tōmi	3.1	Tsu	28.9	Kawanishi	15.7	Akitakata	3.2	Ukiha	3.2	Nishinoomote	1.8
NIIGATA		Iiyama	2.4	Suzuka	19.7	Sanda	11.4	Takehara	2.9	Miyawaka	3.1	**OKINAWA**	
Niigata	81.3	**GIFU**		Matsusaka	16.9	Takasago	9.4	Ōtake	2.9	Buzen	2.8	Naha	31.4
Nagaoka	28.1	Gifu	41.3	Kuwana	14.1	Ashiya	9.3	Etajima	2.9	**SAGA**		Okinawa	12.8
Jōetsu	20.6	Ōgaki	16.3	Ise	13.4	Toyooka	8.8	**YAMAGUCHI**		Saga	23.9	Uruma	11.4
Shibata	10.3	Kakamigahara	14.5	Iga	9.9	Miki	8.3	Shimonoseki	28.6	Karatsu	12.9	Urasoe	10.8
Sanjō	10.3	Tajimi	11.5	Nabari	8.1	Tatsuno	8.1	Yamaguchi	19.2	Tosu	6.7	Ginowan	9.1
Kashiwazaki	9.4	Kani	9.9	Ueno	5.7	Tanba	6.9	Ube	17.6	Imari	5.8	Nago	6.1
Tsubame	8.3	Takayama	9.5	Kameyama	5.0	Akō	5.1	Shūnan	15.0	Takeo	5.1	Itoman	5.6
Murakami	6.9	Seki	9.3	Inabe	4.7	Minamiawaji	5.1	Iwakuni	14.7	Ogi	4.6	Tomigusuku	5.5
Sado	6.5	Nakatsugawa	8.3	Toba	2.2	Ono	4.9	Hōfu	11.6	Kanzaki	3.3	Miyakojima	5.3
Minamiuonuma	6.3	Hashima	6.7	Owase	2.1	Sumoto	4.9	San'yōonoda	6.6	Kashima	3.1	Ishigaki	4.6
						Hagi	4.9	Ureshino	2.9	Nanjō	3.9

※The statistics on this chart are from 2008 and therefore do not include cities that will merge after 2009.

3 Other Statistics of Prefectures

(figures in **bold red** are ranked first amongst the prefectures: figures in red are ranked 2nd - 5th.)

2008 Basic Resident Register Population Directory
Advance Report of Statistics on Agriculture, Forestry and Fisheries, others

No.	Prefecture	Prefectural Capital	Population (10,000) 2008	Area (km²) 2007	Population Density (persons/km²) 2008	Primary Industry	Secondary Industry	Tertiary Industry	Agricultural Production (100 million yen) 2006	Area of Agricultural Land (km²) 2007	Rice (10,000t) 2007
1	HOKKAIDŌ	Sapporo	557	**83,456**	67	7.7	19.0	73.3	**10,527**	**11,630**	60.3
2	AOMORI	Aomori	143	① 9,607	149	14.0	21.4	64.6	2,885	1,581	29.9
3	IWATE	Morioka	137	15,279	89	13.7	25.9	60.4	2,544	1,551	31.0
4	MIYAGI	Sendai	233	7,286	320	6.2	23.5	70.3	1,929	1,371	40.8
5	AKITA	Akita	113	① 11,612	97	11.1	26.7	62.2	1,861	1,513	55.0
6	YAMAGATA	Yamagata	119	9,323	128	10.9	30.3	58.8	2,152	1,240	42.0
7	FUKUSHIMA	Fukushima	208	13,783	151	9.2	30.7	60.1	2,500	1,518	44.5
8	IBARAKI	Mito	298	6,096	489	7.4	30.3	62.3	3,988	1,766	40.4
9	TOCHIGI	Utsunomiya	201	6,408	313	6.8	32.6	60.6	2,609	1,290	36.1
10	GUNMA	Maebashi	201	6,363	316	6.5	32.8	60.7	2,250	774	9.0
11	SAITAMA	Saitama	707	3,797	1,861	2.2	26.8	71.0	1,900	830	17.5
12	CHIBA	Chiba	609	5,157	1,181	3.7	21.7	74.6	4,014	1,309	32.9
13	TŌKYŌ	Tōkyō	**1,246**	2,188	5,697	0.4	18.7	80.9	278	81	0.1
14	KANAGAWA	Yokohama	880	2,416	3,642	1.0	23.7	75.3	736	209	1.6
15	NIIGATA	Niigata	241	12,583	192	7.5	31.1	61.4	2,964	1,764	65.1
16	TOYAMA	Toyama	111	4,248	260	4.3	34.8	60.9	726	598	21.2
17	ISHIKAWA	Kanazawa	117	4,185	279	3.9	29.6	66.5	590	440	13.7
18	FUKUI	Fukui	82	4,189	195	4.7	33.1	62.2	495	411	14.1
19	YAMANASHI	Kōfu	87	4,465	195	8.5	30.6	60.9	832	255	3.0
20	NAGANO	Nagano	218	13,562	161	11.4	30.8	57.8	2,322	1,123	22.4
21	GIFU	Gifu	210	10,621	197	3.7	34.7	61.6	1,236	589	12.0
22	SHIZUOKA	Shizuoka	378	7,780	485	4.9	34.5	60.6	2,443	735	9.3
23	AICHI	Nagoya	719	5,165	1,391	2.8	34.4	62.8	3,108	823	16.0
24	MIE	Tsu	186	5,777	321	4.9	33.2	61.9	1,142	623	15.6
25	SHIGA	Ōtsu	138	4,017	343	3.7	34.4	61.9	638	541	17.6
26	KYŌTO	Kyōto	256	4,613	555	2.7	25.0	72.3	710	325	8.2
27	ŌSAKA	Ōsaka	867	1,898	4,569	0.6	26.2	73.2	336	144	3.1
28	HYŌGO	Kōbe	558	8,396	665	2.5	27.1	70.4	1,462	773	19.4
29	NARA	Nara	142	3,691	385	3.2	25.3	71.5	476	230	5.0
30	WAKAYAMA	Wakayama	105	4,726	221	10.4	23.1	66.5	1,095	365	3.7
31	TOTTORI	Tottori	60	3,507	172	10.9	24.8	64.3	685	354	6.7
32	SHIMANE	Matsue	73	6,708	109	10.1	25.2	64.7	625	389	9.6
33	OKAYAMA	Okayama	195	7,113	274	6.4	29.2	64.4	1,255	704	17.4
34	HIROSHIMA	Hiroshima	286	8,479	338	4.3	27.2	68.5	1,069	597	13.9
35	YAMAGUCHI	Yamaguchi	148	6,113	242	6.8	26.9	66.3	684	509	11.6
36	TOKUSHIMA	Tokushima	81	4,146	194	9.8	25.5	64.7	1,052	317	6.7
37	KAGAWA	Takamatsu	102	1,877	543	7.1	26.6	66.3	796	326	7.4
38	EHIME	Matsuyama	147	5,678	259	9.4	25.7	64.9	1,300	556	7.9
39	KŌCHI	Kōchi	78	7,105	110	12.7	19.2	68.1	987	289	6.2
40	FUKUOKA	Fukuoka	503	4,977	1,011	3.5	21.6	74.9	2,116	883	19.4
41	SAGA	Saga	86	2,440	354	11.0	24.8	64.2	1,194	554	14.2
42	NAGASAKI	Nagasaki	147	4,096	359	9.1	20.7	70.2	1,329	507	6.9
43	KUMAMOTO	Kumamoto	184	7,406	249	11.5	22.1	66.4	2,984	1,191	21.0
45	ŌITA	Ōita	122	6,339	192	9.0	23.9	67.1	1,302	592	12.8
45	MIYAZAKI	Miyazaki	116	7,735	150	12.7	22.8	64.5	3,211	697	7.8
46	KAGOSHIMA	Kagoshima	174	9,188	189	11.6	21.2	67.2	4,079	1,243	11.6
47	OKINAWA	Naha	139	2,276	611	5.9	16.3	77.8	906	391	0.3
	National Total (National Average)		12,707	377,930	(336)	(4.8)	(26.1)	(69.1)	86,321	46,501	871.4

Note: 1. The area of HOKKAIDŌ includes Habomai Islands 100km², Shikotan Island 250km², Kunashiri Island 1,499km², Etorofu Island 3,183km²; SHIMANE includes Take Island 0.2km². They are also included in the National Total.
2. ① Excludes Lake Towada (61km²). However, it is included in the National Total.

Vegetables (100 million yen) 2006	Fruit (100 million yen) 2006	Livestock (100 million yen) 2006	Captured fish (10,000t) 2006	Industrial production (shipment amount) (100 million yen) 2006	Retail annual sales (100 million yen) 2007	Convenience stores per 100,000 persons (stores) 2004	Foreign workers per 10,000 persons (persons) 2008	Electricity usage per person (kWh) 2004	Air conditioners per 1000 households (machines) 2004	Passenger cars in use per 100 households (cars) 2008	Amount of waste per day per person (g) 2006	Park space per person (m²) 2007
1,712	62	**4,918**	**140.6**	57,944	61,565	**46.0**	9.5	5,349	187	103.0	**1,199**	**19.03**
653	**771**	704	23.0	16,325	14,400	33.9	6.9	5,926	611	121.5	1,131	12.76
267	128	**1,330**	20.2	24,854	13,198	35.3	11.9	5,995	656	136.7	1,013	9.84
268	23	674	39.7	38,359	25,318	**40.6**	13.6	6,184	1,274	130.1	1,111	8.08
265	85	298	1.1	15,953	11,404	37.4	11.2	6,186	1,313	137.8	1,123	**14.73**
327	461	316	0.9	30,397	12,222	35.4	14.4	6,102	1,727	**165.7**	974	13.55
523	284	537	12.6	59,401	20,389	37.4	15.2	6,877	1,287	151.5	1,093	10.00
1,512	139	956	28.4	115,264	29,588	**39.1**	41.5	8,444	2,500	162.8	1,022	8.00
730	87	872	0.1	87,634	21,362	36.4	39.1	8,506	2,429	164.2	1,069	12.43
819	92	925	0.1	78,261	21,258	34.1	52.6	8,211	2,550	**168.8**	1,177	12.15
814	68	325	0.01	143,665	**63,378**	29.9	25.8	5,547	2,709	106.3	1,061	5.52
1,570	167	**1,003**	22.5	130,099	57,550	34.4	23.9	6,151	2,556	104.5	1,113	4.60
155	31	21	8.3	106,198	**172,789**	44.1	**95.1**	6,587	2,585	52.0	1,174	2.12
355	92	176	4.8	202,407	85,481	34.8	31.2	5,971	2,353	79.1	1,066	2.31
337	89	525	4.2	48,737	25,766	29.2	13.9	6,763	2,527	154.5	**1,261**	9.98
37	15	93	3.9	37,455	11,754	37.1	38.8	**9,886**	2,676	**172.8**	1,073	**13.65**
90	22	98	8.1	26,937	13,394	32.5	33.5	7,190	2,594	151.7	1,161	11.19
59	11	43	1.6	20,421	9,047	31.0	48.0	**9,328**	**3,134**	**175.5**	1,067	13.31
111	**514**	75	0.1	25,804	8,735	**38.6**	43.1	7,256	1,599	153.9	1,089	7.99
671	**532**	311	0.2	64,135	23,736	30.8	47.3	7,143	927	159.4	966	9.83
347	60	437	0.2	55,860	21,121	31.0	**88.6**	7,084	2,502	**168.1**	1,060	8.34
605	334	419	21.0	**183,502**	40,782	31.6	**83.3**	8,272	2,297	145.8	1,107	6.63
934	203	782	9.7	**439,112**	82,915	34.7	**84.0**	8,353	2,815	135.7	1,114	4.99
159	89	335	21.5	108,226	19,325	24.5	**79.9**	8,730	**3,168**	149.4	1,123	7.79
73	6	114	0.1	68,604	13,608	29.2	53.1	**9,479**	3,009	145.0	1,004	8.06
248	19	123	1.7	53,748	30,225	29.7	19.9	6,189	3,091	89.4	1,129	4.46
139	61	28	2.5	168,799	96,505	29.5	27.8	6,864	2,776	71.1	**1,315**	3.43
370	30	483	6.3	145,286	54,873	24.6	19.2	7,151	2,685	95.9	**1,227**	6.29
129	74	75	0.003	23,562	12,503	23.2	13.6	5,470	3,019	114.8	1,034	11.29
162	**675**	58	4.4	28,491	9,348	21.0	6.5	6,158	**3,116**	118.8	1,143	5.94
169	77	220	6.3	11,427	6,356	23.3	20.4	6,289	2,535	142.2	1,068	10.53
95	39	203	11.7	11,210	7,318	20.2	19.7	6,470	2,413	137.7	995	13.58
180	172	454	3.2	83,197	20,439	28.9	31.1	8,753	2,931	138.4	1,091	12.29
177	143	379	13.0	86,201	31,151	28.8	46.1	6,753	2,505	111.9	1,028	6.37
124	40	204	5.3	66,678	14,856	26.4	14.7	8,142	2,478	121.5	1,174	10.56
376	100	292	3.2	16,531	7,320	24.2	25.5	7,678	**3,287**	133.9	1,044	6.47
245	59	256	5.5	25,806	11,073	28.0	24.8	7,363	**3,165**	132.6	1,010	12.07
207	**466**	307	16.9	37,532	13,654	26.9	24.4	6,461	2,586	110.6	1,009	9.67
568	102	78	10.4	5,579	7,494	23.2	9.9	5,758	2,443	106.0	1,029	7.55
637	213	370	9.5	82,023	53,562	33.1	19.1	6,102	2,438	110.1	1,169	3.87
343	150	308	9.4	17,193	8,181	35.6	16.2	6,763	2,786	147.7	936	8.53
359	151	453	29.3	15,262	13,874	31.0	14.5	5,159	2,284	105.6	1,033	9.82
975	343	873	9.1	28,453	17,527	36.9	14.3	5,870	2,641	128.8	953	7.18
292	154	452	6.9	38,999	12,094	25.3	17.2	6,705	2,084	126.6	1,060	9.19
669	118	**1,843**	11.8	13,417	11,473	30.1	10.1	6,066	1,915	124.3	1,059	16.29
424	100	**2,382**	16.7	18,630	16,065	33.1	9.3	5,469	2,077	111.2	956	10.27
118	61	383	4.1	5,364	11,078	32.2	10.3	5,293	1,664	124.3	911	8.97
20,400	7,710	26,512	566.9	3,168,941	1,347,054	(33.5)	(38.3)	(6,778)	(2,347)	(110.0)	(1,116)	(8.83)

INDEX

Letters in blue : Place names
Letters in black : Subjects

A

Abukuma Highlands 105,120
accelerated cultivation 115
afforestation 73
aging 33,67,126
agritourism................96
Aichi Canal 93
Ainu 130,134
air pollution 28,49
airline hubs 31
airport(s).....30,31,53,79, 106,107,128,135
Aizuwakamatsu 128
Akabira 139
Akaishi Mountains..8,88
Akita Plain 123
alluvial fan(s) ..10,89,94, 121,124
Amagasaki..................77
aquaculture 64,67
Ara River 104
Arctic..........................14
Ariake Bay............46,48
Ashikaga 113
Ashikaga Yoshimitsu 23
Asuka 21,80
Asuka period 20
Atsugi 112
Atsumi Peninsula..89,93
automobile(s)...30,31,34, 50,124
autumn rains..............15
Azuchi-Momoyama period....................23

B

baby boom....................29
baiu season ..14,15,17,43
basin(s) 7,9,10,28,94, 121
bay(s)..........................43
beaches 12
Biei 140
Bōsō Peninsula...13,105, 115
brand(s)............33,66,68, 107,124
Buddhism 21,22,23
Bungo Channel...........67
burial mounds 21

C

caldera 43
caldera lakes.............132
car(s) 30
castle town(s).........24,60, 65,100
central city...........45,100
Central Highlands...89,96
Chikuma River 0
Chishima Islands 13
Chita Peninsula 93

Christianity 24
Chūbu International Airport 90
Chūbu Region.........38,86
Chūgoku Mountains ...8, 17,59,61,66,73,83
Chūgoku/Shikoku Region 38,56
Chūkyō Industrial District 77,90
Chūō Expressway..94,95
civil warfare................23
climate 16,20
cloudbursts 43
coal 31,49,50,139
coalfield(s).................139
coastlines 12
cold (sea) current(s) ...13, 33
cold summers............121
cold weather damage ..18
complexes....................63
Confucianism 21,25
continental shelf(-ves) 13,48
convenience stores.....27, 35,82
coral reefs 12,43,54
crop rotation 137
crude oil 31
cultivation............33,138
cultural assets 81
currents 13

D

dairy farming........32,137
dams.................9,97,101
deep-sea fishing..........67
delta(s) 10,11,60
depopulation..........29,69
desertification.............66
development 134
Dōkai Bay....................49
downtown ...108,109,110
droughts........17,18,43,47

E

earthquake(s) 18,76, 79,121
East China Sea............13
Ebetsu......................139
Echigo Mountains 105
Echigo Plain 9,89,98
Economic Sphere for the Northwest Pacific Region................100
ecotourism 54,96
Edo 24,25,106
Edo period.............23,24
electronic industries...34
electronic(electrical) machinery 128
Emperor(s)...21,22,25,80
endangered species 54
energy revolution 139

erosion.........................10
eruption(s) 18,43
Etorofu Island 6,131
Eurasian continent 14
Exclusive Economic Zones 33,138
expressway(s) 28,30, 31,61

F

farming 47
fast(high)economic growth 28,69
fast food 27
feudal lord(s) 23,24
fief(s) 23,24
field farming (non-irrigated)...137
fish farming 84,121
flat land......................59
floods 9,15,19,92
forestry.......................84
four major industrial districts................49
four seasons 14,26
fruit cultivation 32, 121,124
Fudoki........................21
Fuji River...................89
Fujiwara family..........21
Fukuchiyama.............83
Fukui Plain................98
Fukuoka.................44,45
Fukuyama 63
Furano 140
Furano Basin...........137

G

Genji Monogatari (Tale of Genji)........22
geothermal energy..19,43
glaciation 20
Gotenba......................92
government-designated city 100
greenhouse(s)...33,46,48, 93,115

H

Hachimantai.............120
Hachirōgata 123
Hagi 65
Hamamatsu................91
Hanamaki.................128
Hanshin Industrial District 49,77
harbor settlements.....60
Harima Plain..............73
headlands 12,43
heavy and chemical industry................63
Heian period..........21,81
Heiankyō..............21,80
Heijōkyō.................21,80
Heisei 25

Hida Mountains ...8,9,88
Hidaka Mountains ...132
Higashiōsaka..............78
high tides 18
highlands 59
highway(s)...63,77,82,96, 106,113,122,128
hills 76,78,92,93,110,111
hiragana 21
Hirosaki 124
Hiroshima...................63
historical heritage 27
Hitachi 113
Hōfu 62
Hokkaidō Region 38, 130
Hokuriku Area..97,98,99
Honshū 6,20
Honshū-Shikoku Bridge Expressways 61
hot spring(s) ...19,43,51,65, 89,116,120,132,140

I

Ibi River 92
Ibuki Mountains.........73
IC(s) 50,95,128
ice floes................133,140
Imperial court........21,22, 23,80
Ina 95
industrial complex(es) 31,109,127
industrialization.........25
infrastructure.............25
inlets 12
Innoshima..................63
Internet......................35
Iriomote Island..........54
iron 34,49,63,77,112
iron ore..................31,49
Isahaya Bay................48
Ise Bay 91
Isesaki 113
Ishikari Coalfield 139
Ishikari Mountains ..132
Ishikari Plain 133
Ishikari River 132,136
Iwaki 128
Iwaki River 124
Iwakuni......................63
Iwami Ginzan.............65
Iwami Highlands........59
Izu Islands 104
Izu Peninsula 89

J

Jinzū River 89
Jōganji River 9
Jōmon period 20

K

Kaga 99
Kamakura...................22
Kamakura period 22

Kameyama....................91
Kamikawa Basin......133
Kamisu.........................115
Kanazawa....................100
Kanazawa Plain.........98
Kanda............................50
Kansai International
　Airport......................79
Kansai Science City...75
Kantō Mountains......9,105
Kantō Plain..........11,104
Kantō Region........38,102
Karafuto.............132,134
Kariwa..........................101
Karuizawa....................89
Kasanohara..................47
Kashima......................113
Kashiwazaki...............101
katakana.......................21
Kawagoe.....................112
Kawasaki..............55,112
Keihin Industrial District
　..............................49,77,112
Kesennuma.................125
Kibi Highlands............59
Kii Channel..................67
Kii Mountains.........73,84
Kii Peninsula...............73
Kinki Region..........38,70
Kiryū............................113
Kiso Mountains......8,88
Kiso River.........89,90,92
Kitakami.....................128
Kitakami Basin.........121
Kitakami Highlands...8,
　120
Kitakami River.........121
Kitakyūsyū............49,55
Kitakyūsyū Industrial
　District...................49
Kitami Basin.....133,137
Kitami Mountains....132
Kōbe........................75,78
Kōchi Plain............67,68
Kōfu Basin............10,94
Kofun period...............20
Kojiki............................21
Kojima Bay..................64
Konsen Plateau.133,137
Kōriyama..................122
Kōshū............................94
Kumamoto Plain........46
Kurashiki......................63
Kure...............................63
Kurobe River...............89
Kuroshio...13,17,43,52,89
Kushimoto....................84
Kushiro.......................139
Kyōto..22,23,24,25,81,82
Kyōto Basin............73,81
Kyūsyū Mountains.....43
Kyūsyū Region......38,40

■ L ■

Lake Biwa..........73,74,85
Lake Fujigoko.............89
Lake Suwa...................95
land reclamation...12,59,
　62,64,78,85,104
landslides..........15,18,43

leisure........................129
lowlands......................92

■ M ■

Maebashi...................113
Makinohara.................93
Makuhari New Center
　..................................109
Makuranosōshi............22
mangroves..............52,54
Man'yōshū...................21
market gardening..53,93
Matsue..........................65
Matsumoto............95,96
Matsumoto Basin........9
meadows...................137
Meiji Irrigation Canal
　....................................93
Meiji Restoration........25
metropolitan area(s)..73,
　74,102
Mikatahara...................93
Minamata Bay............55
Minamata disease......55
Minamitori Island........6
Minamoto no Yoritomo
　....................................22
Minato Mirai 21.......110
Miura Peninsula.105,115
Miyake Island...........105
Miyawaka....................50
Miyazaki Plain...........48
Mogami River...........121
Morioka..............122,126
motor vehicle(s)....63,77,
　91,110,117
mountain ranges.....7,88
mountains......................7
Mt.Akagi...................104
Mt.Asama.................104
Mt.Aso..........................43
Mt.Fuji...............8,89,104
Mt.Hakkōda..............120
Mt.Hakone................104
Mt.Hakusan.................89
Mt.Haruna.................104
Mt.Iwate....................120
Mt.Norikura...........89,96
Mt.Ōdaigahara............73
Mt.Unzen(Mt.Fugen)
　...............................18,43
Mt.Zaō.......................120
Muromachi period......23
Muroran....................134
Muroto..........................67
Mutsu Bay.................125

■ N ■

Nabari...........................76
Nagano Basin..........9,94
Nagara River...............92
Nagato..........................66
Nagoya....................90,93
Nansei Islands......12,13,
　14,17,43
Nara.........................21,80
Nara Basin...................73
Nara period.................20
Naraha.......................129

Narita International
　Airport..................107
national park(s)...96,116
national treasures......81
natural disasters...18,19
natural gas.................101
new town..............76,111
Nihon(Japan) Alps..8,88
Nihon Shoki................21
Niigata.................100,101
Niigata Chūetsu
　Earthquake..........97
Nōbi Plain........89,90,93
Noboribetsu..............140
Northern Territories
　..........................131,138
Noto Peninsula
　Earthquake..........97
nuclear power plant(s)
　..................................101

■ O ■

Oda Nobunaga............23
Ōdate..........................126
Ogasawara Islands...104
oil crisis........................34
Okaya...........................95
Okazaki Plain.............93
Okinawa......................53
Okinotori Island..........6
Ōsaka..................24,74,76
Ōsaka Bay...75,77,78,79
Ōsaka International
　Airport....................79
Ōsaka Plain.................73
Ōta..............................113
Ōta River......................60
Ōtake............................63
Ōtsu..............................85
Ōu Mountains....120,121
overpopulation............28
Owase...........................73
Oyashio(Chishima
　Current)........13,133

■ P ■

Pacific high pressure..15
Pacific Belt..................34
Pacific War..................25
pasture lands..............66
peat land....................136
petrochemical(s)...34,63,
　91,110,112,113
petroleum.............50,128
plain(s)...........7,10,19,28,
　60,62,73,89,102,104
plankton......................13
plateau(s).........10,11,92,
　104,114
plates..............................7
pollution.................49,55
population..............24,28
Port Island.............78,79
precision machinery
　industry................34
primary industry(-ies)
　....................................32
primeval forests.........54
Prince Shōtoku Taishi
　....................................21

prolonged cultivation..115
pulp...............................91
pulp and paper mills..92

■ Q ■

quasi-national parks..96

■ R ■

Ramsar Convention...85
reclaimed land......64,98,
　110
recycling facilities......55
redevelopment.........109
reservoirs............17,59,73
ria coast(s).............12,43
rice........20,46,93,94,98,
　121,123,124,136
Rokkō Mountains........78
Rokkō Island................78
Roppongi...................109
Russo-Japanese War.....25

■ S ■

Sabae............................99
Sagami River............104
Sagamihara...............112
Saitama New Center
　..................................109
Sakaide.........................62
Sakaiminato................66
Sakurajima..................43
salt evaporation pan
　...............................59,62
sand dune(s)....12,66,73,
　101,115
San'in...........................65
Sanjō............................99
Sanriku Coast.....13,121,
　125
Sapporo..............134,135
satellite........................66
satellite centers..........74
Sayama.....................112
Seagaia.........................51
Sea of Japan................59
Sea of Okhotsk...16,133,
　137,138,140
seaports.......................53
seasonal jobs............127
seasonal wind(s).........14,
　17,43,52,59,73,89
second crop.................98
secondary industry(-ies)
　....................................32
Sendai.................118,122
Sendai Plain......121,123
sericulture..............83,94
Seto..............................91
Seto Inland Sea....12,59,
　60,62,63,64,73
Setouchi......................17
Shikoku Mountains...17,
　67
Shima Peninsula........84
Shimanto River..........67
Shimōsa Uplands......11
Shinano River.........9,89
Shinchitose Airport..135
Shingū.........................83

151

shinkansen 6,28,30, 90,96,97,122
Shintōism.....................22
Shiogama 125
Shirakami Mountains 121,141
Shirakawagō...............26
Shiraoi 139
shirasu 47
Shiretoko Peninsula..141
shōgun................23,24,25
Shōnai Plain........121,123
shopping malls 30,45, 91,109,116
Shōwa 25
Shūnan 63
Silicon Island...............50
silk-reeling industry ..95
single-crop region(s) ..98, 123,136
Sino-Japanese War.....25
Sōya Strait................132
steel........34,49,63,77,91, 112,113
stockbreeding 47
subarctic zone..........133
suburban agriculture 32,114
suburbs 28,30,108,110
Suruga Bay..................93
Susono 92
Suwa 95
Suwa Basin.................95

■ T ■

Taishō..........................25
Tajimi..........................91
Takaoka 99

Tama River 104
Tanba Highlands.......73
Tango Peninsula.........83
Tateyama 89,105
temple 21,22,23,80
Tendō...................126,128
Tenryū River.......89,91,93
terracing for cultivation 69
tertiary industry(-ies) 32,35
textile(cotton) industry (-ies).............34,77,90
thermal power plant(s) 101
three metropolitan areas.....................28
Tōhoku Expressway 127,128
Tōhoku Region.....38,118
Tōhoku shinkansen..127
Tokachi Plain....133,137
Tōkai Area.............89,92
Tokugawa Ieyasu........24
Tōkyō Bay..........104,109
Tōkyō International Airport..................106
Tomakomai 139
Tōmei Expressway.....92
Tomioka 113
tonden-hei................134
Tone River...............104
torrential rain............15
Tosashimizu................67
Tottori 12,65
tourism........100,116,140
Toyama Plain..............98

Toyokawa Irrigation Canal 93
Toyotomi Hideyoshi....24
trade friction.............34
traditional handicrafts 27,52,100
traditional industries 82,99,126
traditional culture(s)..26, 27,100
tropical forests............54
Tsugaru Plain...........124
Tsugaru Strait...130,132
Tsukuba 109
Tsukuba Express......109
Tsukuba Science City 109
Tsukushi Plain 46
Tsumagoi 115
tsunami..............18,121
Tsushima Current.....13, 43,89
Tsuyama Basin..........63
23 wards of Tōkyō ...110, 111,112
two crops a year 46
typhoon(s)...15,17,18,26,43

■ U ■

Uchiura Bay 138
ukiyoe.........................24
Utashinai.................139

■ V ■

valleys 59,89
volcano(es) ..18,19,43,89, 105,120,132

■ W ■

Wajima 99
wajū..........................92
Wakayama 74,83
warm (sea) current(s) 13,33
waste 49,55
water pollution 49
World Cultural Heritage 21,65,81,84
World Natural Heritage 121,141

■ Y ■

Yahata.......................34
Yaku Island.............141
Yamagata................128
Yamagata Basin 121
Yamanote Line 108
yamase.................18,121
Yayoi period 20
Yodo River............73,85
Yokkaichi 55
Yokohama 110,112
Yokote Basin.....121,123
Yonago......................65
Yonaguni Island 6
Yonezawa 128
Yonezawa Basin 123
Yūbari 139
Yufuin 51

■ Z ■

Zen 23
Zushi 105

Photographs

Akita City / Akita Prefectural Institute of Fisheries / amanaimages / Amano Taro / Asahiyama Zoo / Canon / Central Japan International Airport / Ehime Gyoren / Ehime Prefecture / Genki Sushi / Haga Library / Hatakeyama Shigeatsu / Historiographical Institute The University of Tokyo / Hitachi Zosen / Honda / Imperial Household Agency Sannomaru Shozokan / Ishihara Marine Products / Japan Agricultural News=PANA / Japan Meteorological Agency / Jiji Press / JTB Photo / Kaga Zome Promotion Cooperative Association / Kagoshima Berkshire Producer Conference / Kami Town / Kanasaka Kiyonori / Kanazawa City / Kansai Electric Power / Kansai Science City / Kimura Shigeru / Kobe City Museum / Kobe Port Promotion Association / Kōchi Prefecture / Kodansha / Kyodo News / Mainichi Newspapers / Matsumoto Electric Railway / Minabe Town / Minamata City / Minami-Nippon Shimbun / Miyagi Prefecture Souvenirs / MO Photos / Nagasaki Prefectural Tourism Federation / Naikai Zosen / Naracity Tourist Association / NEC Semiconductors Kyusyu Yamaguchi / Nidec Sankyo / Nishinippon Shimbun / NOA NOA / OCVB / Ogasawara Whale Watching Association / Okinawa Prefecture / OPO / Ōta City / PANA / Panasonic / PPS / Roku-on-ji Temple / Rural Culture Association / SABO Publicity Center / Seiko Epson / Shirakawa Village Office / Shishido Kiyotaka / Shizuoka Prefecture Tourist Association / Shosoin / Snow Brand Milk Products / STV / Suisan Aviation / Teijin / Tohan Aerialphotographic Service / Tohoku Hundred<Vegalta Sendai> / Tokai University Research & Information Center (TRIC) / Tōkamachi City / Tokyo National Museum / Tokyo Waterworks Museum / Toyama Prefecture / Toyota Motor / Toyota Motor Kyushu / Uniphoto Press / Wajima City / Weathernews / Yokohama Plant Protection Station / Yomiuri Shimbun / Yonezawa City Uesugi Museum / Yukobo

Discovering JAPAN
A New Regional Geography

定価　本体 1900 円（税別）
平成 23 年 12 月 15 日　印刷
平成 23 年 12 月 20 日　発行

監　修　者 Editorial supervisors	伊藤喜栄 Yoshiei Ito	中村和郎 Kazuo Nakamura	金坂清則 Kiyonori Kanasaka	編　集 edited by Editorial Department of Teikoku-Shoin	帝国書院編集部
著　作　者 Authors	金坂清則 Kiyonori Kanasaka	宮町良広 Yoshihiro Miyamachi	関戸明子 Akiko Sekido	発　行 published by Teikoku-Shoin Co., Ltd.	株式会社　帝国書院
	松井圭介 Keisuke Matsui	荒木一視 Hitoshi Araki	小岩直人 Naoto Koiwa	〒 101－0051 東京都千代田区神田神保町3-29	
	天野太郎 Taro Amano	土屋　純 Jun Tsuchiya	梅田克樹 Katsuki Umeda	電　話　03（3262）0830（販売部） 　　　　03（3261）9038（開発部）	
		武者忠彦 Tadahiko Musha		振替口座　00180－7－67014	
英語版監修者 English editorial supervisor	ジョン・サージェント John Sargent			URL http://www.teikokushoin.co.jp/	

ISBN 978-4-8071-5844-7

Printed in Japan